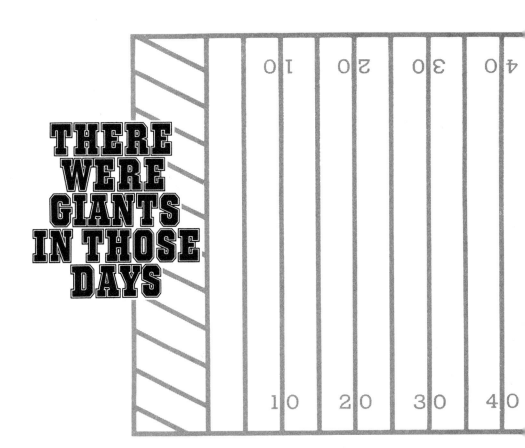

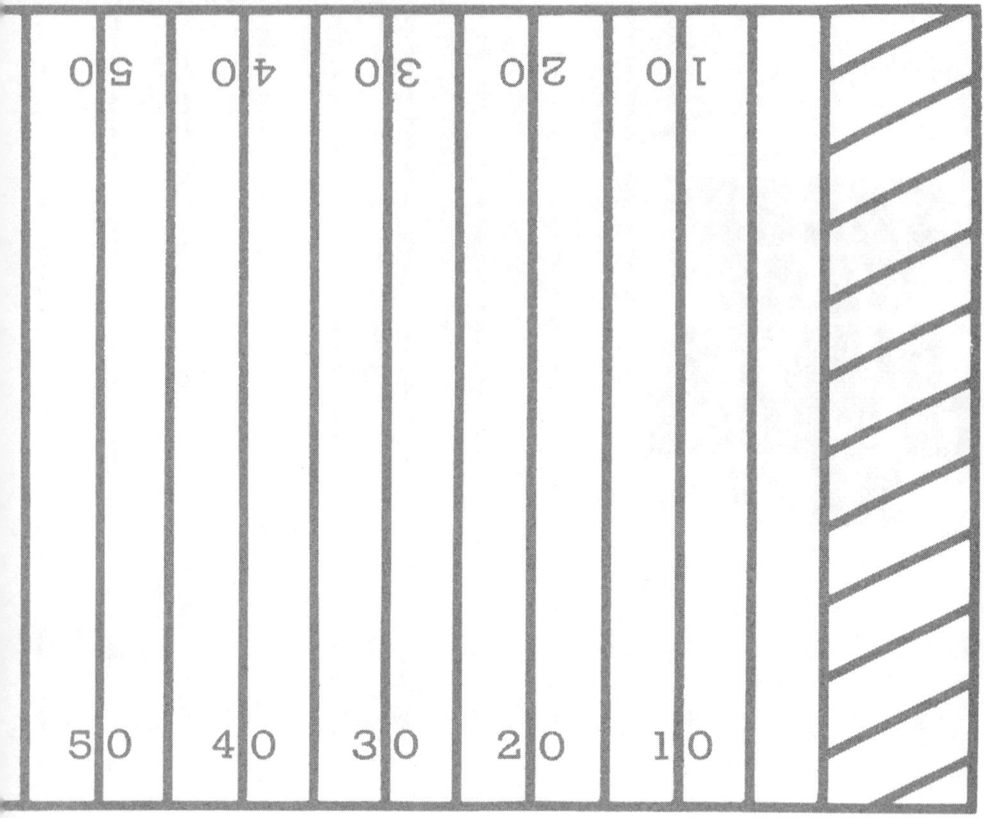
50
40
30
20
10
10
20
30
40
50

THERE WERE GIANTS IN THOSE DAYS

GERALD ESKENAZI

Publishers · GROSSET & DUNLAP · New York
A FILMWAYS COMPANY

This book is for Michael, who wears No. 12 on his pajamas.

Acknowledgments

It is not necessary to be a hypnotist to make a football fan regress. Throw a name—"Tittle," "Gifford," "Robustelli," "Huff"—and the fan will tell you what he was eating, the time of day, and what the temperature was when his particular memory of his particular hero was evoked.

For that was a magic time for many of us—even those of us who were not part of the magic era of football's coming of age.

And because so many people like to remember, they have helped in the making of this book. Most of the Giants and the Giants' officials, past and present, written about gave me their time and enthusiasm. All the reminiscences were given directly, so I thank each of them without repeating all their names here. Also, the necessary technical help was provided by Jim Rooney of the NFL, whose Don Weiss and Joe Browne also served.

Ed Croke of the Giants, a storehouse of information, discovered long-lost facts, figures, and phone numbers; and Ed Uhas of the Cleveland Browns, the greatest living authority on Jim Brown, offered important statistical help. Of course, Don Smith, thanks. And Dave Klein, Barry Gottehrer, Joe Durso, Jack Mann, and Smith wrote books that proved helpful in my research.

As for the Giants and the Giants' officials: I hope this book brings you some enjoyment.

Friends and jocks and colleagues who, invariably, were at a key game and gave me an additional bit of information— my thanks. Special applause goes to Bob Markel, editor-in-chief at Grosset, who thought it might be nice to look back on this era. Now, finally, I will take my wife on a vacation.

Gerald Eskenazi
Roslyn, New York

From 1954 to 1963 a football team named the Giants loved—and was loved by—New York. On Sundays starting in September, when the New York haze would begin to disappear as fall winds blew sulphurous exhaust out to the Atlantic, through the biting wintertime, the Giants mattered more than most things. It was a decade that started well, with AT&T selling for $169, President Eisenhower playing golf, and Roger Bannister running the mile in under four minutes.

The beginning of the Giants' great decade coincided with the manufacture of millions of twelve-inch and sixteen-inch television sets. The future had arrived. Americans were becoming accustomed to a sort of instant sensationalism in their entertainment.

For New Yorkers, touched by people, buildings, smells, and sounds more than most Americans, the changing patterns of behavior were perhaps heightened. They were ready for a new outlet, especially in the games they enjoyed. Baseball was dominated by the Yankees. They had won five straight championships. They were good and predictable. There were rumbles that baseball's Giants and Dodgers would leave New York. There were basketball and hockey, in the Knickerbockers and Rangers. But the Knicks maintained a bush-league image because they were forced to perform in an armory during the playoffs, when Madison Square Garden was showing the circus. And the inept Rangers were also forced out of the Garden during playoff time to play ''home'' games in places such as Toronto.

The Giants played in the National Football League, a professional loop of twelve teams divided into an Eastern Conference and a Western Conference. In 1954 professional football was hardly removed from the days when the NFL was termed ''postgraduate football.'' Indeed, even today—but much less than in former years—the television announcer often follows a player's name with the name of the college the player attended. It was almost as if the athlete had played his *real* football in college, as if he still needed that collegiate identity to make his profession legitimate.

There remained a touch of, well . . . country, in pro football even into the 1950s. The Giants' coach since 1931 was Steve Owen, a product of the Cherokee Strip in Oklahoma, who enjoyed ''rasslin' '' as a test of man-to-man skills. When Owen was asked his opinion of the coaching techniques of the innovative Paul Brown or what he thought of the new T-formation, he would smile and drawl, ''The game is played in the dirt.'' He had been thrust from the trench warfare of World War I into a new world he had never made, where there were new rules, new machines, and new armaments. And there were also new people, differently motivated and better educated.

Owen's last year with the club was 1953. Everyone hoped that the men who controlled the Giants had fired him gently. They realized that a new era was starting in professional football. It needed new coaches, new coaching techniques, and new players who could adapt to the more fluid style that the second half of the twentieth century demanded.

Few people could have envisioned the impact on New York life that the Giants would make over the next ten years, when Vince Lombardi was only an *assistant* coach, along with the cerebral Tom Landry. It was a time when the head of the Parke-Bernet Galleries (who also hired Emlen Tunnell as a guard in the rare books section) would show up at the games, as well as Toots Shor, network executives, priests and nuns, and generals. Before sidewalk cafés became fashionable in Manhattan, there was al fresco dining under the shadow of the Bronx elevated at Yankee Stadium, tailgate parties before the big game.

The shouts, the demands, really, of "Dee-fense! Dee-fense!" started with the football Giants' fans. More than 60,000 of them, the largest season's ticket-holding group in the world, would bellow for the most famous defensive unit in sports— probably in the history of sports in this country. Even today, the names have a magical connotation, taking in a time, a place, and a definite part of one's mind: Rosey Grier, Andy Robustelli, Sam Huff, Dick Modzelewski, Harland Svare, Em Tunnell.

People had never before come to sports events to root for a defense. Had baseball fans gone to Yankee Stadium to see Babe Ruth make great catches in the outfield? Did they want to see George Mikan grab a rebound? Did they want to see Maurice "Rocket" Richard poke the puck away from an opponent? No, they had wanted to see Ruth smash a home run; Mikan bank in a hook shot; or Richard sail down the ice with his eyes flaming like torches from a cave, zero in on a goalie, and score.

The offense had stars of its own, more names that are a part of nostalgia: Frank Gifford, Kyle Rote, Y. A. Tittle, Charlie Conerly, Rosey Brown, Del Shofner, Alex Webster. But the defense had captured the imagination of a public hungering for a new thrill. Or perhaps it simply wanted relief on Sundays from the ever-present reality of the real world, where there was a real bomb. Through the 1950s, the public believed it possible that the Soviet Union would unleash an atomic bomb on the United States. When estimates of A-bomb destruction were issued, they often were based on "how many people would die if the bomb were dropped in Times Square."

Out there on Sundays, though, the bomb was tossed by Tittle. And when the opposition threw it, it often was quenched by the Giants' defense, a remarkable unit that was forced to keep a team without scoring punch in contention. The defense liked to refer to itself as the DVW, which stood for Defense Versus the World.

From 1954 (when a big Arkansas farmer named Jim Lee Howell, to his great surprise, became the Giants' head coach) through 1963 (when the team won its last championship under Allie Sherman, a Brooklynite with a Southern drawl), the New York Giants won the Eastern Conference title six times. They won the world championship once; they never finished below third. Over that remarkable stretch, they yielded the fewest season points in the NFL three times.

Likely, pro football would have burst upon the American consciousness sooner or later. But because the New York Giants fielded the best team in the United States over such a long stretch, and because it was a New York Giants team involved in what has become known as "the greatest football game ever played" (the 1958 championship with the Baltimore Colts), it seems that the Giants were the catalyst.

Ironically, professional football was hardly a big city game. It had belonged to the mill and coal towns of Pennsylvania and Ohio and upstate New York. A town's honor often depended on how fiercely its football team played. For the most part, these clubs, which flourished at the turn of the twentieth century, were sponsored by local companies. They were, perhaps, the forerunners of the Little League, in that a corporation hoped to spread goodwill while selling its product.

But organized sport in this country had been the domain of the amateur, except for baseball. The idea of being paid to play, well, it just did not sit right with many Americans.

Football especially was a game to be played among gentlemen. It was a test for fun. Before the rise of acknowledged professional teams, there were amateur clubs composed of postcollegians (or even collegians) and workers who received a salary in the privacy of an office. The concept of amateurism had carried over from England, where there were gentlemen farmers, amateur rugby players, amateur polo players, gentlemen jockeys. The principle took hold over all North America. Indeed, Joseph Seagram, the founder of the great whiskey empire, caused a scandal in 1893 in Montreal when, in a joyous moment after his favorite hockey team won an important game, he gave gold pieces to each of his players.

But practicality won out for Americans. It was they, and not the Canadians, who fielded the first confessed professional team, a squad in the upper Michigan peninsula mining town of Houghton. Called Portage Lakes, it began play in 1903—with Canadians as players.

By then, professionalism in the States had been accepted. Does anyone know when it began? Perhaps the only way to start is from the time people admitted they were paid. By reaching back to what seems pristine to us, the lure of the Giants and the time they were a part of take on a newer meaning. One can appreciate Rosey Grier's tossing a Cleveland Browns' lineman out of the way to get to Jim Brown. But perhaps it is more fun to know that if Grier had played fifty years before, he might have pulled the lineman's hair.

Based on reports from people who were there, the first professional football game in this country was played in Latrobe, Pennsylvania, some forty miles southeast of Pittsburgh, on August 31, 1895. The sponsor was the local YMCA. And of course they would not dream of playing the game on Sunday. It was a Tuesday game against a team from Jeanette, a city ten miles away. The game, say local historians, was the start of a ten-year-long winning streak for Latrobe.

It took only courage to play. The players wore shin guards and some sported nose guards. But no one wore a helmet. Players never took haircuts—their thick hair helped absorb blows to the head. Unfortunately, it also made hair-tackling easier.

Rules were, at best, stretched like a pig's bladder. There were no rules to protect kickers or those who received the kicks. If a player looked skyward, he was either waiting to receive the ball or praying. This was the time of the flying wedge, and the team was given three tries to gain all of five yards. There was no line as we know it. Players went into a huddle, all folding their arms as if each was snuggling the football. Then they suddenly would break out screaming and sending the opposition into a panic. Often, the ball-carrier hooked his free hand into the belt of the man in front.

Even into the 1930s, a form of the wedge persisted. "We had one boy," recalls Jim Lee Howell, "who went into the wedge feet first. Maybe that was the only way to go."

That first pro game in Latrobe saw a practice that was to be repeated many times. One of the players was John Brallier, who happened to be the quarterback for Indiana Normal. Forty years later, Dr. Brallier recalled that he was paid $10 for the game. A week later he enrolled at Washington and Jefferson College, played quarterback at the school, then returned at the end of the year to perform again for Latrobe for, as he said, "ten dollars and cakes."

The next year, Brallier, a would-be dentist, went to the University of West Virginia, which refused to pay him to play football. So he returned to Latrobe to play on weekends and picked up $150 for the rest of the season.

Rules were broken even before recruiting violations. And among the most sacrosanct were the Sunday Blue Laws, which outlawed sports on Sunday. There had always been an exception taken to those laws. That took place in the coal-mining regions, where the miners hungered for a day off after a six-day work week. If their leisure included watching a football game, that was the way it was, and the local police did not enforce the laws. The YMCA's objected, but no one heard.

Does anyone remember the Greensburg–Latrobe rivalry? It was as heated in its time, with mutual hate, as the Giants–Browns warfare was more than fifty years later. The people of Greensburg were obsessed with stopping their neighbor, Latrobe, from another victory. Saloonkeepers, gamblers, factory owners were called on to bankroll a team that could stop Latrobe.

They wound up, incredibly, with Lafayette College's entire backfield: the alliterative Best, Barclay, Bray, and Wallbridge. The four-man backfield was more or less standard. It came about, in the words of an observer, because a team needed "three to tote the oval and one who can kick it a mile."

It was the habit of football players then, as it is now, to run to the right—or at least to feel more comfortable running in that direction. So a defensive left end, a good one, was the key to halting the opposition's offense. For three out of every four plays was a run to the right, which is the defensive team's left. The other plays were a run to the left or a kick—there was no forward passing.

The best defensive left end around? He was Doggie Trenchard of Princeton, who was selected for Walter Camp's all-America team. Actually, the all-America teams, which made Camp one of the most famous names in football history, really were made from the narrowest of selections. It surprises people to discover that from 1889, when Camp began his selecting, until 1900, he picked only four players who had not played for Yale, Princeton, Harvard, or Pennsylvania.

Trenchard by now was coaching at West Virginia, and Brallier, who was becoming something of a secret agent, knew how good he was. Brallier discovered that Greensburg had offered money to induce Trenchard to play for its team. The information was leaked by a telegraph operator, who had broken his sacred trust to keep telegrams confidential. When Latrobe made the discovery, it made Trenchard the beneficiary of the first player auction in pro football.

Latrobe won out for $75, but Greensburg bettors would not give up. One saloon owner was dispatched to the Latrobe train station to meet Trenchard, presumably to pluck him off or to make believe that he was a Latrobe operative. But Latrobe had some people with more than a casual interest in seeing that the all-American played for their side. So two people from Latrobe met Trenchard at a station up the line, took him off, and drove him by horse over the back roads.

The game itself, in Greensburg, attracted 5,000 fans—including a contingent of sportswriters from Pittsburgh. They saw Greensburg boot the opening kickoff beyond the goal post and into the creek that bordered the end zone. Three players dived in after the ball.

Greensburg's money appeared well spent by half time, when Barclay scored a touchdown, worth 5 points. Coupled with the 1-point conversion, Greensburg had a 6–0 lead. Soon after the second half began, though, Ed Abbaticchio, who was also the second baseman for the Philadelphia Phillies, tied the score. A Pittsburgh writer refused to learn how to spell Abbaticchio, though, and referred to him in print as "awful name." Latrobe won, 12–6.

They were bad winners. A drunken revelry spilled over into town, and the Greensburg courthouse steeple was knocked out of line by Latrobe followers that night.

The New York football Giants had not been invented yet. But the "postgraduate" football tradition in the New York area went back to 1890. Clubs composed of college men, supposedly amateurs, abounded; there were the Manhattan Athletic Club, the Orange A.C. in New Jersey, the Crescent Club in Brooklyn, the Staten Island A.C., the Knickerbockers.

It was the sort of "amateurism" in which everyone winked at the name. One of the players, whose name was Parke Davis, described its workings this way: after a game each player got a watch. Somehow, they all would wind up at the same pawnbroker's after the game, where each player hocked the watch for $20. Then the player would go to the promoter, who bought the pawn ticket back for $20. In other words, each player made $40 a game. The promoter then retrieved the watch, which would be kept in circulation. It was said that some of these watches became so accustomed to certain players that they refused to tick for anyone else.

From 1897 to 1920 the face of football metamorphosed into today's game: the value of a field goal was changed from 5 points to 3 points, a team received four downs, the field was shortened to 100 yards, the value of a touchdown went up to 6 points, the game was divided into four quarters. One area remained backward, though: player safety. There was no mandatory protection for the pros. Amateurs—the collegians —by now were well-padded and even wore helmets. The pros? Well, they were getting paid, weren't they? And they wore their hair long anyway.

During this burgeoning period of growth, clubs sprouted across the country. They included the Duquesne Country and Athletic Club, backed by W. C. Temple of Pittsburgh, whose

Temple Cup preceded the World Series and was awarded to the top National League team following a playoff. The Duquesne club lured a fullback named Christy Mathewson from Bucknell.

In those early days there was a zany atmosphere to the game, as there seems to be at the outset of so many other sports. The orchestration of today's teams—a time to practice, a time to eat, mandatory taping of ankles—appears almost dull by comparison to some of the pioneer efforts.

There was, for example, David Fultz, coach of a team called the Homestead Library (owned by Temple), whose contract stipulated he would not play or coach on Sundays. The Library broke up when it could not find any teams to play.

Meanwhile, in Philadelphia in 1902, teams were organized to grab the pro championship from Pittsburgh. One of the teams was coached by a Dr. Roller of Seattle, who had come to Philadelphia to study medicine. He was a good athlete. But while playing football, he wore kid gloves to avoid damaging his fingers. He also wore a Van Dyke beard.

A football team in Philadelphia called itself, tongue in collective cheek, the ''Athletics.'' This was to show it was an invader, just as the baseball team named the Athletics had invaded the territory so long held by the Phillies. The Athletics baseball team was referred to as a ''white elephant'' by Establishment owners. Hence, the A's symbol of an elephant.

The football A's manager was Connie Mack, who also happened to be the baseball A's manager. One of his problem baseball players was the great Rube Waddell, the major leagues' strikeout leader, a twenty-game winner, and future member of the Baseball Hall of Fame. Waddell, though, allowed himself to be swallowed up by other diversions, such as drinking. So to keep him occupied during the off-season, Mack decided to let Waddell play football. Waddell saw action in the 1903 season, receiving about $1,000. He helped his football team get to the state championship. But first, incredibly, the A's staged three warm-ups: on a Friday night in Elmira, on Saturday in Athens-Sayre, and on Monday in Williamsport. The championship was to be played on Thursday.

Elmira was a fine place for Waddell, since it had a fire-engine factory. Waddell liked fire engines. He did not like the field, though. Neither did any of the other players. To light up the field, overhead lights were strung up along the sidelines, as if it were an outdoor party. Behind the goal posts there were giant searchlights. The players could not see when they looked up. So they looked down during the whole game and confined all their plays to runs in the line.

Waddell was back in shape by Monday afternoon, though. And Mack wanted to drum up interest for that night's game. So he asked Waddell to walk around Williamsport with a sandwich board to advertise the contest. One can hardly imagine Sandy Koufax passing out leaflets on Flatbush Avenue asking fans to attend a baseball game in Brooklyn.

As part of the tour, Waddell passed the local high school wearing his board during lunchtime. No one went back to class, as a few hundred students followed him back to his hotel. Under the marquee he raised his hands and asked for quiet. Then he did handsprings to the delight of the students.

The night before the championship game Waddell went to Pittsburgh for the logical reason of seeing Willie Hoppe give a billiard exhibition. He got drunk and lost a lot of money betting. He returned to his hotel and woke up Connie Mack and asked for money. Mack instead ordered him to bed.

What happened next is clouded in the mists of history, which often happens when a superstar athlete gets in trouble. Supposedly, Waddell went to the room clerk to get his key. He told police that he reached into his rear pocket for his handkerchief but that the handkerchief somehow got hooked around the loaded revolver he packed. The revolver fell to the floor. It went off, the bullet whizzed inches past Connie Mack's head.

Mack retained enough of his senses the next day to be suspicious about getting paid for his championship game with Pittsburgh. He knew that the Pitt University football team was playing its traditional rival, Washington and Jefferson. He knew, too, that the collegians would outdraw his pro game. That meant there was just a limited number of fans—and money—available that day.

So he told his team's bus driver to park on the outskirts of the field where the title game was to be staged. Then he refused to permit his players to leave. He dispatched a messenger and asked for his guarantee money. The messenger returned with the announcement that the players would be paid out of gate receipts. Mack's narrow eyes squinted even more as he surveyed the stands.as game time neared. The place was virtually empty and his suspicions were confirmed. The Pittsburgh pros took the field to warm up, but Mack's A's did not budge.

A distinguished, well-manicured man rapped on the door of the bus and asked to be let in. "What's the delay?" he asked Mack. "Money," replied Mack.

"What's your guarantee?" he asked Mack.

"Three thousand," he replied.

"If that's all, I'll give you a check," the man responded.

"Well, who are you? How do I know it's good?" Mack asked.

"William Corey, if that means anything to you," replied the president of United States Steel.

After the game, Rube Waddell quit football. But apparently, the pistol incident had not traumatized him. The next season he blithely reported to baseball training and wound up having a sensational year. He led the league with 349 strikeouts (a Major League record that lasted for sixty years). He also led the league in games started, posted 26 victories, completed 39 of 46 starts, had an earned-run mark of 1.62, and hurled 383 innings.

Soon after Waddell quit football, pro football was given a stamp of approval. It received the imprimatur of Madison Square Garden, which staged its first indoor football game. Even then, the Garden was the world's most famous arena. Anything that was held there automatically took on a big league image. The first indoor football game, on December 15, 1903, was part of a three-way playoff. Franklin halted the Orange Athletic Club, and then two days later, it defeated the Watertown Reds and Blacks. Our old friend, Dr. Roller, scored for Franklin when a teammate literally threw him five yards to cross the line.

The game attracted curiosity seekers from all over the United States, as well as New York's sports fans. One of the players was Glenn Warner of Cornell, a well-spoken young man who met some of the administrators from the Carlisle Institute, the Indian school. Warner impressed them, and a year later they asked him to coach the school's football team. It was there that Pop Warner began more than fifty years of coaching, and it was there that Warner and Jim Thorpe impressed themselves forever on America's football consciousness.

The indoor game was officiated by Frank Hinkey (who was renowned as an end for Yale) and Bill Edwards (a guard from Princeton). Each wore full evening dress—top hat, white gloves, patent leather shoes. Hinkey's decisions, coupled with his superior airs, angered Franklin. For the last play of the game, the team decided to run—right over Hinkey. Which is what it did.

The fact that a pro football game was staged in New York's showplace indicated that it was ready to take off. Although the major pro teams remained in the Pennsylvania area, the rest of the country heard about this unusual contest in the Garden, and pro football suddenly became a part of the sports scene.

Ohio soon got into the sport in the grandest way yet seen. It became the major game in the state and set up a tradition that continues until today: the production of rock-hard football players from Ohio and Pennsylvania, especially in the stretch of land from western Pennsylvania through eastern and central Ohio.

Just a few miles west of Pittsburgh is Stark County, Ohio. It is the home of Canton and Massillon. It was the home of the Gish sisters and of Jacob Coxey, who led a ragtag collection of hobos on a March to Washington in the 1890s to lobby for good roads. Massillon and Canton were to establish a football rivalry that was vicious, long-lasting, and yet a prod to the growth of the pro game.

The Professional Football Hall of Fame is in Canton, which is where the first meeting was held of the group which was to become the National Football League. Canton was named for the Chinese city by Bezaleel Wells. He had migrated to Ohio from his native Baltimore, where one of Wells's heroes in the early nineteenth century was Captain John O'Donnell, famed for sailing from Baltimore to Canton, China. Canton, Ohio was a heavy-industry town, making steel, vacuum cleaners, and safes. Massillon also was a busy industrial city. Like many towns dependent on machinery, it found itself awakening from the slumber induced by years of working six days a week, ten hours a day. The Industrial Revolution was becoming automated in the early days of this century, and that meant more free time. Not free time as we know it now, especially not in Canton or Massillon, but time for people to relax a bit more.

Relaxing and leisure times were alien words to an ambitious youngster named Timothy Mara. In 1900 he was twelve years old, but he was already a newsboy in Manhattan's hub—along Broadway, from the old Wanamaker's north to Union Square. He lived in nearby Greenwich Village, attended P.S. 14 in the mornings, delivered papers in the afternoons, and worked as an usher in a movie theater at night.

It was difficult for a youngster living on the southern tip of Manhattan to see many sports events. The Giants played baseball up at Coogan's Hollow, on Eighth Avenue between 155th and 157th Streets.

Young Mara was too young to play the horses, which ran in such out-of-the-way places as Sheepshead Bay and Brighton Beach in Brooklyn, Aqueduct in Queens, and Jerome Park in the Bronx. But he noticed a group of well-dressed men, who gobbled up his papers every day as they waited impatiently for him to make his rounds. They were the bookies that lined Broadway. Later, he was to recall, "They seemed to dress the best and work the least of anyone I knew." That appealed to him. He was given further insight into the profession one day when he made his first bet, a one-dollar hunch bet on a horse ridden by a jockey who happened to be an ex-newsboy. The horse lost, and the bookie kept his money.

Soon, he was running bets between bookies and his newspaper customers, many of whom were hotel guests. When the guests lost, the bookies gave Tim five percent of the bet. However, he got tips from the bettors when they won. By the time he was fifteen he was finished with school. Horse racing was burgeoning. The Jamaica racetrack opened, and soon racing moved down from the Bronx to open at Belmont Park. Tim Mara left his profession as a runner and went to work for a company in the financial district that made law books. He delivered the books, as well as working in the factory, and soon he got to know many lawyers. They were office-bound, but they found out that Tim Mara could get a bet down for you if you had a hot horse. He was back in business as a runner, although at times he booked some of the bets himself.

As he moved in legal circles he found himself delivering winnings to clubs, where many of the lawyers congregated. These were local Democratic clubs, and the ambitious, friendly young man became a favorite of the politicians. Many went on to high places in the party and in local and national politics, and Tim Mara remained their friend over the years.

Before he was far into his twenties, he was able to open his own place, the New York Law Bindery. Of course, someone remarked, "More bookmaking than bookbinding goes on there." He got wound up in his business and in raising a family with his wife, Lisette. It is doubtful he ever heard of Massillon or Canton or knew that as Americans left the farm in increasing numbers, and as a true middle class began to evolve, football was becoming a mild passion.

The cities of Massillon and Canton became intertwined forever in the fabric of the pro game because a newspaperman did not know what to write about once the baseball season was over. The city editor of the *Massillon Independent*, Eddie Stewart, thought he would organize a football team and went to a local sporting goods store and bought all the leftover jerseys. They all happened to be striped. So he named the team-to-be the Massillon Tigers.

He found players to fill the uniforms and then called a young lawyer friend in Canton, Bill Day, to see whether Day could find a bunch of people in Canton willing to play Massillon. Day, the son of Supreme Court Justice William Rufus Day, accepted the challenge and fielded a team that was glad to play for Canton's honor. Thus, two of the proud names in the sport, the Bulldogs of Canton, the Tigers of Massillon, made their way into the record books. Games have been staged in more favorable surroundings since—this first one was played at the Hospital for the Insane in Massillon.

These two clubs started the true concept of the team, which had been virtually unknown in pro football. Players previously had shuttled in and out, receiving $75 to play for this team, jumping to another club for $80. Players practiced on their own and exercised on their own. Now, for the first time, clubs concentrated on defense and execution, working drills with the same players.

Of course, that included working with a ball. And because Canton practiced with a sixteen-ounce football all week for the 1905 renewal of the instant-rivalry with Massillon, it lost. The contract stipulated that the home club—Massillon—would provide the ball, and Massillon used a ten-ounce ball. Massillon had been practicing with it and could handle the more fluttery variations it would go through. The umpire, Christy Mathewson, was helpless to prevent the ball from being used. The star for Massillon was a fullback named Red Salmon, whose last job had been as a sand-hog working under the Hudson River in New York on the Hudson–Manhattan Tubes.

The United States Commissioner for Indian Affairs was a Canton resident, and he liked football. Perhaps if he had lived in Maine he might not have cared so much about the game. But because he cared, he engineered a game between Carlisle Institute of Pennsylvania and Canton. In a sense, he was responsible for the start of one of the great careers—and great tragedies—in United States sports. Carlisle was only a high school, through the twelfth grade. But it had players who were as old as twenty-two or twenty-three. One of its youngest was the fifteen-year-old Jim Thorpe. The Institute now was being coached by Pop Warner, and it wanted to make a name for itself. It did, in what now seems ludicrous fashion: a high school playing professional teams. Warner spoke of a "boy at my school who has leadership ability. His name's Jim Thorpe. But he's sulky and hard to handle, and that may ruin him."

Thorpe would wind up his career with the Giants almost twenty years later. His retirement, troubled by alcohol, was spent in odd jobs as a bouncer, movie stunt man, and carpenter. He could never manage his private life as elegantly as his on-the-field activities.

Massillon and Canton were joined by Akron in fielding teams, and the center of pro football power was established in Ohio. Canton received further fame by experimenting with a forward pass, which was only a gimmick before. One of the Ohio teams was the Columbus Panhandles, so-called because all the players were mechanics for the Pennsylvania Railroad's Panhandle Division in Columbus. The players even wore the railroad's colors of gold and maroon. The team included the seven Nesser brothers and the son of the oldest brother—eight Nessers in all. The team's manager was Joe F. Carr, who was to become famous as the first president of the National Professional Football League.

It did not cost much to run the Panhandles. Transportation was free, since all were railroad men. They would work until their 4 P.M. Saturday shift was over, then grab a train for their Sunday game. Their mother was the team laundress. Their father was the water boy. The Panhandles claimed that they once played against Knute Rockne on six different teams the same season. He went wherever the pay was best.

The only acknowledged fixed game in pro football forced the sport underground for six years in Ohio. It took place in 1906, between Massillon and Canton, naturally. The Canton manager, named Wallace, asked one of his players to throw a game. When he was found out, he admitted the act to his teammates, explaining, "I always do what coach wants me to."

By 1915 Massillon and Canton had resurfaced and Canton signed Thorpe, a legend after his exploits in the 1912 Olympics. Thorpe had learned a thing or two about professionalism over the years. He knew that games between the rivals were not only heated, but they also brought the bettors' blood to boiling point. He planted the suggestion in a few places, before a game between the teams, that he would be unable to start because of injuries. The odds favored Massillon. He furtively bet $2,500 on his own club. He did play, and he scored 23 points in a 23–0 victory.

The teams and leagues in Ohio and Pennsylvania prospered. The beginning of the war in Europe, meanwhile, sent soldiers around the country, in some cases bringing the pro game with them. By then the sport was established in colleges east and west, north and south.

One fine day in 1918, a barrelly teenager was sitting under a tree on the campus of Phillips University in Enid, Oklahoma, eating an apple. A hulking man named Johnny Maulbetsch, who once knocked over a mounted policeman and his horse which unfortunately were standing too close to the sidelines during a Maulbetsch run, spotted the youngster.

The boy, Steve Owen, was not terribly interested in football, but Maulbetsch, who was the school's football coach, was. Many years later Owen was to recall, probably embellishing the memory, that he was tested as a football player by being asked to stop the club's top lineman. On the first try, said Owen, "I was knocked back." When he learned what he had to do, he picked up the lineman and tossed him over his shoulder, as if baling hay.

Life and football were similar to Owen. Neither was complicated. Appearances were not deceiving. He judged a man by his actions, and it was as simple as that. Owen was born in 1898, part of an era when the last Conestogas still bounced their way west over rutted Indian paths. He was from Cleo Springs in Oklahoma Territory. His mother taught school on the north bank of the Cimarron River, on the Cherokee Strip, a vertical stretch of fertile land down the center of what was to become Oklahoma. He was educated in a tent with six other pupils.

As a boy, he learned not to be hoodwinked by praise, a trait he carried over to the big city where he grew to mistrust fast talkers. His father taught him horse-trading. The pair made their deals, and his father never would tell him who got the better of the deal. It was up to young Steve to figure it out, to learn by trial and error. It taught him to trust his own judgment. And it probably taught him not to listen to anyone else's opinion. With him, self-reliance had become an absolute.

Strangely, he had more respect for outlaws, as he termed them, than for United States marshals. Both passed his farm on their way to no-man's land in the Oklahoma Panhandle. The outlaws worked their way from Missouri or up from the Strip, as they headed for the Panhandle, in the northwest part of the territory. Owen recalled a pair of outlaws named Black and Yeager, who were fed by the Owens and whose horses drank their water. The outlaws, in gratitude, left a $20 gold piece. But the marshals often demanded food and water and did not pay. Owen learned never to ask a stranger where he came from, what his name was, or where he was headed.

His was the world of action, of basics. Yet, his life had prepared him (inevitably, it would appear) for a game and New York. Tim Mara took a different route (inevitably, it would appear), but both were to wind up bound together, forever a part of the New York experience.

The formation of a pro football league was inevitable also. Semi-pro teams were the vogue by the time the Great War was over. There was a club called the Duluth Esquimaux; there were the Malted Milkers of Racine. The pros had become such a factor that the great Amos Alonzo Stagg called for a conference among midwestern colleges "to break the pro football menace."

But in 1920, the pros organized. On September 17, they met in Hay's Hupmobile showroom in Canton. Out of that meeting came the American Professional Football Association. The thirteen teams were the forerunners of the National Football League.

Organization gave the pros a readily identifiable image. The teams agreed not to raid one another's players. Thus, the team you saw on one Sunday was the same team you saw the following week. Not one club survived in name to the NFL as we know it now, even with the $100 franchise fee.

Football did not create much excitement for Tim Mara. There was not much betting on it. In 1921 he opened his own betting area at Belmont Park. These were the days when bookies were legal, and each had his own site at the racetracks, where he would put the odds up on blackboards using white chalk. While Mara continued to hob-nob with the New Yorkers who knew how to get things done—the Tammany politicians, the Broadway shrewdies—the American Professional Football Association renamed itself the National Football League in 1922. It had no team in New York, and New York did not seem concerned about that.

Bookies had cash. Money was an object in short supply in the fledgling NFL, where some clubs played ten games and others played thirteen or fourteen (depending on how attractive they were as road draws). There were no season ticket sales to keep a club going. Indeed, some clubs played only road games. Cash flow was a week-to-week proposition, if you had a game week-to-week.

Whenever possible, the other NFL owners looked for bookies or gamblers to join their league. This was the day of a minuscule income tax, and bookmakers were constantly looking for investments. Some became antique collectors, others bought baronial estates, and still others became patrons of the arts. Timothy James Mara remained close to his roots. One of his great friends along the Great White Way was Billy Gibson, a fellow-bookie and manager of Benny Leonard (the world's lightweight boxing champion).

The New York football Giants were created because the president of the NFL, Joe Carr, sweet-talked Mara into investing his money in it. Mara had never met Carr, a former sportswriter, until one day in 1925 when T. J. went over to see his friend Gibson. The boxing man was handling a Shakespeare-spouting fighter named Gene Tunney, who called himself a "pugilist." Tunney exuded what passed for class among the coterie of Mara's friends. Although it was outrageous to believe that in another year Tunney would defeat Jack Dempsey for the championship, Mara liked the aura surrounding the fighter. He wanted to talk to Gibson about buying a piece of Tunney as an investment.

Mara was surprised to find Carr with Gibson, along with

Dr. Harry March, a football promoter/doctor from Canton.
Gibson had turned down Carr's pleadings to buy a franchise
from the NFL for New York.

"Maybe you'd be interested in this, Tim," Gibson told
Mara.

They wanted $500 to put a franchise in New York. Mara
would recall later, "Any franchise in New York has to be
worth $500, even if it's for shining shoes." Before the ink was
dry the anomalously named All-Collegian Professional Football Club, Inc., was founded. Gibson, who suddenly became
interested in the venture when his own money was not at stake,
was named president. March was the secretary. And Mara
was the treasurer.

There was only one place to play, really. That was the Polo
Grounds. It was the home of the New York Giants, the glorious
baseball team led by John J. McGraw. The Polo Grounds had
just been refurbished, its seating expanded to 54,000 as a
reaction to the opening in 1923 of the Yankee Stadium. Mara's
team would be named the Giants, too.

It is unlikely that polo ever was played at the Polo Grounds.
It got its name because the baseball Giants often played in
open fields in the 1880s, and in that decade there were plenty
of fields in Manhattan. One of the team's favorite places to
play was James Gordon Bennett's polo field at Fifth Avenue
and 110th Street. From then on, whenever the Giants played,
their home field was automatically called the "polo grounds."

Bennett was the publisher of the *New York Herald*. He did
not live to see the Giants play on his field, and so history
remembers him more for his financing of Stanley's trip to find
Livingstone than as a baseball patron. In 1889, the baseball
Giants moved to Coogan's Hollow, on Eighth Avenue from
155th to 157th Streets. The hollow, looking like a giant excava-
tion, was all that remained of a farm granted by the British
Crown in the seventeenth century to John Lion Gardiner,
whose descendants live still on Gardiners Island.

One of John Gardiner's descendants, Harriet Gardiner
Lynch, married a Bowery upholsterer named James J. Coogan,
who also was to be the first borough president of Manhattan.

Coogan became a dilettante. He enjoyed holding open-air horse shows in the hollow beneath the bluff. He even considered bringing in Shakespearean actors from England to stage the Bard in the hollow. When baseball's Giants moved into the park, Coogan's Bluff field became known as the Polo Grounds.

The only football man in the front office was March, and the team he selected was largely his. Few of Mara's friends would buy a piece of the team. It might have cost only $500 to get a franchise, but it would cost thousands more to rent the Polo Grounds, pay players, buy equipment.

March hired the first Giant coach. His name was Bob Folwell, who was best known for being a professional wrestler and for being dismissed as the Navy coach because of his bad temper.

The players included, incredibly, Dr. Joseph Alexander, who practiced medicine during the week and played center on weekends. Jim Thorpe also was hired on a special deal. Thorpe was thirty-seven years old and hard used. He really could not play a full game. So he was signed to play half-games. His salary was $250 for each performance. If he would be able to play a whole game, he would be paid $500. The players, for the most part, held full-time jobs. How could they practice for the season at 10 A.M? The problem was solved by starting workouts at 4:30 P.M.

The first game of the New York Giants was staged in Providence, following an all-night boat ride aboard a cargo ship that listed badly the entire voyage.

Then the Giants came home to their first game at the Polo Grounds. Mara was beginning to have his doubts, as were the few friends who had invested with him, most of them fellow gamblers. It looked as if this operation would require about $40,000. How to get the people in? First, Mara gave away 5,000 free tickets. Perhaps if they showed up, even for free, they might want to pay to see the product again. Perhaps. And then he priced the tickets even cheaper than the colleges were charging. The four ticket prices were 50¢, $1.10, $2.20, and $2.75.

There were 25,000 people on hand in the Polo Grounds for the Giants' debut. On the bench, T. J. Mara sat with his nine-year-old boy, Wellington. Meanwhile, seventeen-year-old John Mara handled the yard markers.

The Giants' bench was on the shady side of the field for the first and only time. Wellington's mother asked that the team switch to the other side so that her little boy could get some sunshine. Dr. March did not get any sun, either, that first day. He was arrested by police after a minister swore out a complaint against playing football on the Lord's Day.

Thorpe hardly earned his half pay. His leg was braced and he could not even last the thirty minutes his contract called for. He did pick up a few yards on the Giants' first play from scrimmage ("Now, isn't that the greatest run you ever saw?" T. J. Mara asked his coach), but limped off in the second quarter.

Thorpe's knees symbolized the Giants' underpinnings: shaky. If it were not for Red Grange, who never wore a Giants' uniform, it is likely that Gifford, Tittle, Robustelli, Huff, and all the others who followed never would have. The Giants simply would not have existed. But Grange's appearance in an exhibition game at the Polo Grounds (he was a one-man barnstorming operation, picking up players to complement him in different cities) attracted more than 70,000 people, who somehow were shoehorned into the Polo Grounds. As the co-promoter, Mara made enough money to wipe out his Giants' losses. Grange had finished college only a few months before, but he had become a legend, one of the 1920s larger-than-life heroes alongside Babe Ruth, Bill Tilden, and Jack Dempsey.

Blissfully unaware of the Great White Way, Steve Owen, a man of unheroic proportions, had found himself a pro football player. He had become fascinated with the intricacies of how an "X" on a blackboard became a human being on the field, and how that "X" could really be taken out by the man who was an "O." The chalk sprung to life on the gridiron. And since he was getting $50 a game to play for pickup teams in the early 1920s, and since he enjoyed football more than working the oil fields and being covered with a slimy film that never came off, Owen decided to see how far football could take him.

He once described a blind-side hit by Thorpe in a barnstorming game in 1922 as "firing my imagination." In 1924, Owen made it to the NFL by joining the Kansas City Cowboys. It took him three days by jalopy to drive from Enid, Oklahoma, to Kansas City 300 hard miles away over unpaved roads.

He didn't make it to New York until 1925. Naturally, people in the big city expected a team named the Cowboys to have real-life cowboys. For all their reputed sophistication, New Yorkers have always been pushovers for the outrageous lie, or fib, at any rate. (So in 1926, when the New York Rangers hockey team was created, the child of Tex Rickard and thus Tex's Rangers, a smart publicity man actually sold the public on the fact that many of these players were descendants of the Texas Rangers.)

In any event, when Owen and the Kansas City Cowboys hit town in 1925, the first thing they did was head for a theatrical costumer, who provided the sixteen or so players with chaps, Stetsons, vests, boots, and spurs. The players dressed in Mara's office in Times Square.

Dressing in cramped quarters was not unusual in the National Football League's early days. Most players did not even change after a game until they got back to their hotel. The memory of years of playing and years of walking around in mud-caked, sweat-soaked uniforms became indelibly impressed on Owen. He was always to abhor poor dressing facilities afterward. He had always found it embarrassing to clomp back into a hotel lobby with his filthy uniform clinging to him, and walk past the stares of hotel guests. Once, he overheard one old woman tell another, "It's a shame these fine looking young men never got an education." When he was to become a coach, he insisted that the floors and walls be scrubbed sparkling clean.

After the 1925 season, Dr. March asked Owen to play for the Giants in an exhibition game in Palm Beach, Florida. The game was in a sense an interview for Owen. March and Mara wanted to get to know Owen better. They liked his jovial, straightforward manner. And the next year, 1926, they bought

him from the Cowboys for $500. The price, Owen said later,
"was staggering for those times." Yet, he could recall fatted
hogs bringing more in Kansas City.

Pro football was not a profession to the pioneers. They
did not devote all their energies to playing a game on Sundays. Between games their time was mostly their own. Their
off-season time was spent in serious work, and for many,
serious eating and drinking. Even while he ran the Giants as
sort of a general manager, Dr. March referred to the sport as
postgraduate football. His players took it about as seriously.

Even after joining the New Yorkers, Owen barnstormed
about the country. During one springtime he got involved in a
fabulous cross-country foot race called the Bunion Derby. His
job was to start the runners each morning at about five o'clock,
usually with a shot from a pistol borrowed from the sheriff of
whatever town they happened to be in. Many Giants worked
as marshals or starters or cooks on this zany trip that took
eighty days after starting in Los Angeles and winding up in
Madison Square Garden. The winner was an Oklahoma Indian
who captured a $25,000 prize and became a court clerk back
home.

But the event did not make any money for the promoter, the
fabulous C. C. Pyle. He was probably the first players' agent,
an occupation which made him the instant *bête-noire* of every
owner. The initials "C. C.," they said, stood for "Cash and
Carry." His greatest coup was plucking Grange off the campus
just after his final football season ended, and making Grange
virtually a millionaire within a few months. It was Pyle who
talked Mara into staging the Grange game at the Polo Grounds.

After Pyle's Bunion Derby drowned, Pyle rose from the sea
of red ink like Poseidon. He decided that if the marathon
would not make any money going from west to east, well,
maybe it would make money going from east to west. So he
got Owen back again the next year, along with a bunch of
other football players, and started out from the Astor Hotel.
It was another fiasco. Yet, the winner got paid. He went back
to his hometown of Passaic, New Jersey, where he resumed his
job as a policeman. He was killed at a sandlot baseball game.

A line drive hit him in the back of his head as he attempted to keep the crowd off the foul line.

The Giants have had a natural distrust of the flashy promoter since Pyle's day. For Pyle, unable to bring a National Football League team to New York, organized the American Football League in 1926, only thirty-four years too soon. He set up a team called the New York Yankees, and they played in Yankee Stadium. History forgets events like that. When it is repeated in sports, it becomes a "first." Unfortunately for Pyle, his American Football League had the name, but none of the success, of the league that was to follow within two generations. In fact, his AFL was more spiritually aligned with the World Football League. He raided the Giants and relieved them of Coach Folwell, who jumped. Then he induced one of the fabled Four Horsemen of Notre Dame—Harry Stuhldreher—to play. Even with Stuhldreher as a drawing card in the backfield, poor Cash and Carry was doomed. It rained five of the seven Sundays the Yankees took the field (just as it did when the New York Stars of the WFL were created).

The old Yankees died within two months. Still, C. C. had developed yet another tradition, one that was to imbed itself somewhere in the back of the Mara family's collective psyche. For when Pyle formed another league, he also started a bidding war for players. Salaries tripled and quadrupled, and the long-term contract was born. The Maras also remembered who had remained loyal.

To replace Folwell as coach, Mara hired Dr. Alexander. But Alexander really did not have enough time to practice medicine and football and to find someone to cover for him on Sundays. Also, there was a near revolt by players. Their coach was never around. Dr. Alexander only lasted for the 1926 season, and for the next two seasons Earl Potteiger was the coach. After a bad season in 1928, Dr. March went around looking for a new coach and new players. The best player available was Benny Friedman, the former Michigan quarterback, who was considered the game's smartest player. Friedman was playing for the Detroit Wolverines and he refused

Dr. March's offer to come to New York. But he enjoyed playing for his coach, LeRoy Andrews. So Dr. March enticed
Andrews to come to New York as coach. Friedman followed.
And Andrews pocketed a $1,000 bonus from New York for
getting Friedman to join him. Andrews stayed around for one
and a half seasons. His propensity for taking a piece of his
players' action did him in.

Friedman complained to T. J. Mara about Andrews' temper.
Mara was not enchanted with Andrews anyway, especially
after finding out that the club had lost the great Ken Strong
in a bidding war after Andrews had offered Strong only
$3,000. Mara had authorized Andrews to bid as high as $4,000.
Friedman finished out the 1930 campaign as coach.

The Giants did not know it then, but their era of solidifica-
tion was about to start. After five coaches through their first
six years, the men of Mara Tech, as the club had become
known, would be led through the Depression of the 1930s,
World War II, and the upheavals of the 1940s into the modern
era of the 1950s by the same man: stout Steve Owen.

Actually, Owen was to be only the interim coach in 1931. He
continued to split the duties with Friedman. After the 1931
campaign Mara asked Friedman to take over the club. But
Friedman wanted a piece of the team. "Benny, I'm sorry,"
replied the old man. "But this is a family business and the
Giants are for my sons." The year before, T. J. had turned
the team over to his sons. He was having some legal battles
because he had foolishly, although out of friendship, cosigned
a note for Al Smith. The note was due and Smith could not
pay. Meanwhile, Mara also was suing his old friends, Billy
Gibson and Gene Tunney, over a piece of a fighter. So T. J.
wanted to make sure that, in case he lost his suits, his assets
were not attached. He made Jack Mara, aged twenty-two, the
president of the club.

Between the off-seasons of 1931 and 1932, Owen was working
in T. J. Mara's coalyard, happy as always to be gainfully employed after the football season. Mara needed a permanent
coach after Friedman quit over not getting a percentage of
the team. Owen was stunned when Mara phoned him and said,

"I'm sick of looking for uniforms for you to fit into. You're our coach." And he was—until 1953.

There were only six losing seasons in the twenty-three campaigns that Owen led the Giants. There were eight championship-game appearances and two National Football League titles. There were the "forever" stars: Mel Hein, the redoubtable center who played that curious position through all of Roosevelt's presidency; there was Strong, who returned as a Giant and played Mr. Everything; and there was Emlen Tunnell, the first player inducted into the Pro Football Hall of Fame purely for his defensive status.

And leading up to the modern era, there was a host of the comic and the absurd, the events that people swore they saw but probably only read about. Yet, the event had been recorded and discussed so often, that memory blurred proximity—were we there or did we only read about it?

Under the Owen reign, the Giants established themselves as a force almost immediately. Once a team becomes known as a dynasty, it remains locked in that high plateau in one's thinking. Thus, it still surprises some people when Green Bay muddles through a losing season. And baseball fans still think it strange that the Yankees have not won five-straight World Series lately.

The Giants played in the league's first championship playoff, losing to the Chicago Bears in 1933, the first year there was a realignment into Eastern and Western Divisions. The next year the Giants put the phrase "sneaker game" into football's vocabulary. The game was on December 9, 1934, and it concluded an interesting week.

A few days earlier at Ebbets Field, 18,000 fans showed up to see Madison High School halt Theodore Roosevelt High, 12–0. The star of the game was the speedy Marty Glickman, whose 53-yard touchdown run clinched the victory for Madison. Glickman would spend much of his professional life as the voice of the Giants, broadcasting their games over radio.

While Glickman was dashing around Brooklyn, Alf Letourner was getting ready for a six-day bike race at the Garden; ex-Governor Al Smith was warning a dinner that "lack of

religion'' was the reason so many teenagers were committing
murder on the city's streets; Babe Ruth hit three American-
sized homers in Shanghai as his Yankees defeated a Chinese
all-star team, 22–1.

The 1934 championship again pitted the Bears against the
Giants. Apparently, New Yorkers had other things on their
mind. By Thursday morning, only half the place was sold. Perhaps the stiff price of $3.30 for a box seat and $1.10 for
bleachers turned people away, or perhaps it was the weather.

Game day broke cold and gray. It was eleven degrees in
New York, but almost 40,000 people turned out. They saw the
Giants play badly, sliding over the frozen dirt and trailing by
13–3 at half time. The New Yorkers clomped up the steps of
the locker room at the Polo Grounds, a dispirited bunch made
more miserable by the booing of the fans, who were practically
within whispering distance. The Polo Grounds was not a place
for sensitive-eared ballplayers. The fans were closer, spiritually and physically, to the Giants' players here than any place
else.

The Giants' captain, Ray Flaherty, recalled that when he
had played for Gonzaga in 1925 the team used sneakers in a
game on a frozen field against the University of Montana.
Why not use sneakers here? Sunday in New York. Where to
get a few dozen sneakers, big sneakers? Enter Abie Cohen,
another part of the "sneaker game" legend. Cohen was a
tailor, but he was also a basketball buff and served as the
locker-room attendant at Manhattan College, where he was
also in charge of sewing torn uniforms. Unfortunately, Cohen
never received a key to the locker room. He and some friends
broke into the lockers, scooped up nine pairs of sneakers, and
headed back to the Polo Grounds. They arrived just as the
half-time break was ending. As he watched the Giants pad
down the steps to the field, George Halas, the Papa Bear himself, is supposed to have told the Bears, "Step on the Giants'
toes." But the cold hurt Strong more than the Bears did.
When he kicked off for the second half, he lost the toenail of
his big right toe. The Giants went on to win, of course, by
scoring 27 points in the last quarter.

It was a result sure to be appreciated by an interested spectator at the game, Casey Stengel, manager of the Brooklyn Dodgers. Another who was interested was the Manhattan basketball coach, Neil Cohalan, who was told about the sneakers stolen from his locker room later that day.

"I'm glad the basketball shoes did the Giants some good," he said. "The question now is, did the Giants do our basketball shoes any good?"

Through the 1930s, the New Yorkers' attendance picked up each year. The acquisition of better players helped, of course, and the man who discovered many "hidden" collegians was none other than Wellington Mara. He was still a teenager when he induced collegians older than he was to sign with the Giants. He read, digested, and synthesized and finally knew more about the college scene than any other person in professional football. He was so astute that other owners often asked him for advice. Indeed, in 1939, only two years after he graduated from Fordham University, he drew up a master list of 300 collegians for the league to consider. In his wisdom, he kept a fullback from Arizona off the list. The Giants drafted the back first.

Wellington's precocity led to his nickname of the Duke of Mara. In his honor, the name "The Duke" was inscribed on National Football League's official ball for many years, until the big merger.

Ideas tumbled out of Mara's head. He received a movie camera for a Christmas present in 1935, and the next year the Giants began studying movies of themselves, thanks to Wellington Mara, who had become the official cameraman. Years later, when the Polaroid Land camera had been invented, Mara attached a longer lens to the contraption and shot pictures from the press box of alignments during the game. Sixty seconds later the finished picture was wrapped in a weighted sock and tossed onto the field. An assistant picked it up and showed it to Owen.

The post-World War II years were slow ones for Owen and

the Giants, who played through indifferent seasons. But the team survived its only betting scandal in 1946. It also survived the temporary invasion of two teams from a new league, the All American Football Conference. The AAC placed teams in Brooklyn (called the Dodgers, of course) and in Yankee Stadium (known as the Yankees).

The Giants' star in 1946 was Frank Filchock, an old-fashioned run-and-pass threat. He helped turn around the losing season of the year before, and the New Yorkers reached the title game with the Bears. The week of the game, Owen announced that Filchock had been playing with a sore arm all season, a revelation which made all the more remarkable his accomplishment as the club's leading rusher and passer. A few days before the game, Mayor William O'Dwyer launched a massive drive against corruption in the New York Police Department. The city was waiting for new scandals to unravel, and many citizens wondered whether any area of the city's life had escaped tainting.

At least the sports fans' minds would be taken off evil doings. The post-war boom had elevated the Giants' attendance to such a degree that crowds often approached 50,000. In 1946, though, the greatest attendance in football was not recognized by anyone from the Establishment. It belonged to the Cleveland Browns, one of the AAC upstarts, which averaged 57,000 people a game. One of the Browns' heroes was Otto Graham, a quarterback whom the team paid $250 a month while he was in the army so he wouldn't sign with the NFL. There was also Marion Motley, the all-around fullback. And there was Paul Brown, the big name in Ohio coaching, whose Massillon High teams were 80–8, whose Ohio State teams were 18–8, and who led the Great Lakes Naval Training Center teams to a 15–5 mark during the war.

Some people thought that the Browns, in their first year of operation, were the equal of any NFL team. The Browns posted a 12–2 mark while outscoring the opposition by more than 3–1 as they led the new league in offense and defense. Remarkable. But unrecognized.

The Maras and Owen were thinking only about Sunday, De-

cember 14, and the championship against the Bears. But on
Saturday, Mayor O'Dwyer called his old friend, T. J. Mara,
and told him to get to City Hall. It was there that Mara learned
that Filchock and Merle Hapes, another Giant, were being in-
vestigated for not reporting a bribe offer from a gambler
named Alvin J. Paris. Paris was a heavy bettor who spent
much of his time in his florist shop on the telephone with
bookies.

Some bookie friends of Paris' from New Jersey asked
Paris to act as a go-between and offer Filchock and Hapes
$2,500 apiece, plus a $1,000 bet each, plus an off-season job.
The players simply had to make sure the Giants lost by more
than the 10 points the Bears were favored by. Paris had gotten
close to the pair by working his way into their confidence, by
taking them to nightclubs and parties. Paris' friendship with
the pair might have gone unnoticed if it were not for his dealings with a Jersey bookie named Moish. The police tapped
Paris' phone, and wound up with a collection of recordings
they called the ''Al and Moish tapes.''

The night before the game, Filchock was on a radio show
receiving an award as the Giants' most valuable player. He
was told to leave the station and go to the mayor's. There, he
met T. J. Mara, who was joined by Wellington and Jack, and
Owen. Filchock and Hapes did not have a lawyer with them,
of course. Paris had one, a partner in the firm that had de-
fended Lucky Luciano.

In true police fashion, the suspects were separated, Hapes
in one room of Gracie Mansion, Filchock in the other, neither
knowing that the other was nearby. The mayor made repeated
trips from one room to the next attempting to get a confes-
sion, or at least some understanding of what had taken place.
Finally, Hapes admitted the bribe offer. Bert Bell, the NFL
commissioner whose first year had been busy with a rival
league, now faced the threat of scandal. He acted quickly by
suspending Hapes. Since Filchock's involvement was not so
clear-cut (Filchock did not admit to receiving an offer), Bell
permitted Filchock to play in the championship.

If fate had been more historical minded, it might have

permitted Filchock to lead his team to a startling upset. As it
was, he played brilliantly considering the circumstances. He
did not leave the mayor's office until three o'clock in the
morning. He showed up at the Polo Grounds less than seven
hours later. Before the game, Father Dudley delivered his
usual pregame prayer. Father Dudley was the ''offensive''
priest. Whenever another priest would tag along with the
team, he would be dubbed the ''defensive'' priest.

''You will see one of our boys is missing,'' Father Dudley
told the players. ''He is Merle Hapes, at the moment, under a
cloud. No matter what happens, I know you will go out and
play the game for all it is worth.''

In the first quarter, Filchock's nose was broken. Still, he
played fifty minutes and threw for both New York touchdowns.
The Bears won, 24–14. Ironically, all bets were off since the
ten points were the amount the Bears were favored. No one
won a bet. Filchock lost, though. After the game, Bell suspended him, too.

The Giants slumped to their worst season the next year, but
they rubbed their hands in anticipation of 1948, when they
would try to make a deal for Charley Conerly, a Marine veteran hurling himself into the record books at Ole Miss, as the
headline writers liked to refer to the University of Mississippi.

With Conerly's arrival in 1948, the beginning of the end of
the Steve Owen era was underway. For football had started to
change. The T-formation was becoming the most popular form
of attack. In this newfangled setup, the quarterback stood directly over the center and received the ball from him. It was a
game designed for passing, a game in which Owen was uncomfortable.

Over the next few years, Owen selected the personnel that
was to take over the club and to move it into the modern post-
war era. Ironically, he brought along the seeds for the new
flowering himself.

In 1954 an advertisement promised you could find uranium in your backyard with a mail-order gadget. You could see *The Solid Gold Cadillac* on Broadway; improve your mind with *The Power of Positive Thinking;* laugh to Martin and Lewis in *Living It Up* at the Criterion; marvel at Ted Atkinson riding his 3,000th winner.

You could also become a TV star on "So You Want to Lead a Band"; see Bobby Riggs play in the Eastern States Professional Tennis Championships; chuckle that the woman sports editor of *The Cornell Sun* was granted a seat in the Yale Bowl press box; wonder whether that light-heavyweight from Bedford-Stuyvesant, Floyd Patterson, would make it; nod in agreement when the vice president of the baseball Giants, Charles "Chub" Feeney, contended, "I can think of nothing more ridiculous than the rumor that the Giants will go to San Francisco."

You could also celebrate with Lou Little his twenty-fifth anniversary as football coach at Columbia; stay up late with a new show called "Tonight," with Steve Allen; bite your nails after The Mad Bomber injured four people at Radio City Music Hall as they watched *White Christmas;* think how absurd that charge was against Aristotle Onassis, who supposedly made a Saudi Arabian deal signed in disappearing

ink; become curious about an eighteen-year-old pitcher at the
University of Cincinnati, Sandy Koufax of Brooklyn, who was
signed by the Dodgers.

The 1953 season was over. It showed only 3 victories and
9 defeats. In those 12 games the Giants scored only 179 points,
the fewest in the 12-team league. It was a league in which some
profound changes had taken place, with the Cleveland Browns
admitted to membership from the hated AAC and establishing
themselves as the class.

It was the end of another season for Jim Lee Howell, the
club's 6-foot 4-inch, 220-pound end coach. Another season
ending; another one beginning. This one back home at Lonoke,
Arkansas. He worked his father's rice farm and his cattle
farm, and he had been doing that most of his life.

He would work the farm, as always, then report back to
New York for the summer of 1954 and tutor the Giants' ends
in the proper way to catch a football. When college began, he
would also coach Wagner College over on Staten Island. It
was a simple, uncomplicated life. Howell was a simple, uncomplicated man.

Even today he laughs easily at himself as he describes his
job title. He sits in one of the many rooms at the Giants' office.
To his left a wall is filled with names of collegians, the current
crop. He does not appear overworked.

"I'm supposed to be the director of player personnel," he
says. "That's supposed to be college and pro. But specialization has set in now and it's just college. I don't like to travel,
though. The regular scouts are out six days a week. Me? I go
out once a week."

Howell would probably be the first to tell you that his job
is for long and meritorious service, sort of a gold watch
souvenir of a company. Except that in this case the company
still pays.

Howell has no trouble remembering his years as a coach
with the Giants or his years as a player. One has the feeling
that he has fun in recollecting them. He enjoys chuckling at

his private jokes or the absurdities of some of the people he played with and coached. And he is fond of insisting, as he has since 1954, "All I did was pump up footballs."

He begins:

"You know, I never thought I'd get the Giants' job. I had been with the club for some time, playing end for them, then coaching the ends. I was the first end coach they ever had. Before the war, they didn't specialize in coaches. One coach taught everybody everything.

"Well, the 1953 season was over, and I packed my bags and gave up my lease. I was clearing out to get back to Arkansas when the Maras called me and told me to come to the office. I told them I was getting ready to go back home, and unless it was very important. . . . They said I'd better come over.

"So I told my wife to wait outside the office and I'd be right down. When I got in, they said sit down, and then told me they wanted me to be the coach. And I was flabbergasted. I thought they'd go with some big name or someone with head coaching experience.

"My roots were in Arkansas, and I didn't know about coaching here. I remember when I was clearing out my locker after the last game, and we all knew Steve wasn't coming back, someone asked me whether I'd return and I told them I didn't know—unless it was some coach I could work with.

"I was delighted to take the job. But first I went up to see Steve. Steve Owen. He thought people were always trying to get his job. I wanted him to understand I hadn't gone looking for it. And he said, 'Sure, go ahead and take it. But you might get some surprises one day like I just did.'"

Being named coach was about the biggest surprise Howell ever got. He was an unknown to some players and to many writers who traveled with the club. He had no credentials of success. Some people, in fact, were unhappy with his selection. They wanted the innovative Allie Sherman to take over or perhaps Tom Landry, the introspective defensive genius.

There was the beginning of substance on the team. There were Kyle Rote and Frank Gifford, the college Golden Boys of 1951 and 1952 now having to adjust their styles to the

demands of the pros; there was Conerly, a commanding figure
who had been molded into a T-quarterback by Sherman; there
was Landry, the last remaining gift from the defunct Yankees
of the AAC, which included Arnie Weinmeister, Harmon
Rowe, and Otto Schnellbacher. There was Emlen Tunnell.

Sherman left when Howell got the job. Howell had to find
a new man to run the offense.

"I knew about Vince Lombardi," says Howell, with none of
the reverence that a generation of coaches and players would
surround him with. "He came down to see me on the farm.
He was a sort of up and down person, high and low, very
brilliant, very smart. Vince knew what he could do with players.
He was very basic in his thinking. He was just a fine coach.

"He was older by this time, you know. He'd been kicking
around. But he had all the confidence in the world. What would
he get low about? Mostly, he thought he should have been
somewhere else. He should have been a head coach somewhere,
but he wasn't. He wasn't even a college head coach. He was low
about Red Blaik's boy getting caught in the cribbing scandals
at West Point. Vince was the assistant coach at West Point.
But he had always wanted to be the head coach of Notre Dame.
Then he wanted to be the head coach at Fordham—that's
where he played and was one of the Seven Blocks of Granite—
but that job went down, too. Whenever a head coaching job
came up anywhere, Vince was always asking about it. He
always wanted to be the head coach.

"Once in Texas I made a speech somewhere, and Vinnie was
there and he asked me how come I didn't mention who the
offensive coach was. He was always writing letters around the
country asking for a head coach's job. I don't know how many
letters I wrote for him. I was always trying to help him get
a job."

Howell's other key choice was to retain Landry as a defensive back—but also to use him as defensive coach.

"Landry was brilliant, very, very smart," recalls Howell.
"He could size up a situation very quickly and get it right.
Him and Lombardi could get to the bottom of it right quick.
If this went wrong, then he'd do this. Landry on defense was

very basic. He could do something in thirty minutes that would take me an hour and a half.

"I was never jealous of Tom and Vinnie. Not ever. I remember my first year at Arkansas as an assistant coach, and that the head guy always had his way. At Arkansas the head guy said to me, 'When I'm talking don't you open your mouth.' Some of these head coaches think they're like god, that they're the only ones who know anything. And I said to myself that if I ever got to be head coach the one thing I wouldn't want, wouldn't do, was that. If I had assistants I'd want them to run their departments. I want their ideas; I want the benefits of their experience—not just me calling all the shots."

Howell used to brag around the league that he had "the two smartest assistant coaches in football." He oversaw Lombardi, "who shouted, screamed, kicked, ranted, jumped up and down. But he knew how far he could go."

And he watched over Landry, "who never raised his voice. He would just sit there and burn inside. He'd tell his players what to do and one would say, 'Well, what are you gonna do if they try this?' And Tom would say very quietly, 'Well, we'll just take care of it.' Tom had this smile with him all the time."

It was a nice feeling for Howell to know that he would begin coaching a club that had Lombardi in charge of the offense and Landry heading the defense. Despite his rosy feeling, he was wondering about Conerly.

Conerly would be thirty-three years old for the 1954 season, although he was listed as two years younger. He probably felt two years older than his true age. He told Howell he would not return for the 1954 season, that he was "tired of getting hit."

"I tracked him down, and I caught him in Missouri or Iowa, something like that," relates Howell. "He was putting out fertilizer on his farm, you know wearing those high rubber farm boots. And I asked him about coming back, and he told me he didn't want to be hurt anymore. I told him I'd get him protection, and he said, 'That's all I want to know.'"

So Conerly would be coming back. Once again he would face the fans, to whom he had been the symbol of the Giants' failure. As the quarterback, he was the most visible man on the offense. And because he was unemotional, because the only gesture he ever made after being tackled on third down was to toss the ball back over his shoulder to the official, it appeared from the stands he didn't care.

He cared. The night before a game he took a tranquilizer. After a game, after he painfully removed his gear and steeled himself for the inevitable post-loss questions, he would answer ''Yep'' or ''Nope'' and never make much of the thrashing he took.

Since he took over as quarterback he had waited in vain every year for offensive linemen to protect him. Each January he and his wife, Perian, would search the papers after the college draft to see which guards the Giants had drafted. Each season a new young quarterback would come along, groomed to replace the old man. And each one was put down by Conerly. As a rookie in 1948 he beat out Paul Governali of Columbia. Two years later, in 1950, Travis Tidwell of Auburn came along. In 1952 it was Fred Benners of SMU, and the next year it was Arnold Galiffa of Army.

Well, that was okay, too. No one ever said it would be easy. Certainly not in Clarksdale, Mississippi, where Conerly was born in 1921 and where his nose was broken for the first time in high school. He had started to make a name for himself at the university, but he was soon in the Marines. On Guam, his rifle was shot out of his hand by a sniper. But while he was on Guam, he learned the Washington Redskins had drafted him. He decided to return to school and became the country's top passer.

He was, in fact, one of those larger-than-life college heroes that the two-platoon system and the era of specialization has done away with. In 1947 he set NCAA records by hurling 133 completions in 233 attempts for 18 touchdowns and 1,367 yards. He also carried 104 times, averaging 4 yards a run. He scored 9 touchdowns. And he was eleventh nationally in punting with a 40.1-yard average.

The trouble was Washington did not know what to do with him. The Redskins had Sammy Baugh, the quarterback, and a promising youngster named Harry Gilmer. Despite how

Conerly's age read in the record books, the Redskins knew that he'd be a twenty-seven-year-old rookie. So they traded him to the Giants.

He had a great rookie year. In some ways he never matched his success of that first season, even though he played until 1961 and retired as the league's oldest player. In that first year Conerly had to switch from the old A-formation to the T, mostly because the Giants were not gifted with a great center after Mel Hein's retirement. The "A" required more from a center than the new "T" did. Yet, Conerly wound up with a 54.2 percent passing average, picking up 2,175 yards. The 22 touchdowns he threw were five more than he ever tossed in the thirteen seasons to follow. He was intercepted only 13 times in 299 throws.

Although 1948 was still part of the era of the relatively unsophisticated attack, in which the pass was not yet the ultimate offensive weapon it became for the Cleveland Browns, the Giants scored 297 points that season. They were not to score that many points again until 1961, when Allie Sherman returned as head coach after Howell retired. In other words, Conerly played through all the 1950s with an offense that could never generate the points it had in a simpler era. Little wonder that the Giants' defense became better known than the offense.

In 1949, Owen had brought in little Allie Sherman, a football oddity, as his man to install the T-formation for keeps. Sherman had impressed people around the league with his knowledge of quarterbacking, even though he had never progressed beyond the second string in Philadelphia. Sherman approached Conerly one day in training camp and interrupted his reading a Western paperback.

"Charlie, we're going to make a T-quarterback out of you," said Sherman. "I know this is a big step for you."

"Okay," replied Charlie. "Whenever you're ready to start."

Howell also was blessed with Kyle Rote, a pulp writer's hero in the flesh. If, at latest count, 654,000 people swear they saw

Babe Ruth point to his home run, and if 6 million people were
at the Polo Grounds the day Bobby Thomson's ninth-inning
homer won the pennant for the Giants over the Dodgers, then
all of Texas saw Kyle Rote step in for Doak Walker and
almost upset Notre Dame.

Until that day in 1949, Rote had been a Texas hero, which
is a big enough aspiration. But ever afterward, he became a
national figure. Notre Dame was a 27-point favorite. Southern
Methodist's great senior back, Doak Walker, was out with an
injury. His place would be taken by Rote, a junior. And by
half time there was nothing to suggest the bookies had been
wrong in their picking, since the Irish led 13–0.

Then Rote got hot. In the third quarter SMU drove 71
yards, all but 18 figured in by Kyle. At the end of the third
quarter Notre Dame led by 20–7. Soon after the final quarter
began, Rote scored and the score was 20–14. Then another
drive and again Rote scored. Notre Dame pulled the game out
to win 27–20, but what Rote had accomplished made people
marvel. He had run for 115 yards on 24 carries; he had passed
for 146 yards by completing 10 of 24 attempts; he had caught
one pass for 15 yards; he had scored the three SMU touchdowns; he had punted 5 times for a 48-yard average.

There is the same athletic quality now, more than a quarter
of a century later, as he glides into the lobby of his East Side
apartment house. When he opens the door to his apartment,
he says, "Welcome to my bachelor quarters."

He clears a desk, which is the size of an airplane wing, of
its pile of cigarettes, golf tees, and papers. Cigarette butts are
everywhere, next to stacks of papers and unopened mail. Yet
when he speaks there is an orderly progression of ideas, and
he very carefully explains that he wants the listener to understand and to get the facts straight.

"That game, that was the first time anyone outside of Texas
had ever heard of us," he began, using "us" instead of "me."

"In training camp as a rookie in 1951, I tore the cartilage in
my knee. In those years it wasn't like it is today. If a guy gets
a knee injury today, they take him immediately to the hospital

while the muscle is still warm and supple. And they get better results.

"But then, if you had a knee injury you would rest up for a few weeks—you know, salts, hot water, massage, exercise—until you could play again. You'd play until it went out again on you. Then you'd rest again, then play again, then it would go again. So I had the knee operated on after the rookie season. Then in 1952 it was a question of playing on a knee that had just been operated on. In 1953 I got my other knee banged up. And again they didn't operate. So I sort of hobbled through 1953.

"In 1954 Tom Landry was our defensive coach, as well as our cornerback, a respected member of what we called our umbrella defense. I'd run patterns against Tom from my position of flanker. A yard back of the line of scrimmage. You'd be out to what they call wide receiver today. Basically I was a halfback. If they said formation right, the right halfback would go there. After running some patterns against Tom he said, 'Hey, why don't you become an end?' He knew I couldn't run out of the backfield any more because of my knees. I just couldn't do it. And it was the biggest break of my career."

Of course, Rote wouldn't say it, but his was a career of might-have-been. Still, his name and reputation persist. What he accomplished was outstanding no matter what standards are employed.

When he was a senior in high school, he was as well-known in the southwest as any athlete of his time. When Vanderbilt, in Tennessee, was getting close to convincing him to attend, Governor Beauford Jester of Texas wrote a note to young Kyle, telling him not to attend Vanderbilt and closing with, "No young man of your possibilities should sell Texas short."

There was the aura of excitement and of Texas tradition in the handsome, sandy-haired Rote. Why, his grandfather was John W. "El Colorado" Smith, who escaped from the Alamo in 1836 with the message to the world, "God and Texas, victory or death." So Vanderbilt knew it would have a heck

of a time spiriting that boy out of Texas. He was the personal
responsibility of Tommy Prothro, assistant coach to Red
Sanders. In virtually all big-time colleges, one of the assistant
coaches is in charge of doing the personal recruiting.

Sanders flew Rote to Nashville in a private plane. Along the
way they met some famous Vandy alumni, such as the mayor
of Dallas and the lieutenant-governor of Arkansas. Another
time Sanders stayed in Rote's house for eight days with the
boy's "foster parents." They took care of Kyle while his
father worked. His mother had died when he was a child.

Rote enrolled in Vanderbilt in the summer, but he missed
his girl friend, Betty Jamison. He decided to go to SMU, to
the delight of the governor of Texas and the rest of the state.
There was no question that in 1951, when he graduated, he
would be the top draft choice of the National Football League.

How could the Giants possibly get him? In 1950 their 10–2
record tied the Cleveland Browns for the best mark in the
league. The Giants would pick next to last in the draft. In
those years, though, the league had a gimmick which spiced up
the draft, and which gave any team a chance at whomever they
wanted. It was called the bonus pick. This selection was made
out of a hat. Whichever team picked the card with the word
"bonus" on it would get the first choice.

"Let's change our luck," Wellington Mara said at the
draft ceremonies. "Let's have Steve put his hand in the hat."
Owen did, and he plucked out the bonus selection. Without
even taking a breath he blurted out "Kyle Rote." The Baltimore Colts, who had a 1–11 record then went. As the worst
team they had the choice of any player in the country—after
the bonus pick. They chose a quarterback from Louisiana
State with the silly name of Y. A. Tittle.

"When Howell took over in 1954," recalls Rote, "we
started to have separate offensive and defensive meetings.
This was the first time anything like this had happened. Before, we all met in one big room. But the offense and defense
became separate, definitive units under Jim Lee. We used to

say that the reason separate meetings were held was because we didn't want to discourage the defense by making them watch films of the offense. Our defensive unit was just great, and most of it was built around trades—Andy Robustelli, Modzelewski, Svare, Svoboda.''

What about Lombardi, that powerful, driving force with the alligator teeth? The man who was to make his Green Bay players practice without gloves when the temperature dipped below zero? The man who never wavered, whose confidence was supreme? The man who became a synonym for winning?

''When Vinnie first came to the Giants, he was very careful. In 1954 I was going into my fourth year, Conerly into his seventh, Gifford into his third. Vinnie didn't assert himself too much. He wasn't sure what he knew about football was enough for pro football. He was going to wait and see. And as time went by he learned that what he knew was sufficient. It was more than adequate.

''But at first Vinnie found that most of the players had been there for a number of years before he arrived. He was deferential toward us. Now, Charlie Conerly, he tried to get away from exhibitions. Most of the veterans hated exhibitions. Vince would start us, then put in the second offensive unit in the exhibitions, and then he would say to us, 'Are you ready to go back in?' He would ask us instead of tell us. And we would say, 'Not quite, Vince, not quite.' We had told Vinnie that we were concentrating on watching a new cornerback or safety, but it's no great trick to run a pattern on a new man. We knew that. Finally, when we figured we used up as much time on the bench as we could in good conscience, we'd tell Vinnie we were ready to go back in.

''So we'd run a pass pattern against the rookie, the one we said we were 'watching.' And uncannily we must have hit on seventy or eighty percent of our attempts, either a TD or a long gain, and Vince must have thought, gee, these guys really know what they're doing. As he stayed around us more and more, and around the pro game more and more, the mystique wasn't quite what he imagined it to be. He realized what we were doing. Finally, instead of asking us how much we'd

like to play in preseason, he said to us for the first time,
'You're going to play the whole first half and a little of the
second half.' And we realized he'd caught up with us.''

As Lombardi's confidence grew he would take a firmer stand
on such simple matters as his ''chalk talks,'' the blackboard
plays. His dynamism began to show, began to surround the
offense which, curiously, was not to lead the league in scoring
until 1963.

''The fact that we weren't as good as our defense created
a bond between Lombardi and the offense that might not have
existed otherwise,'' says Rote. ''He was so dynamic that he
made you feel that you had a hell of a unit. Yet, we really did
have a great defensive unit. It won most of the games for us,
and it bailed us out of trouble most of the time. We'd cough up
the ball, lose it after not gaining much yardage, and the
defense would get it back for us.''

Lombardi was barking his orders by the time the season
started. ''He'd draw a *zero*,'' says Rote, punctuating the word
and making a punching, circular motion, ''with strength. And
he'd make his *exxes*. He drew his zeros and exxes like he
hoped that's where everybody was. At first he hoped. And
then, when he knew where everybody was, when they really
were in those places on the field, his *X*'s and *O*'s would be
more definite. His voice had a booming quality in the locker
room, and when he made a point, you knew he'd made a point.''

If you were a New Yorker and a Giants' fan, you would be
very optimistic about this new season, even though the club
had posted only a 3–9 mark the year before. The promise that
Howell had made to Conerly, that he would protect him, apparently was becoming true. Roosevelt Brown—6 feet 3 inches
tall, 245 pounds, and an incredible torso that triangled down
to a 32-inch waist—was coming into his own in his second
season as the right tackle on the offensive line.

Jack Stroud, a 6-foot 1-inch, 215 pounder, was also going
into his second year as a guard, and Ray Wietecha, a 6-foot

1-inch, 225 pounder, was the center. Bill Austin, also a 6-foot 1-inch, 225 pounder, was back playing guard in his second year since serving in the military. These men could push some people around.

Meanwhile, Landry was doing some experimenting on defense. The Giants had built quite a reputation as a defensive club, mainly for unveiling something called the "umbrella defense" in 1950, the year the Browns joined the league. The Browns frightened people with their talent and their record. They had lost only 4 of their 58 games in the AAC. Owen was faced with defending against the great fullback Marion Motley, as well as the accurate passing of Otto Graham (whose receivers included Mac Speedie, Dante Lavelli, and Dub Jones). A formidable task. So Owen did something that was really quite simple but at the time gave the appearance of genius. He designed a formation called the umbrella defense.

Instead of a 7-man defensive line, which was good for the rush but inadequate against the pass, he positioned his men this way:

E	T	G	G	T	E
Duncan	Weinmeister	Baker	Mastrangelo	DeRogatis	Poole

C
Cannady

H   H
Landry   Rowe

H   H
Tunnell   Schnellbacher

If you look at an imaginary line from Landry to Tunnell to Schnellbacher to Rowe you see a semicircle, the top of an umbrella. Also, the ends, Duncan and Poole, could drop back for the pass and the Giants would have a 4–1–6. Cannady, meanwhile, would key on Motley. This change shocked the Browns, and the Giants beat them twice that season—the only defeats the Browns suffered.

That umbrella had saved the Giants over the years, alright. But Landry was wondering if there might even be more drastic changes. What about a four-man line? And three men behind them? Call them linebackers. And four defensive backs. Ballplayers were changing physically. Big defensive men now could run, could move quickly "off the ball." If you could put your four strongest men on the line and back them up with stronger and quicker linebackers, then you'd have every "zone" on the field covered. And the people in each zone would be ideally suited to cover their territory.

Two rookies broke into the secondary in 1954, Dick Nolan and Herb Rich. They joined Landry and Em Tunnell, and by the season's end, the Giants had intercepted 33 passes—almost ten percent of all the passes thrown against them. Another rookie, Bill Svoboda, cracked into the linebackers' corps.

Blessed with a new defense, and a new attitude on offense, the Giants staged the greatest improvement of any club in 1954. They began their thirtieth season with a 41–10 victory over the Chicago Cardinals. Those 41 points were 11 more than the 1953 Giants had scored in the first three games. That gave the 1954 edition some immediate attention, for a change. The baseball Giants were winning the National League pennant, led by Willie Mays, who captured the city's heart by playing stickball in Harlem with kids off the street. Because the baseball team had first call on the Polo Grounds, the football Giants, as usual, were forced out of town for the beginning of the season. Their games were shown over channel 5, the local station for the Dumont TV network. The Giants were not even on the Big Three—CBS, NBC, or ABC. NBC, though, did cover the Canadian Football League on Saturdays.

A key move Howell—or more exactly, Lombardi—made in 1954 was to take the fluid Frank Gifford and make him, once and for all, a running back.

"We're through fooling around with you," Lombardi told him. "You're a back now."

Owen had not known what to do with Gifford, the handsome all-American from USC. So he had used him every place—on defense and offense. Gifford was a defensive back and an offensive back. He ran, sometimes passed, sometimes caught passes. For two years he split his skills and his talent. Then Lombardi came along and placed him in the backfield.

Gifford starred almost immediately. His average per rush was almost half a yard better than anyone else's in the conference—5.6 yards. With Conerly finally able to toss long—thanks to a rookie end from Bowling Green, Bob Schnelker—the Giants' offense actually scared some people. Another favorite receiver was Rote, who quickly established himself as the most clever pattern-runner in the game. The year before fewer than a third of Conerly's passes had gone to his ends.

His achievements included a pair of touchdown passes in the opener to Schnelker and four TD passes in a victory over the Redskins. After five games the New Yorkers sported a 4–1 mark and 161 points. That was only 18 points less than they had scored all of the previous season.

Even after losing to Cleveland in the sixth game, the Giants still sported a 4–2 record and they were tied with the Browns for first. They beat the Steelers and then the Eagles and Giants fans began turning out in capacity numbers at the Polo Grounds, which held 54,000 people.

But in the ninth game, against Los Angeles, Gifford got injured. He was out for the season, along with his remarkable rushing average. The stage was set for the tenth game, at the Polo Grounds and against the Browns. Conerly tore ligaments in his knee in the second quarter. But the Browns' Otto Graham could run, and he sneaked over for a touchdown. Lou Groza added 3 field goals, and the Browns won 16–7 and headed securely for their ninth straight divisional title in two leagues. Conerly was out for the season, and the Giants were buried.

Another would-be quarterback replacement, Bobby Clatterbuck, took over the mop-up chores for the rest of the season. He was joined by Don Heinrich, who had been the top college passer at Washington in 1950 and 1952. He had been unable to make it in the pros. He stayed with the Giants though, hanging around, and he got his chance to play for a few minutes backing up Clatterbuck. In the Giants' last game, they had a chance to retain second place over the Philadelphia Eagles. Clatterbuck did not complete a pass during the first half, going 0 for 11. The Giants' offense was minus 9 yards that half. The Giants lost and finished third, losing the $250 a man second place would have meant.

The Giants had a 7–5 record. But they had scored 293 points, which were 114 points more than in 1953. And the 184 points they yielded were 93 fewer points than in 1953. Only the Cleveland Browns gave up fewer points in the whole league. Obviously, the Giants were moving.

After his fourth season in the league, Rote finally was selected for the Pro Bowl, but not for his rushing, which was good for only a 2-yard average. He made it as a receiver. He averaged 19 yards a catch, an average that was unsurpassed in the conference. Other Giants joined Rote in the Bowl— Svoboda, Austin, Gifford, Tunnell. Five Giants on the club. The year before only Tunnell and Gifford made it. And before that, only Tunnell had been selected.

Part of the Giants' 1954 success was tied in with the mangled right foot of the kicker, Ben Agajanian, who joined the club that year at the age of thirty-five. Agajanian's kicking foot had no toes, except for the little one.

He was the Eastern Conference's only perfect extra-point kicker in 1954, though, booting 35 straight. He made good on 13 of 25 field-goal attempts at a time when most field-goal attempts failed. He was very careful about the way he kicked, as he was very careful about the way he walked, so it would not appear he was limping.

Agajanian, who had an Armenian heritage, was born in Santa Ana, California. In the back alleys, he learned to kick a tin can so that it would rise into the sides of buildings. He was captain of his high school tennis team, but because he weighed only 135 pounds—he would grow to 6 feet and 215 pounds—he was on the lightweight football team. He also played soccer and baseball. From Compton Junior College he went to the University of New Mexico on a scholarship. But the scholarship did not pay his way. He was poor. He washed pots and pans, refusing to ask his parents for money. The dishwashing job sapped his strength, and he found himself too weak to work out with the club. So he quit for a softer job in a soda-bottling plant.

One day he took the freight elevator, which was loaded with barrels of syrup. He did not realize that his right foot protruded a few inches over the edge of the elevator floor. Four toes were sheared off when they hit a well extending out. Before the surgeon operated, he told him, "Don't worry, Aggie, I'll square off your stumps and you'll kick better than ever."

Recuperating back home, after twelve days in the hospital, he started to go to the beach day after day. He soaked his foot in salt water to toughen it. He learned that if he walked slowly he wouldn't limp. It hurt horribly when he wore shoes, so he wore tennis shoes all the time.

He returned to school and attempted to kick. The pain stopped him. But he discovered that after about a dozen kicks the foot would become numb and he could kick without pain. Meanwhile, an Albuquerque cobbler devised a leather "box" to serve as his right shoe. Agajanian put on three pairs of socks and stuffed a wad of cotton into the front of the shoe. He was ready to return.

In his first game back he kicked his extra-point attempts 10 yards farther than he had before. But he was off target. So he took a file and straightened out the "toe" of the shoe.

The year 1954 was pivotal not only for the Giants but also for many in sports. George Mikan, basketball's first great big man, quit the Minneapolis Lakers. Otto Graham complained in *Sports Illustrated* that football was getting "too dirty." In Washington, Curly Lambeau was dismissed as coach of the Redskins. That left only George Halas of the Chicago Bears in control of an original National Football League franchise from the beginning, thirty seasons before.

Baseball began its modern wave of moving into new cities

and deserting old ones. It took the Browns out of St. Louis and transplanted them to Baltimore, where they became known as the Orioles. At the same time, baseball turned down a bid by a Texan named Clint Murchison, who wanted to put the Browns in Los Angeles. "Los Angeles won't support a baseball team," said the American League owners. The New York Yankees, meanwhile, who had been playing baseball most of the century, acquired their first Negro—Elston Howard.

The NFL began blacking out its home games. Weeb Ewbank was named coach of the Baltimore Colts. Bert Bell, the NFL president, hired people to tell his players of the benefits of the NFL versus Canadian football, which was raiding players. One of the stars taken was the Giants' Arnie Weinmeister. Another player who left was an unheralded fullback from the Redskins, Alex Webster.

Pop Warner died that year at the age of eighty-three. Frank Leahy quit as coach of Notre Dame. Marion Motley quit the Browns because of his injured knee. "The Yankee baseball era is ended," proclaimed a Cleveland Indians' official after Cleveland won the pennant.

In 1955 people were smiling because Eddie Fisher and Debbie Reynolds married at Grossinger's; the "Mickey Mouse Club" bowed on television; the army commissioned its first male nurse; people frowned when reading a *Saturday Evening Post* article titled, "Can This Drug Cure Insanity?" It was about L.S.D. and was subtitled, "Help for the Living Dead."

Fairy-tale addicts were sad because Princess Margaret decided not to marry Group Captain Peter Townsend; science-fiction addicts were nervous because Moscow confirmed it had tested the H-bomb; meanwhile, the new West German Army began, with 101 young men signing up in a Bonn garage.

People who believed in nature were gladdened because New York State promised to clean up the Hudson River; capitalists saw unending rivers of oil flowing here because Yemen had given a United States company thirty-year oil rights; health faddists were sliding on a Bongo Board, which cost $9.34 at Macy's.

Sports was making big news, too. The East was the only section of the country to show a decline in college football attendance—a 10 percent slump. But for the fifth straight year the National Football League showed an increase.

Yet the Giants did not really pull in the fans. There were perhaps 25,000 fans a game. This distressed the owner of the Skins, George Preston Marshall. He chided the city, its tele-

vision stations, and its newspapers for not supporting the
Giants football team.

"New York is dying as a sports center," he warned. He
turned out to be a bad seer in this respect. But his next statement was uncanny, in that more than twenty years later the
same charges would be leveled against the city over Yankee
Stadium.

"New York spent $22 million for the Coliseum under the
guise of slum clearance," he said back then, "but would not
help the Giants."

Sport fans in New York also concerned themselves with
the fate of Brooklyn College football, which was in doubt (the
Norwich game was canceled). Brooklyn had not won since
1950, when it defeated City College.

The Knicks were attracting fans to Madison Square Garden
with a basketball lineup of Harry Gallatin, Sweetwater Clif-
ton, Ray Felix, Ken Sears, Dick McGuire, and Carl Braun.

A very tall freshman named Wilt Chamberlain got his name
on the sports pages when he led the Kansas frosh to a victory
over the Kansas varsity with a 42-point performance. The
varsity was favored to take the Big Seven basketball title.

The baseball Giants were talking about moving to Yankee
Stadium in 1957, even though Leo Durocher kept insisting
that San Francisco would support major league baseball. The
Giants complained that the Polo Grounds was too old, did not
have parking, and was in a bad neighborhood.

Baseball appeared to be in a bad way. In the National
League attendance fell by more than 330,000 fans.

But the football Giants turned down an offer of a million
dollars to buy their team. "Football is our business, and we
intend to stay in it," said Jack Mara. This million-dollar bid
was the greatest offer ever made for a professional football
team, and it got Bert Bell, the NFL commissioner, thinking.

"I felt depressed for a week after hearing of that offer,"
said Bell. "I bought the Eagles for $2,500 and sold them for
$160,000."

Mara, though, said with supreme logic: "If Nashua, a horse,

alone commanded $1,251,200, how could anyone think we'd accept only $1,000,000 for the Giants?''

A huge, genial man who blocked out the sun showed up at the Giants' preseason camp in the summer of 1955. His name was Roosevelt Grier, but he liked to be called ''Rosey.'' He was not quite sure how to spell his nickname. He experimented with ''Rosie'' and ''Rosy'' and ''Rossee.'' None seemed quite right.

He was 6 feet 5 inches tall and weighed 290 pounds, some days. He was also the first link in what was to be the great backbone of the Giants of this decade, the Front Four of Grier, Robustelli, Modzelewski, and Katcavage.

There was a great big teddy bear air about Grier. He wore glasses and strummed a guitar and told jokes and had a black wit that was edged with irony rather than anger.

Mostly, though, he could play football. Not as often as Jim Lee Howell would have liked. (''You had to give him an incentive,'' Howell was to recall.) When he felt the stakes were sufficient, Grier was at his Sunday best.

Grier's life these days is geared toward nonviolence. Since that day in 1968 in the Ambassador Hotel in Los Angeles, when he stood next to Robert Kennedy and watched him get shot, he has made his life over. Now he has an office in the Los Angeles mayor's office and a title: Consultant to the Mayor on Youth and Senior Citizens. He may be out at midnight attempting to cool a potential gang war. He may be out on Sunday afternoons sitting in a rocking chair next to an old woman in a nursing home who has no one else to talk to.

''I played hard and I wanted to win,'' says Grier of his football days. ''But I didn't have a lot of emotion as far as winning or losing. We won some, we lost some. I was happy inside. I never displayed the emotion, jumping up and down.''

What was important?

''Chasing chicks, I guess. I fooled around. I didn't bother working in the off-season. I had no commitments. My commitment those days basically was just learning how to talk.''

That seems a strange statement. Today, Grier is a television personality, a Buddha-like figure who appears on talk shows and laughs and tells jokes and does needlepoint and plays a guitar.

''I was a team guy,'' he continues. ''The team was the most important thing. If the team needed a clown I'd be a clown. If the team needed somebody to stand up and talk seriously, I'd stand up and do that. I didn't make an awful lot of money. Just a little. I made $6,500 that first year. I climbed up the wage scale very begrudgingly.''

Until the moment Robert Kennedy was assassinated, Grier went through life with a sort of shoulder-shrugging acceptance of the way things are. Perhaps his early life had taught him the futility of attempting to rise beyond the level that society expected of him. Perhaps he simply made his accommodation with society. Here is how he tells part of his story:

''My father left us in the South to go north. I was the big man in the house at the age of ten. This was in Cuthbert, Georgia, not far from Waycross. At the age of five, I was working in the fields getting paid as much as grown men. What did I do? Working, shaking peanuts, picking cotton. So basically my childhood was very short. All my life I wanted a bicycle for Christmas, and now my kids have bicycles and so many toys. They get to be kids a long time now. I was a kid a short time, three or four years maybe.''

Grier spent most of the next thirteen years attempting to catch up. He could never make up for the lost time. When he was eleven his father brought his family up north, to Roselle, New Jersey.

''I was so far behind the other kids in school it wasn't funny,'' says Grier. ''I had to catch up somehow. I wasn't a grade-A student in school.

''There was an Italian kid named John Grossie, a good friend of mine. I used to see his report card in the seventh grade and he used to get all A's. I used to get like C's—not D's—but just all C's. And I said, 'John how'd you get all A's?' And he said, 'I'm smart.' I asked him how I could get smart and he said I had to study like heck. Some people get along fast, without studying. I had to study. So this fellow, this John Grossie, made me competitive. I didn't get all A's, but I got A's and B's.''

Curiously, John Grossie was to become one of the three people in Rosey Grier's life whom he searched for, and never found.

''I've been looking for John Grossie so long, ever since the seventh grade. John Grossie dropped out of school in the eighth or ninth grade. He had to quit. I can't find him.''

At Roselle High, Grier was still shy about his ability to speak, and he received special help. He also was singled out by the principal, who called him into his office and told him, ''You're an athlete. You can be a leader because a lot of kids look up to you.'' Grier decided then, he says, ''to be good as opposed to deciding I should be bad.''

In high school, Rosey set the state record for the shot put, and he also starred as a javelin and discus thrower. He got a track-and-field scholarship to Penn State, where he also played offensive and defensive tackle on the football team.

After hours he hooked up with a remarkable Penn State runner named Lenny Moore. They roamed the campus at night like wandering minstrels, singing at the top of their lungs, often serenading favored young ladies outside the girls' dormitory. The pair dubbed themselves the Mystery Singers.

Did they get paid?

''Are you kidding?'' asks Grier with a bellowing laugh as punctuation. ''If you get paid, then you aren't a mystery any more, are you?''

He was somewhat of a mystery when he reported to the Giants. He was the most massive player that had ever worn a New York uniform. ''They had no idea of the longevity I had,'' he says now. ''Or the determination or the kind of person I was. You see, there was my size—but there was also a man who was in my body.''

The man had some quirks that are accepted by teammates when a player is good. When a player is not good or not well liked, the quirks earn him the nickname of ''flake.'' Grier was

well liked, so his teammates would watch with detached amuse-
ment when before a game Grier spread a horse-blanket-sized
collection of towels out on the floor in front of his locker and
stretched out in contemplation. And because Grier could be
so good when it really mattered, they accepted his cavalier
attitude to a game that for many was a metaphor of life.

Oh, there were times, in years to come, when Andy Robustelli would scold Grier, call him a "fatso" and "lazy." But
that was just to psyche Grier up for the big ones. Anyway,
Jim Lee knew that when it mattered, Grier would play. To
make sure, Howell would tell Grier, "They say this fellow on
Baltimore whom you're up against claims you're nothing but
a big stiff. He says he can take you with a hand tied behind his
back." Good old Rosey, he'd respond.

"If I wanted to, I could've been a Hall of Famer," says
Grier. He says it not bitterly, just as a simple matter-of-fact
statement. "If they told me a guy opposite me was great, I
played. Look, I was never in top shape. Not because I didn't
care. It's just that it was a game. A game. I knew that in the
game I'd be in shape. Sometimes, though, I played harder
than at other times. Sometimes I didn't play hard at all."

Yet he often becomes emotional when speaking of his playing days and of the second person whose life had an effect on
him and whom he has been unable to find.

"It wasn't that I didn't . . . you know what I'm saying?
I loved it. I enjoyed it. And so if I beat a guy, I didn't try
to make him look awful. If one of our guys hurt another guy
he'd get a punch from me. I'd tell them you don't try to hurt
a guy deliberately. I saved Jimmy Brown. I saved Johnny
Unitas. I saved Ollie Matson. I saved so many guys out there
because I didn't want to hurt them.

"And still, of all the guys I didn't want to hurt, there was
one guy I hurt a lot. His name was Lowell Perry. I put him
out of the game permanently his first year. Remember Lowell
Perry?"

Actually, no. But the record shows that Lowell Perry played
four games for the Pittsburgh Steelers in 1956. But in those

four games as a receiver he averaged a remarkable 24 yards a catch. He ran only twice, for an 18-yard average.

"The President just gave Lowell Perry a government job," continues Grier. "I was the guy who put him out of the game as a rookie. Forever. And he was great. He ran a reverse. I caught him on the sideline and fell on him, and he dislocated a hip, got a fractured pelvis, a whole bunch of injuries like that. He went on to become a lawyer. It was an accident. . . . I never would have . . . I felt awful that this happened to a guy I admired so much. I used to watch him play. I loved to see him get that football. And then I went in and hurt him. Guys told me, 'Forget about it, man.' But I always kept up with him. I knew he was a lawyer. I never got in touch with him, but I always kept up with him."

After his second year Grier made it to the Pro Bowl, but soon he was drafted into the army. Now, he wonders why. "I guess it was because they wanted me in the army. I had flat feet. I was 290 pounds. But they swore me in before they took a physical. They were just determined I was gonna be in the army. A lot of guys didn't go. A lot went in for six months. I couldn't get that deal. I went for two years. The year before I went in, Fran Rogel, guys like that, they played on weekends even though they were in the army. Paul Hornung played on weekends."

Still, he was able to return for the 1958 season. By then, the pros were becoming more and more racially integrated. Grier noticed more and more of a pattern.

"I came from the South, so being segregated didn't bother me. It was the way things went then. We knew only six black guys would make the team no matter how good they were. If they came with thirty guys, and they were all O. J. Simpsons, we knew only six were going to make it. Number Six. That's what it was. And that guy on Washington—Marshall?—he wasn't going to have no blacks on his team." Another belly laugh begins rumbling from somewhere in Grier's huge body and he says, "Sometimes I look at pro basketball and everyone on the whole court is black and I say, wow, this is unreal."

Today, he concedes, racial discrimination is disappearing in football, "Because the black guys are beginning to get as wise as their white brothers. They get their own lawyers."

In his career with the Giants, which lasted until 1962, Grier had only one confrontation with management over racial matters. That was in 1959 in Dallas during a preseason game with the Baltimore Colts. The Cowboys had not yet come into the league, and this was a game to show Dallas just what the NFL was all about. But the black players were not permitted to room in the hotel where the white players stayed.

"There was a pre-game party at the hotel to meet some businessmen, and we were invited too. We weren't allowed to eat at the hotel, but we were supposed to go to a party there —to be gazed at."

Some of the Colts' players called up some of the Giants' players and a miniboycott was organized. Grier recalls that he went to management and told them, "Me and Tunnell and Rosey Brown, and some of the rookies aren't for this." Management then told him, "You never said anything about this before."

"We shouldn't have to," Grier replied.

"For the good of the rookies," as the leaders were told, everyone should show up at the party. The rookies' chances would be hurt if they weren't there or if they held out. So Grier and the others gave in. The next year, though, there were no more separate facilities in any city where the NFL played.

His Giants years ended after the 1962 season, and he closed out his career with the Los Angeles Rams. He became a talk-show personality, an anomalous-looking character in his horn-rims and strumming his guitar, singing songs and not worrying about his weight any more.

The pounds hung around him, it seemed, like a cloud. Some training camps he would turn up at 330 pounds, bringing a frown to Jim Lee's face. Then Rosey would get serious and try one of a series of diets. There was only water for thirteen straight days and there was the "teensy-weensy diet," in which he ate candy and ice cream but only in teensy-weensy portions. "It satisfied my mind," he explained, "but didn't expand my body."

That didn't work, either. So after the 1962 season he was traded to the Rams for John LoVetere. When Grier went, the Front Four, which had savaged opposing backs as a unit since 1956, was broken.

Grier hoped to return for the 1968 season with the Rams. He had become interested in politics because of Robert Kennedy and went with him, combining the role of disciple and bodyguard. He loved listening to Kennedy's talk of brotherhood and respect. And then, on June 4, 1968, Kennedy was assassinated. Grier tore the weapon from Sirhan Sirhan, tossed it to Rafer Johnson (the former Olympian), and then sat on Sirhan until the police arrived.

"His death made me realize," Grier recalled years later, "that unless we started to act for the things we believed in, what was the sense of traveling the whole route? I could not waste the time living the life I had led for nothing. It must amount to something."

Grier is married now for a second time and lives in Brentwood. His job with the mayor, he says, is "more than just a nine-to-five job. I believe I should do some good with my life. I can go all out on this—to serve my fellow man."

Grier's celebrity status grew when he took up needlepoint, published a book on it, gave demonstrations to Dinah Shore on needlepoint methods. He was taught the craft by Babs Shoemaker, wife of the jockey.

"The television shows you see me on, everyone wants to make jokes. That's beautiful. But I'm a human being. I am a person." Finally, says Grier, "I am more than just Number 76 that chased quarterbacks. There was a human being in me all the time."

There was no question about it: the Giants were getting a new look in 1955. They did not know it when the season began, but they also would be getting rid of an old stadium. For this was to mark their last season in the Polo Grounds, where they

had been ensconced since 1925. They were to give the Polo
Grounds' fans something to remember with the last NFL
game at the old place.

For the first time anyone could remember, the Giants found
a running back who weighed more than 200 pounds. He was
Alex Webster, a fellow who had grown up across the river in
Kearny, New Jersey, a little north of Newark. Big Red, as
the 6-foot 3-inch, 210-pounder was affectionately known, had
torn up the Canadian Football League in the previous two
seasons after flunking a tryout with the Washington Redskins.

Canada might as well have been the Soviet Union as far
as Wellington Mara was concerned. The Canadian Football
League had stolen his great tackle, Arnie Weinmeister, who
had become the great proselytizer for the CFL, having almost
induced Frank Gifford to jump across the border.

"We will go for the Canadians' best," said Wellington,
"and bring them back here."

Actually, the Giants already had an extraordinary complement of talent, which would be noticed as the club continued to
win. Protecting Conerly and throwing blocks for Webster was
an offensive line of Rosey Brown, Ray Wietecha, Jack Stroud,
Dick Yelvington, and Bill Austin. Brown, Wietecha, and
Stroud were in their third year, and they would play together
many more.

These were nice names, but it took Giants' fans a bit longer
to get excited in those days. One reason was the club's lack
of proximity. It trained in such non-Big Apple locations as
Winooski, Vermont; St. Peter's, Minnesota; and Salem, Oregon. Also, the club always opened on the road. That usually
meant coming back for the home opener with a losing record.
And, quite simply—but perhaps most importantly—baseball
simply pushed pro football off the sports pages. The Giants
had a hard time because they were competing against three
baseball teams. Not only that, but the Dodgers, the Giants,
and the Yankees were in contention, if not at the top, every
season. So newspapers did not send reporters to Winooski to
cover training camp in July while the Bombers' Mickey Mantle
was stroking homers at Yankee Stadium. And newspapers

did not always cover the football team's opener on the road in late September when there were stretch drives going on in baseball's pennant races. And, finally, since one of the clubs usually was in the World Series, the football Giants would play in obscurity. Baseball was, beyond a doubt, the ''National Pastime,'' a sobriquet it had given itself after President William Howard Taft tossed out the first ball on opening day in 1910, giving the game the Presidential Seal, as it were.

In the obscurity of Philadelphia on a Saturday, only a few days before a ''Subway Series'' between the Yankees and the Dodgers opened, the football Giants opened their 1955 season with a dismal 27–17 loss to the Eagles. Mercifully for Conerly, he heard no boos as he completed only 9 of 24 tosses for a pitiful 57 yards.

It did not help Conerly that Kyle Rote had been shifted to the end position with Webster playing right halfback. The defense was letting the club down. The second game was no better, a 28–17 loss at Chicago to the Bears. This time Conerly produced, statistically, one of his worst efforts. Only 13 of his 34 passes were completed, and those 13 gained only 120 yards. But Webster, who moved like a steam shovel, made people gasp with a 71-yard run.

Howell knew he had to shake up his team or it would be out of the playoffs before the season was a month old. Still another road game loomed against the Steelers. Although T. J. Mara and Art Rooney (the Steelers' president) were old friends, the rivalry had been a sort of gutter warfare. Old Man Rooney had nothing but affection for the Giants and especially for Old T. J. For it was T. J. Mara himself who got beaten for much of Rooney's killing that day at Saratoga when Rooney produced the biggest day in the history of horse race betting. Legend has it that Rooney won more than $300,000. He spread his bets around that day, but the bookie he hit the hardest was Mara. That same week Mrs. Rooney gave birth to a son. Art Rooney went over to Mara and said, ''In your honor I'm naming him Tim.'' (Ironically, Tim Rooney became president of Yonkers Raceway, and few people knew he was named for a bookie, even a legal bookie.)

Friendship didn't stand in the way of the 1955 Steelers, though. They believed they would have a contending team and they were ready for the Giants. Howell then made one of his most difficult decisions. He decided to bench Conerly, who had started every game, except when injured, since 1948. He was going to be replaced by Don Heinrich, once the country's leading passer at Washington. Now, he was a second-stringer who stayed near the Giants even though he had once been cut. He had the feeling a job would open for him eventually.

The change did not help the Giants, though. They lost by 30–23 and began their home season with an 0–3 record. The powerful Browns, led by Otto Graham, who had been coaxed out of retirement by Paul Brown, obviously would have first place to themselves.

Yet this new fellow, Webster, was plugging along picking up yardage. In fact, he quickly moved up among the rushing leaders, and his average of more than 5 yards a carry was easily the best in the league.

Alex Webster is now a grandfather. But he recalls 1953, when was a 22-year-old, and he recalls mostly little ironies.

"You won't believe this," says Alex, "but I was a defensive safety when I tried out with the Washington Redskins in 1953. I played halfback and safety in college, and I guess they needed a defensive back. They never looked at me as a halfback. I made the squad, practically. I was the last one cut. I guess it was five days before the opening of the season when Don Doll was released by Detroit. The Skins picked him up, and I got my walking papers."

As he walked out, he encountered a curious scene, one that probably hundreds of players have been through.

"When I got released, Curly Lambeau, who was the coach, said he didn't want to release me, but that his hands were tied by Mr. Marshall. And as I was walking out the hall, George Preston Marshall, the owner, called me in and said, 'I'd like to keep you, but Curly Lambeau wants to let you go.' "

In any event, Webster was out of a football job. But not out of a job. He was going back to work at the Otis Elevator plant in Harrison, New Jersey.

Work. For Webster it seemed that work was all he had ever known. He was delivering newspapers at the age of nine ("that's when Dad died. He was thirty-three years old.") If he was not delivering newspapers, he was delivering milk or ice. In the 1940s around Kearny, you were a celebrity if you had an electric icebox.

A few days after the Skins cut him, Webster had an idea. Perhaps the Canadian Football League would be interested in him. He wondered how he might find out. At ten o'clock one night he telephoned an old friend, Paul Durkin, a budding newspaperman. Durkin now is the associate sports editor of the *New York Daily News.*

"Luckily for Alex, I was in bed at the time," says Durkin. "I was home from the service, that's why I was in so early. That's probably the last time I was in bed that early. Alex wanted to know if I knew anything about the Canadian League. What crossed my mind was that the coach of the Montreal Alouettes was Peahead Walker, who had been the coach at Wake Forest. And Alex had played for North Carolina State and had some big games against Wake Forest. Walker was sure to remember that. So I told Alex to get in touch with Walker."

"Maybe I'll write him a letter," suggested Webster.

The pair decided to send a telegram.

"The next morning my mother answered the phone and said 'there's a foreign gentleman who wants to talk to you.' Walker had this Southern accent, and he asked me how the hell I expected to play football if I can't even put a phone number or address on a telegram. I had forgotten to tell him where to reach me. Anyway, he asked me to come down that same day. You see, there was a deadline for signing American players, and it was that midnight, September 30. They were allowed to sign only ten of us. So I grabbed a plane and got there when it was dark. But they always used to work out at nights in that league because the guys had jobs during the day, so I went out and they watched me run and they were satisfied I could play with them."

The sports world is filled with stories about the scout who

went looking for a player on a team and suddenly spotted someone else and said to himself, "Hey, who's that?" Supposedly it happened in baseball with Willie Mays and in hockey with Bobby Orr. It also happened to Alex Webster.

He was not an unknown, though. He played the final half of the 1953 season with the Alouettes, and the next year he became the greatest runner that Canadian football had seen. He had the touchdown record "and some others. I don't know all the stats. I really forgot them."

As usual, though, the Giants were looking for a quarterback. They had heard a lot about Sam Etcheverry, and they dispatched Al DeRogatis, a serious, insightful student of the game, up north to take a look at Etcheverry. DeRogatis was a successful insurance salesman, but he enjoyed working with the Giants, a team he starred with before a damaged knee made him quit in 1952. It was remarkable he made it at all. How many English majors from Duke were there in the league?

"Well, I saw Alex in the game. And it seemed that every big play, every clutch situation, he made," says DeRogatis. "When I came back I told the Giants that this was the big back they'd been looking for. I always believed in the power-running back. And Alex was their man. Over the years he proved he was a clutch ballplayer."

Webster jumped his Canadian contract, which ran through 1955, to join the Giants. Yet he was not even a starter. He was listed as the Number 2 right halfback behind Rote.

"We were training in Salem, Oregon," says Webster. "Kyle tripped one day coming out of the dormitory, and he twisted his bad knee. Then, in our second preseason game, we played the 49ers up in Seattle. I had a pretty good day. A couple of touchdowns, had a lot of yardage, and from that day I became the back on the right side and Kyle went to the flanker spot."

This interesting new alignment attracted more than 12,000 fans when the New Yorkers played their home opener of 1955. The crowd was huge considering the weather. More than 17,000 seats had been sold, but an extraordinary rainfall, heavy and long, kept most fans home. The Maras even considered calling off the game. Only one game ever had been postponed at the Polo Grounds, when a snowstorm in the late 1920s cut out service on the Sixth Avenue el. Even trolley cars did not move then.

But the Maras decided to let the Giants play this time. It was a strange sight. When a ball hit the ground it never actually touched the mud—it would hit the water and float. Water splashed five feet in the air when a player fell. This was a day for defense, and the Giants' defense finally held. The 10–0 victory was the club's first of the season.

A week later they lost again, and again to the Steelers. Now the club was only 1–4, and it was obvious that a major problem was in the linebacking corps. The Giants were getting picked apart by tosses over the middle or by runs that should have been stopped by the secondary.

A victory over the Redskins at the Polo Grounds helped the Giants forget some of their problems, but in the seventh game of the season they met the Browns. The Browns were en route to their tenth straight divisional title in two leagues. They had also beaten the Giants four straight times. They made it five in a row now, with a 24–14 decision at Cleveland in what some people termed the dirtiest game they had seen.

Graham was helped off the field while running at the Giants' line, and later he charged them with "dirty football." Webster, meanwhile, was taken off on a stretcher. On the last play of the game, with Conerly backpedaling in a futile effort to unload a touchdown pass, the Browns' defensive captain, Don Colo, took a swing at Conerly. Colo stood 6 foot 3 inches tall and weighed 250 pounds. He claimed afterward that Conerly, 65 pounds lighter, had threatened him.

The brutality of the game stunned, and yes, impressed, many fans. For days afterward people wondered what the final confrontation of the season would be like.

The Giants were at a 2–5 mark, and more than half the season was over. They only played 12 games, so there wasn't much time to begin the sort of streak that could carry over into the next season. It began right away, against the Colts at the Polo Grounds.

It was not unusual in those days for upwards of 5,000 people to travel from Baltimore to the Polo Grounds. Only 6,000 season tickets were sold at the old stadium that last year, and they were in the hands of a small number of people— only 2,000.

The Colts were in the second year of a rebuilding program under a crew-cut, barrelly coach with the odd name of Weeb Ewbank. When he took over the club he spoke of bringing Baltimore a championship within five years, by 1958.

He was able to get Alan Ameche, an overpowering running back who was the nephew of a great Giants' fan, Don Ameche, and the Colts were making unexpected noises in 1955. They came into New York, in fact, only a game behind the Western Conference-leading Los Angeles Rams. Ameche was only a rookie, but he was leading the league in total rushing yards and averaging almost 100 yards a game. The Colts' defense, meanwhile, was anchored in the backfield by a small but clever player named Don Shula.

By special trains and buses the Colts' fans poured into the Polo Grounds. They bore Confederate flags and hip flasks and silly hats—there were more than 6,000 of them. That was more than the Giants had in season tickets. The visiting fans made up about a fifth of the total crowd that day. And they were disappointed. For the Giants began a streak, began to play the kind of ball that they would demonstrate for the rest of the decade and into the 1960s. The New Yorkers held the usually irrepressible Ameche to only 40 yards. The Colts were held to their lowest point total of the campaign, and the Giants wound up on top by 17–7.

It began a stretch that would see them wind up unbeaten in their last five games of this pivotal season, with 4 victories, 1 tie. Each of those decisions was, in its way, unexpected. The unexpected would mark the Giants' fortunes for many years.

As the season wound down, the Giants were faced with another big test. The Philadelphia Eagles, the leading offensive

team in the league, were coming to town. Landry, in charge of
the defenses, knew what everyone else knew: the Eagles threw
the ball a lot, more than anyone else. They had the best
quick-strike capabilities in the league, and few clubs had been
able to handle it. The Giants did. In one of their most rousing
defensive efforts, they intercepted six Philadelphia passes
from Adrian Burk and Bobby Thomason. They forced six
Philadelphia fumbles. And they destroyed the Eagles 31–7;
the Eagles had averaged 310 yards a game, but they were held
to 155 this time.

Most of the Giants did not realize that they would be closing the Polo Grounds to the National Football League in a
few days. Even if they had, there was no time for feeling
nostalgic. The Browns were coming, the Browns of Otto
Graham and Dante Lavelli and Lou Groza. They were a
cerebral bunch, too, with such clever linebackers as Walt
Michaels and Chuck Noll.

Columnists began to wonder whether this game would turn
into a grudge match. Would the Giants try to get even because Colo had swung at Conerly, or because Webster had
been carted off on a stretcher? And how was Graham going
to handle the Giants' defensive line, which he had charged
with dirty play?

A press lunch would herald the week's activities, and the
press would be given a rundown on the opponent. That job
usually fell to Jack Lavelle, a 300-pounder who was the Giants'
chief scout and who made every paper in the city once a week.
He was the man who told the press, which told the public
what to expect.

So if a generation of sports fans grew up with the understanding that "on any given Sunday any team can win," it
is because Lavelle often used this cliché when talking about
an opponent that was obviously inferior to the Giants. In
fact, in reading Tuesday's papers week after week, year after
year, one realizes Lavelle's genius in saying something positive about everyone the Giants faced became a sort of art
form.

Lavelle saved his finest adjectives for a club that had just lost. Thus, if the Steelers gave up forty points in losing to the Chicago Cardinals, Lavelle would rave about the Steelers great drive of the opening two minutes, which unfortunately, was halted with an interception. And he would tell the newsmen about how lucky the Cardinals were to get three touchdowns in the span of seven minutes. Since these "neutral" games were not televised to New York, the fans would believe it. More importantly, the players would, too, or at least the coaching staff hoped they would. You did not want to get your players overconfident. If there is anything a football coach would rather face less than a team that has won six straight games, it is a team that has lost six straight games.

Lavalle was one of the most popular people in the New York football scene. He had a robust enjoyment for life, and he was one of the most sought after Communion-breakfast speakers in the city.

His scouting career started at just about the time the Giants moved into the Polo Grounds. Lavelle was a svelte 178-pounder as a guard at Notre Dame, but he was injured before the annual crusade against Army.

Knute Rockne asked Lavelle to scout Army for the Irish. Lavelle did such a good job that he scouted Army for twenty more years. He became such a fixture at Army games that once, without a ticket for an Army–Michigan game, he asked Army's coach, Red Blaik, to take him in with the team.

"Of course, Jack," replied Blaik, "no Army game would be official without you scouting us."

He was so expert at remembering the opposition's plays that he once diagramed the formation a team would use before the team got out of the scrimmage.

He became a man-about-New York; his face was familiar to Madison Square Garden track fans, where he was the official starter for dozens of meets.

Among his dining companions were Herman Hickman (the 350-pound Yale coach who was also, among other things, a gourmet, gourmand, and Latin scholar) and the 300-pound Steve Owen.

A scene that remains vivid for Frank Litsky, the assistant

sports editor of *The New York Times,* was a night at Mama Leone's Restaurant.

"I saw the three of them—Lavelle, Hickman, and Owen—sitting side by side against the wall, napkins under their chins. A great orgy of eating."

Lavelle's most famous scouting report was his one-word recommendation to Hickman. The Yale coach had asked Lavelle to take a look at powerful Princeton in 1950 for the annual Eli–Tiger meeting. Lavelle wrote Hickman: "Cancel."

At the final press luncheon of the 1955 season, Lavelle did not have to frighten the Giants or fans. Howell did it for him. Howell announced, simply, that the "Browns are the best team in football, and Paul Brown is the best coach."

It appeared the Giants would be in trouble, despite their recent positive flurry. Webster could not even walk to get to the Tuesday workout. Without his running the Giants would be in terrible trouble, for the Browns were the best club in the league in stopping the pass. A measure of the relative importance of the football Giants and the Brooklyn Dodgers was apparent when Walter O'Malley received more publicity that week than Howell did.

O'Malley was the president of the Dodgers. That week an unknown architect named R. Buckminster Fuller of Princeton showed O'Malley the model of a domed stadium for Brooklyn. It never got beyond the model stage, but the dome looked like the geodesic dome Fuller constructed for the New York World's Fair near Shea Stadium almost ten years later.

The absurdity of a domed stadium quickly passed as the Giants got ready for their finale. Howell again said he would start Heinrich instead of Conerly, but for the first time he explained: "Charlie will spot flaws in the Browns by observing from the bench."

For the next few years Howell employed that innovation: Heinrich would start and Conerly would, it was thought, mentally diagram the defenses, learn how to beat them, and then take over for Heinrich. For years he came in after Heinrich had "probed" the opposition. This was a very clever idea, fans believed.

Yet, twenty years later, Conerly finally admitted, "You can't see a damn thing from the bench. It's the worst seat in the place. I don't know why they did that."

The Giants–Browns game drew 45,699 fans to the Polo Grounds—the largest crowd of the year there. Another 50,000 people will tell you they were there. Everyone who heard it or saw it, remembers that game.

The great Cleveland defense found itself fumbling and stumbling as Heinrich brilliantly engineered drives in the first two quarters that gave the New Yorkers a 14–0 lead. First Webster scored on a 1-foot plunge, and then Bobby Epps ran 14 yards.

The Browns, though, had a ground game of their own. It was not as frightening as it had been under Marion Motley, or as relentless as it would be under Jimmy Brown, but it led the league in touchdowns running and it amassed more yards on the ground than any team except the Chicago Bears.

The Browns' leading rushers were Curley Morrison (who averaged 5.3 yards a carry) and Ed Modzelewski (Big Mo, who was returning after two years in the service and was to pick up more than 600 yards).

And, of course, the team also had its coach, Paul Brown. He made Landry's fertile mind work overtime by concocting a devilish plan: he would use five receivers to work on the four Giants' pass defenders. Otto Graham employed his favorite target, Darrell Brewster, on a 15-yard touchdown toss, and the Browns cut the edge to 14–7 at halftime. The Browns continued moving after the half as Graham threw a 42-yard touchdown pass to Ray Renfro, followed by a 41-yarder to Brewster. Now the Browns led 21–14. But Bob Schnelker tied the game at the end of the third quarter by recovering Eddie Price's end-zone fumble.

The points continued to pile up on the scoreboard in the final quarter. Modzelewski plunged over for a 1-yard touchdown, and it was Cleveland by 28–21. Rote snatched a 16-yard pass from Conerly, and it was 28–all.

More histrionics: Chuck Noll intercepted a Conerly pass and dashed 14 yards for the touchdown. Cleveland was ahead by 35–28 with the third touchdown of the quarter and time running out. The Giants took the kickoff to their 15. They had 85 yards to go. Coolly, with the fans delirious and screaming as they had not for most of the first thirty years, the Giants made their way toward the Cleveland goal with Conerly in charge. And finally, with fewer than 3 minutes remaining, Gifford took a 23-yard pass from Conerly to score. It was 35–all. Each team had scored 14 points in the period. But the game was not over.

Graham began his final attack from his own 27-yard line. All he had to do was to get to about the Giants' 30-yard line. From there, Groza, who kicked more field goals than anyone else that season, would be well within his range. The goal posts were on the goal line then, not 10 yards farther back as in later years.

First, Graham bootlegged the ball and a 28-yard run brought him to the Giants' 45. Then Morrison ran to the 29, and next time took it to the 19. Big Mo brought the ball to the 14. With only 25 seconds remaining, it was time for Groza to come in. The attempt would be a 21-yarder, 7 yards behind the line of scrimmage.

The snap went back, the ball was placed down, and Groza drove forward, with one of the 405 field-goal attempts in his NFL career. From out of the pack, above the mass of twisted bodies and groping fingers and flailing knees, the Giants' Pat Knight leaped—and blocked the attempt. The game was saved, and it wound up a 35–35 tie.

It was not until the final gun that the crowd streamed out of the Polo Grounds, which was not to see a big-league professional football game again until 1960. That was when a team called the New York Titans began with as much hope of succeeding as the Giants had when they opened the old place to pro football in 1925.

But the Titans were in the future for the happy fans who waited for the subway or for buses home as they discussed Webster's miraculous recovery and spoke of how clever it was

of Howell to bring Conerly in late. Conerly completed 15 of
27 passes, gained 187 yards, and threw for a pair of touchdowns.

The Giants went on the road the next week. They had lost
their first four road games. But they continued to show the
greatest improvement in the league. They toppled the Washington Redskins 27–20 and helped the Browns clinch their
sixth straight title since joining the NFL. In the season's
finale, the Giants won again on the road, this time 24–19 over
the Lions. It was the first time since 1945 that the New Yorkers had halted Detroit. They closed out their season with 4
victories and a tie for their last five games.

Their overall record was a mediocre 6–5–1, and they finished
third in the Eastern Conference. But the Giants knew that the
second half of their season was more indicative of what they
could do.

An invisible curtain descended over the Giants, as well as
the world of pro football, when 1955 ended. Shortly after the
New Year, to extend the metaphor, the curtain rose to a
glittering new performance. The Giants were coming to
Yankee Stadium in 1956, and maybe, they would find a place
on the roster for a rookie named Sam Huff.

Optimism gripped New York and much of the United States in 1956. Why, felonies had dropped by 32 percent on the city's subways. And on television, "The Millionaire" was making some selfless person wealthy every week.

If you were an engineer, you had a choice of jobs anyplace in the country. The want ads rambled for pages under the heading "Engineers." If you wanted a five-room, air-conditioned apartment in the Bronx you could get one for $200 a month.

Of course, you wanted to exercise, and the hula hoop filled the need. Perhaps you smiled when you read that Grandma Moses was celebrating her ninety-sixth birthday.

Reading tastes were of the uplifting sort. *Profiles in Courage* was a reminder of how men performed under pressure.

Yet, you might have wondered about what effect comic books had on children. The comics, charged critics, pandered to violence. Everything would be all right, though, since an administrator of the Comic Books Code was selected. Her name was Mrs. Guy Percy Trulock. She was paid by the Comics Magazine Association of America.

Truth was stranger than fiction when a 167-year-old man from Colombia, Javier Pereira, the oldest person in the world, was discovered. The 4-foot 4-inch, 87-pounder was brought to

New York by the "Believe It or Not" people and promptly punched the president of the organization at a press conference.

The press soon discovered another wonder: Maria Callas made her Metropolitan Opera début in *Norma*. Another début was made, this one in a movie called *Love Me Tender*, by Elvis Presley. If you wanted to stay home, RCA made it attractive with this ad: "If you earn $5,200 a year—or more—your family is ready for COLOR TV."

Things were settling down not far from our shores. An exiled student leader in Cuba named Fidel Castro, who had led raids in Oriente Province, was reported killed.

The sports world had its share of surprises, too. In the summer a Brooklyn Sports Center Authority was formed to build a new Dodgers stadium for 50,000 people costing $9 million. They were also talking about a controversial all-weather dome.

At Columbia, Lou Little announced he was retiring as football coach. But Willie Shoemaker decided to stay around for a while and became the first jockey to go over $2 million in purses for a year. His most famous mount, Swaps, broke a bone in its leg and was put in a sling to keep him elevated while he healed.

Madison Square Garden scheduled twenty college basketball doubleheaders. If you were a student in the city, your G.O. card would get you in for 40 cents.

Ebbets Field was sold to make way for a housing development. However, that was to be five years away. The Dodgers could stay in Brooklyn through 1960.

The Los Angeles Rams were considering using closed-circuit TV, from the spotter's booth to the field, to aid Coach Sid Gillman.

The Pittsburgh Pirates were threatening to move because of bad fan support, and the Pittsburgh Steelers were offered the use of Buffalo's stadium for $1,000 a game. Louisville, meanwhile, wanted to get in on big-league sports and offered the Redskins, Steelers, and Eagles a free place to play if they would move. The leverage allowed the Steelers to renew their lease for a rent of 12½ percent instead of 15 percent.

New names included Paul Hornung, who was Green Bay's surprise bonus pick. Green Bay had needed a halfback and Hornung was Notre Dame's quarterback. Don Drysdale was named the Brooklyn Dodgers' top rookie. And Bill Russell made his pro début with the Boston Celtics.

In January the Giants signed a twenty-year deal with the Yankees to lease Yankee Stadium for 15 percent of the gross receipts. "The uncertainty of the Polo Grounds' future and Giants' future" made the move necessary, said Jack Mara. Also, Bert Bell had urged the Maras to make the shift to ensure the continuity of an NFL team in the city. There was no guarantee, after all, that a new stadium would be built, and once the Polo Grounds was torn down for apartment houses, the football Giants might not have a place to play.

The new season would begin in a new ball park, the most prestigious ball park in the United States. It was probably the most famous outdoor playground in the world. The Giants had finished 1955 with a surge, but 1956 was the year that the backbone of the team would become firmly implanted. For Andy Robustelli, Jim Katcavage, and Dick Modzelewski joined Rosey Grier on the defensive line. They were to remain as a unit until 1962, when Grier was traded.

Sam Huff, meanwhile, joined the club and made it as middle linebacker, a post he yielded only after being traded following the 1963 season. Bill Svoboda and Harland Svare teamed with Huff at linebacker. The three were a unit through 1959.

Another newcomer, Ed Hughes, replaced Landry in the defensive backfield as Landry retired as a player to become a full-time coach. Landry was not only the defensive coordinator, setting up all the alignments to use against the opposition's defense, he was also the individual coach of the defensive line, the linebackers, the secondary, the place-kickers, and the punters.

Ray Wietecha remembers 1956 well. Hardly a day goes by without his being reminded of it.

"I've still got myself a picture of the 1956 championship team," he begins. "I had it blown up originally for my tavern. It's a beautiful thing, must be six feet across. It's bigger than I am. I've had that everyplace I go. I put it in my den. So all I have to do is look at television and look up, and there's the picture. I reflect on that time almost every day when I'm in my den. Anytime something happens to one of the ballplayers, I look at it."

In 1956 Wietecha was in his fourth year as center of the club. He went on to become a ten-year man and now is the Giants' offensive-line coach. He played with Rosey Brown all his years, as well as with Jack Stroud.

"The coaches at that time stood on the side of the picture," continues Wietecha from his Florham Park, New Jersey, home. "And there stands Landry and Lombardi next to each other as assistant coaches. It's quite a picture. I think about fourteen, fifteen people—practically half the team—made it as coaches in pro football. That is amazing to me. Let's see, there was Rosey Brown, Huff, Katcavage, Robustelli, Yowarsky, Modzelewski, Svare, Tunnell, Heinrich, Rote, Schnelker, Wietecha. The guys who became head coaches were Webster with the Giants, Hughes at Houston, Dick Nolan with the 49ers, and Swede Svare with the Rams. And the assistant coaches, Landry and Lombardi, of course. So let's see. That's twelve made it as assistants, four made it as head coaches. Sixteen guys out of a thirty-three man roster.

"Those were golden years for the Giants. Yet, I don't know why so many of us wound up coaching. Now you take Harland Svare, for instance. He and I were roommates. Time after time, when we'd discuss what we would do in the future, Swede would say, 'One thing I'm not gonna do is go into coaching.' Me, I always said I wanted to. That's all I ever liked and all I know. Swede would say that coaching is for the birds. He would say you got to be stupid to want to coach. So you know who ends up coaching? Swede. He had two jobs as head coach.

"Alex Webster was another one. He used to visit me and the Swede a lot. We were single guys, and whenever Alex could get away from his wife, he'd come over to our apartment and we'd talk about the future and Alex would say, 'No. No coaching for me.'

"Another was Dick Nolan. We always called Dick Nolan the little rich boy. He was from New York, and all of us guys were from Chicago or down South, and during our little sit-downs in spring training—when we all lived together and we'd play cards together—we'd always cheat him and try to take his money because we heard his dad was with DuPont, and we thought he was loaded."

In an era when legal battles in sports were virtually unheard of, Wietecha inadvertently became a minor celebrity by jumping leagues—but in two different sports.

As a Marine captain, after graduating from Northwestern in 1950, he became a baseball player. "Babe Ruth was my hero," he explains. "At Quantico all I did was play sports. I played against Willie Mays, Johnny Antonelli, guys like that, and I did well. I made the all-star team, got my weight down to 200 pounds. The Washington Senators saw me, since Quantico was right near Washington. They offered me a contract. I got discharged in March 1953, and went right to spring training.

"They sent me to Charlotte, North Carolina, in the Sally League. I played baseball for two months. I was only hitting about .263, but I was leading in home runs, things like that. I was twenty-three years old, but I couldn't hit the curve ball, which you had to do in the Major Leagues. I began thinking that was going to be my last year in baseball."

Meanwhile, the Giants had sent Wietecha a football contract. The timing was decisive. He knew he could hit the fast ball, but he did not see a career for himself as a baseball player because of the curve. So after playing in the Sally League all-star game, he quit. He left immediately for the Giants' camp in St. Peter, Minnesota.

"I was in camp one day when Clark Griffith—he was the president of the Senators—called up Bert Bell and said, 'Hey,

what's going on? You don't want to start no wars.' Bell called
the Giants and told them to send me back until the baseball
season was over. Well, there was no sense in that for me. I
couldn't make the football team in September. So I just went
home and went to work. I got a job with Standard Oil, in
their training program.

"I lived at home with my grandmother. The Giants used to
call me all the time to come back to them, but I figured, what's
the use? I missed the whole training camp because baseball
wouldn't let me play football. Eddie Kolman—he was the line
coach—he could speak Polish to my grandmother—he used
to call her all the time and talk to her about me. I wasn't no
great shakes. But it was a time when pro football was still
looking for players. The players weren't going into pro football like they are today, for the money.

"Me and Rosey Brown once kicked around how much money
we got paid. I think I got $5,500 the first year. A bonus? No,
no. Anyway, the last week before the football season was
supposed to start they got me to come. I almost left my first
day there. The first scrimmage, Steve Owen was showing me
which way to block—straight ahead, to the left, to the right.
It was so rough. But just when I was ready to go home, someone said, 'That's it.' And Owen said to me, 'We like you and
you made the club.' "

Wietecha was to play in the Pro Bowl four times. In fact,
over the 10 seasons between 1954 and 1963, the Giants sent
players to the Bowl 71 times.

"I prided myself on the fact I could snap a ball very well.
I had a good release. I had good speed, a good spiral, and I
could put it where I wanted it. For a couple of years in practice I put it without looking to Chandler, Summerall, and that
guy from L.A., Agajanian.

"I got to where I could snap it without moving my head or
looking, and so my last few years that's how I snapped in a
game. I would pick my head up, and most guys wouldn't expect it because when you centered the ball you always looked
down between your knees."

Wietecha became one of the first, if not the first, center

to snap the ball backward without looking at his target. The advantage was immense. First, he could start driving forward and do the attacking, rather than simply have to defend. For the opposing linemen did not know when the ball would be snapped back. Because Wietecha was initiating the action, he gave the holder and kicker more time to get the ball off the ground.

"It was like being a pitcher. I found my groove. Once people mentioned it, I took pride in it and then I worked even harder. I used to practice getting the strings [the laces] back in the right position. On field goals and extra points the holder wants the ball, so he just has to put it straight down and the strings face forward. There's a way of doing that. You throw it with the same amount of revolutions.

"Then all you've got to do is find your spot. The strings will always be in the front. Guys used to come around and watch me. I'd go to the Pro Bowl games and I'd snap there without looking and a guy like Tommy O'Connell—he had to hold for Groza—he'd watch. I wasn't even looking and I'd snap the ball to him perfect with the strings in front and he'd say, 'What the hell are you doing? You don't even look.' I enjoyed this attention. I was known as the center who could center the ball without looking."

Wietecha needed every edge he could get. He was only 6-foot 1-inch tall, and he weighed about 225 pounds. He was often outweighed 40 to 50 pounds by the man opposite him.

"I tried never to lose my temper. I made whatever I made through my intelligence. I wasn't that strong or that tough. I'd set a man up for something. I guess I was a finesser. I was quick, and that was essential for me against those 270-pound tackles. Today they have the same size, but they're down to 250 and a lot faster. In my day they were big and slow. I always kept my cool. I needed that to figure out how to get by on the next play.

"There was no question, though, that the Giants were noted for defense more than offense. We were 5 yards and a cloud of dust, or we'd throw the nice little pass. But this was the start of defensive football, when the players started going for

the sacks. We had, for the first time in pro football, continuous good defense, you know, four, five, six years straight.
That was unheard of. I look at that picture in my den and
reminisce. It was quite an era. Yes.''

If there was any glory on that 1956 Giants team, it was apparent to Sam Huff that he would never be part of it. He was
an odd size for the pros of that era. At 6-foot 1-inch and 230
pounds he was too small for the line, too slow for linebacking.
So much for first impressions.

"Jim Lee didn't like rookies, and he was always yelling—
bellering he'd call it. We took so much hell that finally me
and Don Chandler went to Ed Kolman and returned our play
books. I told Kolman I couldn't take it anymore,'' recounts
Huff. ''We saw Coach Lombardi and told him we were quitting
and he gave it to us, about how he had invested two weeks in
us and he wasn't going to let us go and how we couldn't quit
on the team.'' So Huff stayed.

What was to come was four straight years in the Pro Bowl,
eight years as the signal caller of the defense, and more than
a dozen confrontations with the Browns' Jim Brown and
Green Bay's Jim Taylor; a television documentary on the man
and his work; and finally, an image as the most famous defensive football player of his time.

Perhaps it is coincidence, but when he was traded after the
1963 season, the Giants began the slide that kept them in the
sport's lower depths for the rest of the sixties and well into
the seventies.

"Do I remember that time?'' asks Huff. ''Sure. Everyone
does. Even though it was so long ago, ask anyone to name the
front four of the Giants and they'll tell you Grier, Modzelewski, Katcavage, Robustelli. But ask them to name the Pittsburgh Steelers' front four—and they're playing now—and I'll
bet you more people can tell you the Giants' names.''

Huff is a secure executive these days, with the title of Director of Market Development for the Marriott Hotel people. His
big job is to get teams to stay at Marriott hotels.

"You prepare for life and business by playing football. A person competes every day of his life. In football your opponent is on the other side of the line from you. You beat him head to head, you win the game. In business your opponent is out there. But you don't know where he is."

He speaks simply, without wasting words. In a sense, he played simply, without wasting motions. What you saw was what he had to give.

"I was born in a small coal-mining camp near Morgantown, called Edna Gas. Remember that song 'Sixteen Tons'? Well, that's exactly what it was like. I went to a small high school in Farmington, West Virginia. I lived in a coal-mining camp there called Number Nine. You see, coal companies used to own a lot of coal mines, so what they used to do was number them—you know, Consolidated Number One, Console Number Two, Console Number Three.

"The companies built row houses; then they rented them back to the people that worked for them. So all the income, the rent, went back to the company. I was happy as a child. When you're poor you don't realize you're poor. I don't think I'd trade my childhood for any other.

"You know, when we heard of New York, or heard of Chicago, those type of places, California—those were fantasy places. Because all I knew was my father worked in the mine, and we got the Pittsburgh Pirates on the radio and I never traveled out of the state of West Virginia until I went to West Virginia University. So, you know, that's what you grow up with. My father was a coal miner all his life, and he took as much pride in his life of loading coal as I did stopping Jimmy Brown."

Yet, Sam Huff did not want the mine as a way of life. Not that there was anything wrong with labor. It's just:

"My dad would come home with that coal dust and spit it out of his lungs. I always wanted to be a football coach or a history teacher. I never dreamed of playing professional football." He became, though, the only member of his family to leave home.

"We lived on the side of a hill. In West Virginia you live

either in a valley or on a hill. And you might remember about
five years ago there was a mine in West Virginia that ex-
ploded and killed seventy-eight people? Well, that's where I
lived. Console Number Nine. My father worked there, but he
wasn't in the mine. I had three cousins killed in the explosion.
They're still in there.''

How were you able to adjust to New York?

''College was the transition. I got to travel. You know I was
all-American and so forth. And we got to the Sugar Bowl in
1953. We played Pitt, Penn State. I traveled. Then I was
drafted by the Giants. I didn't know what I was getting into.''

History repeated itself in Huff's case. DeRogatis again
figured in it. This time DeRogatis was looking at another lineman and spotted Huff. When Huff made it to New York, he
was lucky in two respects: he was joining a good club, and it
was a club that was to win the ''world'' championship. That
made it easier to adjust to New York.

''We were off and running, winning the world championship. Then I looked closely at the guys around me—you know,
Frank Gifford, Kyle Rote—and at what they were doing and
how successful they were. I watched them, watched how they
operated. I learned.''

Not right away, mind you. For Sam Huff, major league
football player, took an off-season job as a stock boy in a West
Virginia supermarket. He even had the job after he was an
all-pro. It had its advantages. Huff knew the store manager
and was able to avoid joining the union because the manager
gave him fewer than forty hours of work a week.

''I was making a couple of dollars an hour, but I figured
it's better to have some pay check coming in than nothing at all.
My first year with the Giants, I only made $7,000.''

That must have seemed like a lot of money for only six
months of work. As a child Huff always wanted a pony, but
he was one of six young children to feed and a pony was a
frivolity for a coal miner's family in the late 1930s. Sam, especially, personally accounted for a lot of grocery money at
the company store. He was 10½ pounds at birth, and he remained bigger than the other boys through his school years.

He was also more precocious in one other respect: he got married when he was seventeen years old and still a senior in high school. In fact, West Point was interested in him for the Army football team, but Coach Red Blaik did not know Huff was married. That kept him out of the Military Academy.

Now, as the fall of 1956 approached, Sam Huff, twenty-two years old, was going to try to make a name for himself in the big city, a city that had been as real to him as a fairy tale.

Of course, the Giants opened on the road. They started with a victory at San Francisco and a loss to the Cardinals at Chicago. Then came the Browns at Cleveland. Once that meant disaster, but Paul Brown was to taste the first losing season of his coaching career. Graham had retired for good and the quarterback duties were divided among three people—Tommy O'Connell, George Ratterman, and Babe Parilli. It was difficult enough to give a team leadership under a two-quarterback system.

Because of the absence of a throwing threat, the Browns' ground game became ineffective. The quarterbacks threw for a total of only 8 touchdowns in the 12-game season. The club barely averaged 14 points a game. Perhaps because he knew he'd have to try something new, Paul Brown attempted to set up radio communications with his quarterbacks by implanting a tiny receiver in their helmets.

In their opening game the Browns lost by only 2 points to the powerful Cardinals, and in their second game they routed the Steelers. So maybe Brown had discovered something. The Giants knew, naturally, about Browns' plans. They planned to intercept the broadcast.

Bob Topp, a rookie receiver from Michigan, operated a radio receiver on the Giants' bench. Gene Filipski, recently acquired from the Browns, was nearby in case Brown used number signals which had to be translated.

The crisp voice of Paul Brown came over loud and clear on the Giants' bench. But a funny thing was happening on the field. Ratterman was pointing to his helmet, looking to the bench, and then pointing to the crowd. The noise of his home town fans, excited at seeing the Browns' first home game of the season, drowned out the coach. After three plays Ratterman couldn't hear a thing. Topp, meanwhile, was giving Landry the play and Landry was shouting it to the defense. It was an easy 21–9 victory for the Giants, with Webster scoring the three touchdowns. The Giants were 2–1 as they left for New York and their first game at Yankee Stadium.

The stadium had been used only a few weeks earlier—for Don Larsen's perfect game. Now Conerly walked softly on carpeting! The Polo Grounds had had wood floors and toilets that wouldn't flush. This was—well, it was a stamp. A major league image. Conerly took Mickey Mantle's locker. Rote grabbed Billy Martin's. The first time Dick Modzelewski put his foot inside the place he said to Howell, "Coach, my brother was traded to Cleveland last season and they got a championship, and now I've been traded to you and we're gonna get a championship."

Howell walked around the field, looking up at the empty seats, and even though he was a practical man, he recalls: "There was this Yankee tradition. You know. They were the greatest. It helped us."

The two clubs finally joined. Like the football Giants, the Yankees had started in the Polo Grounds. The baseball Giants of the World War I years had not minded sharing the park with them. But the Yanks did not have Babe Ruth. In 1919 the Yanks drew about 600,000 fans to the Polo Grounds. Then they got Ruth and in 1920 attracted almost 1,300,000. That was 100,000 more fans than the Giants attracted.

John McGraw, the Giants' manager, was furious at his club's fame being usurped. He told Charles Stoneham, the Giants' owner: "The Yankees will have to build a park in Queens or some other out-of-the-way place."

The Yanks got the message. But Queens? Nothing there but estates in places with names like Bayside, where Billy Rose lived. No. The Yankees would stay around. Early in 1921 they bought ten acres of land in the Bronx between 157th Street and 161st Street, running from River Avenue to Doughty Avenue. The land was a remnant belonging to the estate of William Waldorf Astor. The running time from Times Square by the elevated was only sixteen minutes.

The site did not please McGraw. For the stadium would be just across the Harlem River—to the eye it would clash with the Polo Grounds. To rival the Yanks' park's opening in 1923, the baseball Giants refurbished the Polo Grounds by adding more than 5,000 seats and bringing the capacity up to 54,000.

The massive building job of erecting Yankee Stadium was given to the company once owned by Stanford White. In April 1922, the Yankees' owners asked if it could be ready in a year. It was turned over to them in 284 working days—on April 18, 1923, when the greatest crowd to see a baseball game (74,200) turned out for the opening. An immediate tradition, one that was to reach full flower during the football Giants' great years, began: two men were arrested for scalping. One hawked a $1.10 ticket for $1.25; the other man was asking $1.50.

More than thirty years later, when the football Giants moved in, the price of a baseball ticket had not gone up that much. In fact, there was little about Yankee Stadium that had changed. There was only parking for 1,500 cars, but that did not seem to matter much since most people came by the IRT subway right outside the place. It was a subway stop familiar to thousands of football followers who had trekked across the Macombs Dam Bridge when the Giants had played in the Polo Grounds. Now they were entering a park so famous that the usually explicit *New York Times* referred to it simply as the "Stadium."

The largest opening day crowd in the football Giants' history saw them open at the Stadium on October 21, 1956. The 48,108 fans were treated to a 38–10 trouncing of the Steelers. It was the first game at the park since the perfect game, and this time the fans saw another type of perfection. The Giants were methodical and Conerly was on target with 3 touchdown passes. That brought their record to 3–1. But they trailed in the East to the Cards, whose mark was 4–0.

In midweek, there was this brief news story: "Robert Lee (Sam) Huff, a rookie, will take over Ray Beck's post as middle guard and linebacker for the Eagles' game this Sunday."

Huff's first start as a Giant had ironic overtones. For he was opposite the symbol of Giants' defenses for most of the club's history: Steve Owen. Owen was now a defensive coordinator for Hugh Devore, coach of the Eagles. It was the first time Owen sat opposite the Giants' bench since he had galloped into town as a member of the Kansas City Cowboys.

Owen, though, proved no match for figuring out how to stop Lombardi's newfangled gimmick, called a "sweep." Although the Giants won handily, 20–3, reporters and fans the next day spoke mostly about Gifford's 37-yard run. The word "sweep" was new to them and in fact, was used with quotes when written about. Gifford's revolutionary dash was a model of simplicity, depending, as did all of Lombardi's tactics, on being in the right place at the right time. This was it:

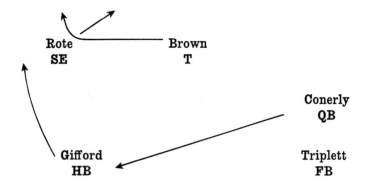

Simple, really. Gifford would take Conerly's pitchout just as the Philadelphia defense would charge up the center. Gifford then ran to his left with Brown running interference for him. This play and others lifted the Giants into a first place tie with the Cards, who were losing their first game to the

Redskins. The Giants and Cards each had a 4–1 mark. Each won the next week and after half a season the teams remained tied at 5–1.

For the first time in years, the Giants had a ''crucial'' game coming up. The Cardinals were coming into the Stadium, and the winner would stand alone on top of the Eastern Conference.

Lavelle, their pessimistic scout, started the Giants thinking about the game early in the week. ''The Cards,'' he announced, ''have a party planned for Sunday night after the game.''

Of course, they did not. Did the Giants really believe Lavelle? Did athletes really get upset when another team bragged it was better? When Walt Yowarsky became a Giants' scout he said before an Eagles' game: ''Philadelphia isn't tough.'' The story was duly noted, clipped out, and tacked onto the Eagles' bulletin board in their locker room.

''The Eagles are mad,'' shouted Howell to his men before the game. ''What are we going to do about it?''

''Maybe,'' suggested Grier, ''we ought to apologize to them.''

Yet, this really was a clutch game coming up. The Cards had an easier schedule for the remainder of the season. The Giants knew they had to take the Cards themselves. No one would do it for them. And to take the Cards, they had to halt Ollie Matson, the East's leading rusher. The Cards, in fact, ran the ball more than any other team except for the Bears in the twelve-team league.

The Cards were easy. Maybe it was because each of the Giants got shots of vitamin B-1 and vitamin B-12 before the game. Maybe it was because the largest crowd to see the Giants play since 1928 (when Red Grange was the attraction) poured into the Stadium. Whatever the reason, 62,410 fans saw what a defense could do. First Robustelli blocked a Cards punt attempt and the keyed-up Katcavage pounced on it for a safety. The final score was 23–10, and the Giants were in first place by themselves. The defense had held Matson to 43 yards.

The five-game winning streak was halted the following

week by the Redskins, but luckily for the Giants the Cards
also lost. The Giants' mark was 6–2, and the Cards were 5–3.
A one-game lead for the New Yorkers. That did not look large,
though, for the Bears were the Giants' opponent in the ninth
game. The Chicagoans were not only 7–1, but they also had
the most powerful attack in the league by far. Rick Casares
was leading in rushing and touchdowns. Ed Brown, replacing
the aging George Blanda at quarterback, was leading in passing, and Harlon Hill, a skinny end, was leading all receivers
in yardage.

This would be a test for the Giants' defense, and especially
for the secondary, which was led by Em Tunnell. This game
would mark Tunnell's 100th straight game as a Giant.

That was not a bad record for a player very few coaches in
pro football had ever heard of until he put on a Giants' uniform back in 1948. Tunnell had been graduated from Iowa, but
nobody drafted him. The reason was simple: he didn't play as
a senior. After his junior year he underwent an eye operation
that sidelined him. He decided to give football a last chance
one day when got a lift from his Garrett Hill, Pennsylvania,
home, not far from Philadelphia. A West Indian driving a
banana truck took Tunnell to the mouth of the Lincoln Tunnel.
The player walked unannounced into the Giants' office and
asked for a job. The name rang a bell with the general manager, Ray Walsh. And Tunnell became the first black man to
play for the Giants.

He was remarkably strong, and especially big, for a defensive back. At 6 feet 1 inch and 190 pounds, he was one of
the most massive defensive backs of his day. When he began
there was two-way football, and defensive backs generally
were not large. Yet, in his first season with the Giants he made
more news by his performance as a punt-return man, and it
was negative news. The conservative Steve Owen did not like
his men to return a punt if there was the least chance of being
tackled. So often Tunnell was forced to signal for a fair catch.
That is seen by some fans as a sign of cowardice. After three
fair catches in a game, with the booing of the Polo Grounds'
fans distressing him, he told Owen, ''I don't want to return

any more punts today." That same game, Tunnell returned a punt for a touchdown.

That was one of 258 punt returns in a career he continued with the Giants through 1958 and then wound up with the Green Bay Packers. That number is a league record, as are his most career interceptions (79), most yardage for interception returns (1,240), and most yardage on punt returns (2,206). In all, he set 16 Giant club records.

Yet he remained a sensitive individual who would never talk badly about an opponent whom he would willingly demolish on the football field. Tunnell always believed he was lucky to be a Giant, and he could never understand new generations of players who thought first about money before they would agree to play.

For many years in the Owen era, Tunnell was the only Giant to make the Pro Bowl. He played in it, against the best of his peers, from 1951 through 1957. He was probably the only player in the league to participate those seven straight seasons. His ability to gain extraordinary yardage on kickoffs, interceptions, and punt returns kept him relegated to the defense. In 1952, though, he gained more yardage with interceptions and kick returns than the league's leading runner, Deacon Dan Towler. Tunnell never led the league in interceptions for any single season. Longevity and consistency were his trademarks.

Tunnell was to become the first black assistant coach in the NFL when the Giants brought him back, and he was the first black selected for the Pro Football Hall of Fame and the first player to get to the Hall purely for defensive talents. As a Giants coach he was a rock for many young, gifted athletes who came up North from all-black schools in the South and Southwest and suddenly found themselves as "representatives" of a race, to make pronouncements on the major racial issues of the 1960s. Rarely did Tunnell ever scold a player, and if he did, he smiled first. One of his groups of backs he called "Emlen's Gremlins," which included Carl Lockhart, who Tunnell quickly termed a "spider" surrounding its prey. The nickname stuck. In later years, when Lockhart had the

first of many salary hassles with the team, Tunnell told him,
"You should be paying them. It's an honor to play here."
This was probably a statement of Tunnell's feelings on being
a Giant.

When he died in 1975, he was fifty years old.

In 1956, playing in his hundredth straight game, Tunnell
was going through an exhilarating time. He was joined by
true stars. They were evolving into a sort of family with a
sort of love, "manly-type love," as Katcavage was to call it
years later. In the Bears, the Giants were facing a team that,
for the first time, was not led by George Halas. Paddy Driscoll
had replaced the Papa Bear. The Giants' confidence was growing. The Cards' quarterback, Lamar McHan, was fined $3,000
by Coach Ray Richards for refusing to work out. It was the
greatest fine ever levied in league history. Perhaps the Cards
would begin to fold. That would certainly be easier than having to stop the Bears.

That is what the Giants did, mostly. The Bears were down
17–3 in the final quarter. But they engineered two long touchdown passes that brought a tie. Still, the Giants held the
league leading Casares to an incredible total of 13 yards in
13 carries. The whole Chicago rushing offense, in fact, got
only 12 yards as the rest of the ball carriers were thrown for
minus yardage.

The last-minute scoring was unsettling, but on Monday
morning the Giants remained in first place. Their record
stood at 6 victories, 2 losses, 1 tie. The Cards were at 6–3.
And, all of a sudden, the Redskins were in the pack. They had
5 straight victories, a mark of 5–3, with a game to be played
after the Giants closed their regular season, and they were
coming into Yankee Stadium the next Sunday. If the Redskins could beat the Giants, they could finish on top, since their
remaining opponents were the losing Eagles, Steelers, and
Colts.

This time Gifford went to work. He scored 3 times. The
Giants had 4 touchdowns. Gifford passed for that other score.
The final was 28–14 and now the New Yorkers' lead was com-

manding. Gifford's running was among the best in the league. He easily had more yardage rushing than any other Giant. But the Giants did not want to make it easy on themselves or their fans. Their final regular season home game was looming, and it was against the Browns. A victory would clinch the Eastern Conference title with one game remaining. But a victory was what the Giants did not get. In the snow and rain the Browns gained an easy 24-7 decision. The only positive statistics were Gifford's 6 catches. They gave him a Giants season record. Now Gifford not only led his club in rushing, he led it in catching, too.

The final game of the 1956 campaign for the Giants was staged at Philadelphia on a Saturday. The Giants were 7-3-1. Washington was 6-4, with two games remaining. A Giants loss would enable the Redskins to finish first by winning their last two games.

Charlie Conerly did not have the honor of leading the Giants to their first first-place finish since 1946. Howell selected Heinrich to start. Conerly merely came in to hold the extra-point attempts by Agajanian. There were three, all good, as the Giants won 21-7. Fittingly, though, the touchdowns were scored by Rote, Gifford, and Webtser. Howell had the distinction of being the only Giants' coach, other than Steve Owen, to lead the New Yorkers to a division title.

The next day the Giants learned they would be playing the Bears for the world championship. To this day, players refer to it as the world championship, not the NFL championship or the North American, or the United States. It was for the best in the world, as simple as that. What did it matter that, except for Canada, no other country had a professional football team?

The title game was set for December 30. Curiously, the last time the Giants had played for the championship, ten years before, they had also met the Bears. Things had certainly changed since then. But they had changed even more dramatically since 1933, when the same clubs met in the league's first championship. Now in 1956 teams were required by league rule to exchange films. The films confirmed what each club knew: the Bears were the most frightening team on offense and the Giants were the finest clutch team on defense.

In boxing, that would be referred to as a "classic" match—the scientific boxer against the slugger. Over the years the Bears had also been known as the roughest collection in football. They still own most of the career records for penalties. In the league's first 50 years they led in penalties 15 times. The closest competitor in this department was the Los Angeles Rams—with 4. Perhaps thinking about the Bears, Gordie Soltau, the 49ers' end, suggested a penalty box should be instituted in football as there is in hockey.

As the Giants prepared for the game at the Stadium, they received further tangible evidence of their growing superiority and stature in the league. Five of them were voted onto the 22-man all-star team. Three of the 11 defensemen were Giants: Robustelli, Grier, Tunnell. Gifford and Brown made it on offense.

It was cold in New York on Sunday. It had been cold for a week, so frozen that the field had been covered with a tarpaulin for days. Still, the ground was like concrete. That gave Wellington Mara an idea. When the Giants won their first championship in 1934, they had played the Bears and they wore sneakers and won. This time there would be no frantic, last minute call for sneakers. Robustelli, who was in the sporting goods business, ordered the special shoes. The day before the 1956 championship the Giants put the sneakers on. The high-topped shoes appeared to work. The players were happy with them.

Something even more unusual took place in the city the day before the game: the National Football League Players' Association was formed. It was a strange coincidence that so much of the NFL's future should be tied up with the two events—the players' union and the Giants–Bears championship. At the time, the association seemed to be anything but a union. One of the driving forces behind the association was

Rote, which doesn't seem so strange. He represented the East. But the man who represented the Western Conference was, in retrospect, startling: Norm Van Brocklin, quarterback of the Los Angeles Rams. In later years as a coach, Van Brocklin was to stand for a reactionary way of doing business and a reactionary way of thinking. Players who were "different" did not get along with Van Brocklin. Yet, he was one of the prime organizers of the association that was supposed to make life better for players in their dealings with management.

"I remember the Bears didn't send anyone to the meeting in New York," recalls Rote. "I guess they were scared. Some of the resolutions we had drafted—such as a minimum wage —were so far below even what they received that they didn't want to jeopardize what they were getting. Halas told them, 'Okay, if you want a union you'll get it, but the other benefits will stop.' Halas used to give them spending money, a hundred bucks for a trip to the West Coast, things like that. And Marshall of Washington told his players that if any of them showed up for the Players' Association meeting they'd be in another uniform next season."

That did not frighten such player representatives as Y. A. Tittle of the 49ers, Bill Howton of Green Bay, and Adrian Burk of Philadelphia. But the Steelers and Bears did not send anyone.

"We had our meeting, we voted, and then later we got ready for a press conference," continues Rote. "And Eddie LeBaron of the Redskins says, 'I'm not going to be in any photos. I'll be here, I'll vote, but no photos.' So if you see the first photos of the Players' Association, Eddie LeBaron's missing."

For most fans who read about the union in Sunday morning's paper, it was a secondary event. The game coming up was more interesting to read about, and the Sunday comics were more fun. There was, in 1956, something faintly silly about big, grown ballplayers forming an association. It was more fun to watch them play than to read about their salary demands.

The wind gusted at more than thirty miles an hour, howling

in from behind the bleachers at the ball park. The Stadium was wide open behind the low bleachers, and the wind came in with a funnel effect, swirling around the place, moving up to the top of the columned rafters and dipping down in crazy patterns. It was cold and one of the most uncomfortable days of the year. That did not stop a few dozen people from taking their accustomed spot on top of the roof of the apartment buildings across the street, behind the bleachers, where they were framed by the H-shaped antennae, and could see a part of the field. Howell sent out Ed Hughes and Gene Filipski before the game. Each wore sneakers. They ran around, did some cutting, and came back to report that they didn't fall. Howell decided everyone would wear sneakers.

The crowd was a remarkable 56,836. They stood and cheered wildly when their team came out, and some of the players sensed an almost collegelike atmosphere. All that remained was to introduce the seniors first. This was the starting line-up the fans saw:

Offense		Defense	
(44) Rote, SMU	L.E.	**(78)** Yowarsky, Ky.	L.E.
(79) Brown, Morgan St.	L.T.	**(77)** Modzelewski, Md.	L.T.
(60) Austin, Oregon St.	L.G.	**(70)** Huff, W. Va.	M.G.
(25) Wietecha, N'western	C.	**(76)** Grier, Penn St.	R.T.
(66) Stroud, Tenn.	R.G.	**(81)** Robustelli, Arnold	R.E.
(72) Yelvington, Ga.	R.T.	**(30)** Svoboda, Tulane	L.LB.
(80) MacAfee, Ala.	R.E.	**(84)** Svare, Wash. St.	R.LB.
(11) Heinrich, Wash.	Q.B.	**(48)** Hughes, Tulsa	L.H.
(16) Gifford, So. Cal.	L.H.	**(25)** Nolan, Md.	R.H.
(29) Webster, No. Car. St.	R.H.	**(45)** Tunnell, Iowa	L.S.
(33) Triplett, Toledo	FB.	**(20)** Patton, Miss.	R.S.

These names did not bring a glow to the bookmakers. They made the Bears a 3-point favorite. The odds did not look half bad to favorite players, either, after they saw that the Bears came out with sneakers, too.

The Giants were loose in their locker room. Too loose. They were joking and living off a giddy high. This disturbed

Howell. "In my time," he told an assistant, "people were pretty quiet before a big game."

Howell soon relaxed. Filipski took the opening kickoff. He had the benefit of extra practice over the rock-hard ground and dashed back 53 yards with the ball to the Bears' 38-yard line. In four more plays Mel Triplett scored on a 17-yard run behind Modzelewski. Hip flasks sprouted from behind raccoon coats as fans celebrated. In the cold, wooden bleachers, fans erected bonfires to keep themselves warm or passed the bottle around.

The Bears got the ball back for only two plays. Casares was popped so hard he lost the ball and the Giants recovered. Before long Agajanian converted that loss into a Giants field goal. The New Yorkers led 10-0. Soon, Jimmy Patton picked off an Ed Brown pass, and this time Agajanian kicked a 43-yarder. It was 13-0 at the end of the quarter.

Before three minutes of the second quarter were up, Webster bulled over from 3 yards out and it was 20-0. The Giants were well on their way to the biggest rout in championship play since the Bears' 73-0 victory over the Redskins in 1940. The Giants' path was blocked momentarily when Tunnell fumbled a punt and the Chicagoans recovered. Casares got the Bears' touchdown on a 9-yard run but the Giants kept pushing. Conerly came in to replace Heinrich. The old man hit Webster on a 50-yard pass play and the Giants capped a 72-yard drive with Webster scoring from the 1 for a 27-7 edge. On the next drive by Chicago, which stalled, Ray Beck blocked a punt attempt, and Henry Moore fell on it in the end zone. At half time the Giants led, incredibly, 34-7. Discretion now became the better part of valor for thousands of fans, and they left at intermission. After all, they could get the game on home television. That season the NFL had signed its first contract with CBS, which gave the network the right to televise all games except those within a 150-mile radius of the city. But the rule was waived for the championship game. So for the first time in the season Giants fans could see a home game on television with Chris Schenkel and Johnny Lujack doing the commentary.

Blanda came in for the Bears in the second half and began
unloading desperation heaves. They fell with a crackling
sound on frozen turf. For the only scoring of the second half
belonged to the Giants—a third-quarter Conerly-to-Rote play
and a final-period Conerly-to-Gifford pass. The final score was
47–7. The Giants were world champions.

The victory was worth $3,779.19 to each Giant. That was
practically as much money as some of them had signed for
in their rookie seasons. Perhaps one of them, in a magnani-
mous mood, might have even offered to provide the Giants
with a new mimeograph machine in the press box. The old
one had frozen during the game.

Later, after celebrating at the park, but before the long
night of revelry to come, Jack Mara saw Tunnell standing by
himself across the street from the Stadium. Mara approached
Tunnell, who was staring at the ball park.

"Someone should put a statue of a Giant on top of that
building," said Tunnell.

Charlie Conerly, the farmer-quarterback, who became the Giants' first T-formation quarterback.

The tactical wizzard, Allie Sherman, paces the sideline at a tense moment.

Kyle Rote, Jack Stroud, Charlie Conerly, and Y.A. Tittle look on as Sherman plays the professor.

Sonny Jurgensen
about to feel the full
impact of Rosey
Grier.

Jerry Hillebrand
zeroes in on Cowboy
quarterback Don
Meredith.

San Francisco quarterback Lamar McHan must have felt the pressure of Tom Scott (82) and Andy Robustelli (81) as his pass falls victim to Giant linebacker Jerry Hillebrand.

Norm Snead, the Redskins' quarterback, about to be hit by 290-pound Rosey Grier.

Norm Snead of the Washington Redskins is seized with fear as
Robustelli and Katcavage burst through his line.

Eagles' Sonny Jurgensen discovers why the Giants' defense was
considered to be the best in pro football. Katcavage (75) and Robustelli
(81) team up to throw him for a big loss.

THE GREATEST GAME EVER PLAYED
THE GIANTS vs. COLTS TITLE GAME OF 1958.

Jim Patton (20) about to pounce on a fumble by Colts' quarterback John Unitas.

A Giant fumble, this time by Frank Gifford, but the Giants recover.

The Colts' place kicker Steve Myra ties the score 17-17 with a field goal.

Victory for the Colts in sudden death overtime, as Alan Ameche plows over from the one-yard line.

Sometimes they got away. Brown runner breaks away from Scott (82), Robustelli (81), and Barnes (49).

Dick Lynch (22) wants to make sure this Steeler is safely grounded.

Kicking specialist Don "The Babe" Chandler warms up at the Stadium.

Jim Katcavage pursues Redskin Taylor from behind.

Del Shofner, one of Y.A. Tittle's favorite targets, brings in a short one against the 49ers.

Shofner watches from the bench alongside Joe Morrison.

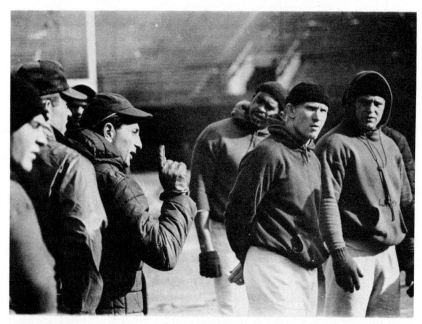

"Now Hear This!" Sherman talks to his offensive starters prior to a game against the Browns to decide the Eastern Division championship.

Sherman gives his offensive players a few pointers at a workout at Yankee Stadium. Listening to Sherman, left to right, are: Joe Morrison, Phil King, Joe Walton, Del Shofner, Don Chandler, Ralph Guglieimi, and Frank Gifford.

GIANT STALWARTS

Joe Morrison

Tom Scott

**GIANT
STALWARTS**

Jack Stroud

Jim Patton

For the first time, sports began making news in nonsports ways in 1957. Instead of people reading about results, they began to read about issues. It was the last year in New York for the Giants and the Dodgers. Althea Gibson became the first black to win at Wimbledon and Forest Hills. And Ted Lindsay of the Detroit Red Wings, hockey's most penalized player, became head of the fledgling Players' Association and accused the National Hockey League of dictatorial tactics.

But other, more cosmic events, were on people's minds that year, too. The Mad Bomber case was closed in New York. President Eisenhower took his first dive in an atomic submarine. There was a boom in Shirley Temple dolls. The Soviet Union sent a satellite into orbit.

Crime became news. Albert Anastasia was murdered in the barber shop of the Park Sheraton Hotel. A convention was broken up in Apalachin, New York, and a policeman in on the raid said, "It looked like a meeting of George Rafts."

The Citizens Budget Committee frightened New Yorkers when it proclaimed the city was on the brink of "a fiscal mess" as a result of extravagant expenses. That shot down any hope for a Dodger stadium. Still, people could improve their minds: if they got up early enough, they could catch Professor Floyd Zulli on "Sunrise Semester."

None of this meant that there were not interesting things going on for the hard-core sports fan. He could marvel at those two old men of baseball, Ted Williams, aged thirty-nine, and Stan Musial, aged thirty-six, who led their leagues in hitting. Williams swatted a .388, the highest since his own .406 season before the war, and Musial batted .351. The hockey fan could frown at the fickleness of the Rangers' followers, who booed Harry Howell out of the team's captaincy. He was replaced by Red Sullivan. It is revealed that Robert Moses had offered to put up a stadium in Flushing, Queens, for Walter O'Malley. The Polo Grounds turnstiles were moved to San Francisco. Dick Lynch's touchdown for Notre Dame ended Oklahoma's 47-game winning streak, the greatest in major college football history.

The Giants–Dodgers rivalry ended at the Polo Grounds after 1,256 games. The Giants won 3–2, on Hank Sauer's two-run homer. The NFL agreed to recognize the Players' Association and to grant its demand for a minimum salary of $5,000 a year and $50 an exhibition game.

Frank Gifford came to symbolize the Giants. He moved smartly around town, from Shor's, to P. J. Clarke's, to television and radio, to the Stadium—all with an easy grace that mirrored the way he played football. People called it "class," as they called the Giants a "class" organization.

Gifford came out of the Golden West, another larger-than-life hero who singled-handedly led USC to an upset over California, which was going for its fortieth straight Pacific Coast Conference victory. While in school he appeared in two motion pictures that might have been named for him: *Saturday's Hero* and *All-American*. He lost out to Tab Hunter in the lead for *Battle Cry*. He came with interesting credentials.

By the time the 1957 season had started, Gifford was in his sixth season. But it had not been until 1956 that he became a heroic, nationally known professional football player. He led the NFL in total yardage. He also led the Giants in rushing and receiving, a feat he was to match for another three straight seasons. His teammates in 1956 voted him the most valuable Giant.

Today, Gifford is probably the most visible ex-pro football player in the United States. He has made it big because he stayed in sports rather than finding success with a TV pilot he once made based on the files of the New Jersey Turnpike Police.

What was so good about those Giants' teams? he was asked.

"It was an unusual group of guys," he says. "First, we had two coaches, Lombardi and Landry, who were the best in the business. What was unusual about the team was that it wasn't that big—but it was smart. That, as much as anything else, contributed to the success. And we had very little distractions. We weren't making a hell of a lot of money. Most of us had come from someplace else, and eighteen of us lived in the same hotel, the Concourse Plaza, and we did things together."

When star athletes today have $200,000 condominiums, white llama rugs, and a Rolls-Royce, it seems strange to think that half the players on a world championship football team lived in a hotel on the Grand Concourse in the Bronx.

Gifford denies that his Golden Boy image hurt him with the team when he was a rookie, although stories persist that the older linemen would refuse to block for him during scrimmages.

"I guess I was sort of a glamor athlete," he concedes. "You know, working in the movies, going to USC. I think a lot of it was just kidding. We had a lot of Southerners and a lot of the kidding came from Jim Lee Howell. He thought Californians were very strange to begin with."

As the Giants' Number 1 draft choice, Gifford received a $250 bonus to sign his rookie contract of $8,000. "I played most of my first season on defense. They used me on offense, too, because they didn't know how long Kyle Rote was going to last. I came up in Kyle's second season and he was having leg problems. Mel Hein was one of my coaches at USC, and he must have told Wellington Mara about me. Wellington came to scout me in the East–West game, and I played sixty minutes and then in the Senior Bowl I played sixty minutes. So I guess they figured I was a pretty good deal. If I did not make it on offense, I could play defense.''

If Lombardi had not joined the team in 1954, it is possible that the Giants would have lost Gifford. They had spread him too thin.

''The last five games of 1953, I didn't come out. I played offense and defense,'' he says. ''I was kicking off, running back punts, kicking field goals. I was really questioning whether to come back in 1954. It was at training camp in Salem, Oregon, and the first thing Vince told me, the first time I met him—in fact, I didn't know who he was; I had never even heard of him—he stuck out his hand and said, 'Hiya, I'm Vince Lombardi and you're my halfback.' ''

Because Gifford could run, throw, and catch, the option play became one of the Giants' most effective weapons. Whenever Gifford ran out to the side with the ball the defense became perplexed. If he spotted a man open, he could hit him with a pass. If the defense lay back for the pass, Gifford could run. Because he did so many things so well, Gifford never was called on to simply run, or simply catch passes, or simply throw, or only kick field goals, or only run back punts, or run back kickoffs. He never ran enough in a season to lead the league in rushing or was employed as a receiver often enough to lead in receiving. Granted, he did not throw the ball as often as a regular quarterback. But he amassed the highest average per attempt of any player who threw at least 25 passes. His average of 13.1 yards an attempt is in a class by itself. Only three others ever averaged double figures. In addition, almost half his completions went for touchdowns. He averaged a touchdown about once in every four throws.

''Well,'' he says, ''I only threw the ball when I saw a man open. And it was usually for a long gain.''

Being in control of the situation has always marked Gifford's career. But once, in a hospital room, he got so shook up he did not know what to do. It was after a leg injury.

''A wild man came into my room at 5:30 in the morning,''

he says. "I had my leg all packed in ice and I couldn't move.
God, he was bananas. He said he wanted to help the Giants.
It was dark in the room and really eerie. He stood at the end
of my bed, and he started to tremble. He said he could make
the team and he could do this well and he could do that. I
wanted to get rid of him and I told him, 'If you're so good,
why don't you go down to the Stadium and tell them that?'
Meanwhile, I grabbed hold of a pitcher of ice water. If he was
going to come at me I was going to clunk him. Then he went
over to the venetian blinds and he began to rattle them. And
I'll never forget—he said, 'You're looking into a dead man's
eyes.' Then he started to talk about Korea and he ran his
fingers up and down the blinds like a machine-gun spray. I
told him, 'Get your ass down to the Stadium if you really want
to help this team.' Which is what he did."

The man somehow sneaked into the team's locker room during a scrimmage, but he ensconced himself in the cubicle belonging to the 260-pound Modzelewski. He was not heard from
again after he was carted off.

Gifford's roommate and good friend was Conerly. Does
anyone remember that in 1959 Gifford attempted to take away
Conerly's job by converting to quarterback? It was one of
the most unusual experiments in professional sports.

"You forget," says Gifford, "that I was a quarterback in
high school and a quarterback at USC for two years. Anyway,
I just felt that the way football was going—and I was proven
right—you needed an athlete to play quarterback. Charlie
was, you know, my roommate. I wrote, telling him what I
wanted to do. Then I flew down to Mississippi to tell him in
person. I thought I'd be more valuable to the team by playing
quarterback. Actually, it wasn't really very well thought out,
because I was also the leading rusher and leading receiver on
the team. Anyway, Jim Lee let me try, I think more to pacify
me than anything else. I really thought an athlete could do a
better job back there than a pure passer. You look at a passer,
when he gets hit he gets hurt. But an athlete gets hurt, he
generally can play in a week or so."

Gifford and Conerly went fishing and Gifford told him of

the unusual plan—a plan that could result in his best friend
losing a job.

"Fine with me," said Conerly. "I'll help you all I can."

Now, almost a generation later, Gifford wonders what really
was behind Conerly's matter-of-fact acceptance of the suggestion. "Actually," says Gifford, "I think Charlie was relieved. He didn't like practices, and now there'd be another
quarterback to have on the practice field."

It's not bitterness, but Gifford seems, at least, miffed that
"Jim Lee didn't believe it would last. I started an exhibition
against Detroit and had a pretty good first half. Then somebody got hurt, and I came in as a halfback and caught a bunch
of passes, and gained a bunch of yards, and that was the end
of it. I don't think I really got a full shot at it."

Was it possible that Gifford was sounding wistful, that his
fabulous career was not satisfying? After all, he set Giants
records for lifetime accomplishments in the following categories:

- Most points—484 (94 more than any other rusher or receiver).
- Most touchdowns—78 (13 more than Joe Morrison).
- Most consecutive games scoring touchdowns—
  10 (1957-58).
- Highest rushing average—4.3 yards a carry.
- Most yardage receiving—5,434 (more than 400
  yards better than anyone else).

He tied Giant records for:
- Most points in a game—18.
- Most catches in a game—11 (tied with Del Shof-
  ner, of all people).

He was second among Giants for:
- Lifetime rushing yardage—3,609.
- Lifetime pass catches—367.

"Well, playing quarterback was one of the things I wanted
to do," he says. "It would have . . . it's one of those things
you can't go back in life to do."

A very experienced Giants offense was now joined by a Giants defense that had a year together as a unit. Things could only be better. The Giants were surprised, though, when the Browns were able to pick up Syracuse's great runner, Jim Brown. He was not chosen first in the draft. At last, Coach Paul Brown would have some leverage in choosing his plays as he did when Motley and Graham starred for him.

Yet the Giants were a confident unit, especially after they halted the powerful Lions 17–0 in an exhibition game. A loss to Green Bay, led by Bart Starr who replaced Hornung as quarterback, did not dampen their hopes. It was the Giants' first victory over Detroit in five years.

The euphoria did not last long. In their opener at Cleveland, they bowed in the final 21 seconds on Groza's 47-yard field goal. The score was 6–3. They met Jim Brown for the first time, too, and the fullback, playing his first regular-season game as a pro, gained 89 yards on only 21 attempts. He left an impression on the New Yorkers and on Sam Huff in particular.

Whether he left an impression on all the writers is unknown. For many newspapers did not assign football people to write about the pros, even in the 1950s. Gifford still remembers that the Giants' opening day stories were pushed to the second sports page, and he remembers how many of the players would collectively pull the leg of the interviewer, explaining, for example, the "set play" that led to a catch while a receiver was falling. The Groza field goal failed to impress one reporter. He wrote: "It wasn't a picture kick. It went end over end." Presumably, he believed that even place-kicks should be aerodynamic spirals.

Although they held the powerful Browns to just two field goals, it was obvious that the New Yorkers weren't the same team without Grier, who packed his 300 pounds (give or take 15 or 20) off to Fort Dix, where he taught physical training. And the statistics bear out the Giants' troubles. In winning the title in 1956, they had the best defense against the run in the whole league, just over a hundred yards a game and an

average of 3.5 yards a carry. Without him, the yards-against
average soared to about 150 yards a game, the average rush
yielded 4 yards against them, and seven other clubs did better
in halting the opposition's running. Year in and year out, the
championship teams are the teams that stop the other club
from running. When you halt the opposition's runners, then
the other club has to try for the low percentage pass play.
That will fail in the long run. By stopping the other team's
runs, you're also stopping them from keeping possession for
any length of time, and that means your own defense will remain fresher.

The Giants barely held on to win their next two games by
24–20 scores. In the third game, at Washington, Conerly again
returned from oblivion. This time he had lost his first string
job to Heinrich again. But Heinrich broke his thumb. Conerly
started, completed 12 of 15 passes. That did not include a 68-
job to Heinrich again. But Heinrich broke his thumb. Conerly
started, completed 12 of 15 passes. That did not include a 68-
yard touchdown toss on the first play from Gifford to Bob
Schnelker, who eluded the Skins' usually reliable defensive
back, Don Shula. The play was designed by Lombardi, who
always mapped out an opening play. The game also was
marked by a club record 50-yard field goal by Agajanian.

So after three games, all on the road (even though they
were not pushed out of town by the baseball Giants any more,
they had to wait for the Yankees' season to end), they were
ready for their first home game with a respectable 2–1 record.
The Browns were 3–0.

What could Lavelle worry the Giants about? The team was
facing the Pittsburgh Steelers. He cautioned them about the
new Steelers' quarterback, Earl Morrall. The young man with
a crew cut was one of three new quarterbacks whom the new
coach, Buddy Parker, put on the team. The others were Len
Dawson and Jack Kemp. In his first year, Parker had made
so many changes that a player remarked, ''Don't send out
your laundry. You may be gone before it gets back.''

All this reslotting could not find Parker some solid running
backs. As a result, he let Morrall throw the ball virtually at

will. Morrall was pretty good at it, too, and he was presenting a problem for the opposition. Landry wondered about how to get as many people as possible into the Pittsburgh backfield. So he came up with something the Giants called the "red dog"—and instantly it became part of football jargon. Quite simply, he sent his linebackers into the backfield like this:

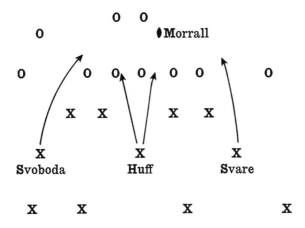

The Giants had shown their fans something new. And the growing sophistication the fans were priding themselves on— the Giants' road games were becoming tremendous CBS attractions in the New York metropolitan area—gave the fans something to look for. Again, a combination of happy circumstances gave an event the impetus it might not normally have received. For the Giants shut out the Steelers, who had scored 69 points in their first three games, 35–0. The Giants not only won, but they suddenly were tied for first with Cleveland, which was upset by the Eagles. Part of the arsenal of football that fans had seen, but had not really taken notice of, became Newspeak. Within a few days of learning about red dogging, fans were deluged with another concept: the "audible." All it means is that the play is changed at the line of scrimmage by the quarterback, who gives a code word and then the new play. The code word—maybe it's "Harry"—

wipes out the old play. The reason for an audible is, of course, because the quarterback suddenly sees something in the way the defense is aligned that tells him another play will work better. Unfortunately, the language took a pounding.

"Audible" simply means something is loud enough to be heard. It is an adjective, describing sound. In the hands of Joe Kuharich, the coach of the Redskins, though, it became a noun, a name for something. It gave an intellectual air to the game. A team no longer stopped another team—it "defensed" it. Here, a noun became a verb. Similarly, a player no longer pursued another—the "player showed good pursuit." This Newspeak was to reach the broadest usage under Allie Sherman and the intellectual jocks of the 1960s, when a player "didn't commit," or was in a "responsibility situation," or "keyed," or tried to gain weight by "beefing up."

The insiders' jargon kept increasing. There were now more than 30,000 season tickets, compared to only 6,000 in the Polo Grounds' final year. A large percentage of the fans were in the advertising business, where ideas were run up the flagpole and which readily accepted anything new. For newness was at the heart of most advertising—you resold a product by adding whiteners or brighteners. In the affluence of the 1950s, the expense account lunch broadened into the day-long entertainment, and when clients came to New York they wanted to see a football game. And since you could deduct the cost of tickets as a business expense on your income tax, why not buy a bunch of season tickets?

Kuharich's Washington Redskins were coming in for the second home game of the 1957 season, and they were led by the 5-foot 7-inch 168-pound Eddie LeBaron, who explained what this newfangled "audible" that Kuharich had started was.

The Giants dared not get overconfident, audibles or no, warned Lavelle. Even though the Skins had just been trounced by the Cards 44–14, the game, according to Lavelle, "was more Chicago brilliance than Washington failure."

On Sunday the game was picketed. This had never happened in pro football before. The pickets were protesting the fact that, in 1957, the Washington Redskins had no black players. They were the only team in big league sports (excepting hockey, a Canadian-based sport) without a black. This time the Giants lost, 31–14, and there was some crystallization of hard feelings. Howell singled out the defense for blame. Landry seethed because he felt his unit was being made the scapegoat. Perhaps at the half-season mark the Giants would begin to play consistently. Their opponent was Green Bay, and although the Packers were last in the West, Lavelle told the weekly news conference, "I can't put my finger on it, but the Packers are good." Perhaps, but not this week. The Giants had an easy 31–17 victory, in which Tunnell grabbed the 69th interception of his career for a Giants record.

After disposing of the worst in the West, the Giants now faced the lowest team in the East—the Cards. But be careful, Lavelle warned, for the Cards "could upset any club on a given afternoon."

The day was not given for the Cards as they were trounced. Another Giants record was established. Agajanian booted his 69th straight extra point. On that same day another more significant record for football was established: the first 100,000 crowd at a pro game. It filled the Memorial Coliseum to see Van Brocklin lead the Rams to a victory over the 49ers.

The next week the race turned even tighter. By halting the Eagles, 13–0, while the Browns were tying, the Giants were only half a game out of first place. They had a 6–2 mark, compared to the Browns' 6–1–1 record. The Giants were being forced to go along without the injured Rote and Webster, who was hospitalized with an ear infection. Webster wanted to leave his bed to play. "I'll only be a couple of hours," he told Mara, "and then I'll come right back."

Injuries did not knock out Katcavage, though. He insisted on playing while hurt, even hiding his ailments from the coaches.

"In them days," recounts Katcavage, "there were only thirteen Giants on the whole defensive unit. That year we went with eleven defensive guys, and the only one we had

to back us up was Cliff Livingston. He was a backup defensive
lineman, a backup linebacker, and a backup cornerman. I guess
we played hurt those days. If you don't think about getting
hurt and play as hard as you can—you don't get hurt.''

Katcavage's Giants playing career spanned 1956 to 1968.
These days he is the pro scout for the Eagles, his home town
team. The Katcavage crew cut remains one of his distinguish-
ing features, sort of a badge that tells you he played in the
days when a banged up knee did not take you out of the game,
especially if your team needed you.

''I was born in Wilkes-Barre,'' says Katcavage, ''but I
moved to Philadelphia in the second grade. I went to Roman
Catholic High School—that was the name of it, Roman Catholic—and I played basketball and football. But I hurt my
shoulder in my senior year—it came out on me six or seven
times in a few months. The colleges found out about it. You
see, they were going to give me a basketball scholarship. I
almost had one to Penn, Cornell, and Maryland. But they
found out about my shoulder and they told me they didn't
have an opening any more. All at once I didn't have a scholarship.

''So I went to my mom and dad and made them get me an
operation for my shoulder, and I got a one-year football
scholarship to Dayton. They told me that if I played well
they'd give me a full scholarship. When I was a junior, Hugh
Devore called me over to the field house and said, 'I want you
to meet somebody named Vince Lombardi.' I didn't know
him from a hole in the ground, but he told me, 'Son, you're
going to make it. You're aggressive. You might even be in
the draft next year.' But that went in one ear and out the
other. I only weighed about two-oh-five.

''But I went to the Shrine Game in 1955 in my senior year,
and I ate real good and I gained about twenty pounds in three
weeks. I was drafted Number Four in the January draft. In
those days they drafted the top three picks in December because they wanted to beat the Canadian League. When I came
up in 1956 I was backup for Walt Yowarsky. Then one game
Modzelewski got hurt and I went in for him. Then, in my sec-

ond year, 1957, Rosey Grier went into the service and I played tackle. After, I played end the whole time.''

Katcavage had one of the more unusual superstitions around football. He had to be first. Always. For everything. Other players might insist on wearing the same socks after a victory, or they always laced their shoes from the left side first. Those were individual hang-ups that did not alter the way a team got around. In Katcavage's case, though, logistics of movement had to be geared to his always being in front.

''I always had to be first—to get my ankles taped, to be the first one on the bus. Once in Cleveland, staying at the Sheraton, I had to leave tickets at the desk for someone. The bus left without me. So they all got way down to the Cleveland stadium and they realized I wasn't in the bus. They wouldn't let anybody off the bus. They came back and picked me up at the hotel. They didn't want to break tradition. I always had to be first, sit in the front, and be the first one off the bus.''

This all-for-one, one-for-all philosophy began with the defense, and the offense, out of necessity, maintained it. ''The whole defense was a close unit,'' says Katcavage, ''but the front four was especially. It just seemed that we helped one another all those years. We were together till 1962. You needed a manly type of love, and friendship, and togetherness. You wanted to help your buddy. How much did they pay me? My first salary was $6,200. To me, it was an awful lot of money. Times have changed.''

The 6–2 Giants heard an unexpected admission as they prepared to face the Cardinals as the 1957 season became gut-tightening. Conerly admitted he was thirty-six years old, not thirty-three as he was listed in the yearbook. ''No one ever actually asked me,'' he explains. ''Since someone asked me how old I was I told him.''

The Cards' game would mark the final positive note of the season for the Giants. Webster insisted on playing despite his bad ear infection. He carried twice and scored both times on short plunges. The Giants won and had a 7–2 mark, still half

a game behind the Browns, who are 7–1–1. But they fell farther
back the next week when they played horribly: Conerly fumbled five times and got red-dogged (and no one shouted "red
dog!" to warn of what was coming), and finally the Giants
bowed to the 49ers 27–17. San Francisco was led by Yelberton
Abraham Tittle, who perfected a play called the Alley-Oop, in
which he looped a pass to the 6-foot 3-inch R. C. Owens, who
leaped higher than the defender for the ball.

The Giants still had a chance to take the Browns. The New
Yorkers were 7–3. The Browns were 8–1–1. If the Giants could
beat Pittsburgh on December 7, and if the Browns fell to the
Lions, then the season would come down to the last game—
the Browns against the Giants at the Stadium. The Lions did
their share by trouncing the Browns, but the Steelers upset
the Giants, 21–10, and the Giants were eliminated.

For most other people, the last game of a schedule in which
the home team does not win would be an anticlimax. But a
strange thing happened in New York that week. The Giants
had the greatest advance sale in their history—50,000 tickets
were gone by midweek. It was more than simply a chance to
see the division champions, the Browns, or their sensational
rookie, Jimmy Brown. A tradition had been established, in
just a few years, of a transcendental rivalry. The Browns–
Giants affairs had become to football what a Knicks–Celtics
contest was to basketball or a Dodgers–Giants game to baseball or a Rangers–Bruins game to hockey. There really was no
such thing as a meaningless game between the football teams.
In 1955 the Giants had closed out their home season with that
memorable 35–all tie with the Browns. And in 1952 the Giants
ended their campaign with a 37–34 victory over the Browns.
Neither game was for a title or crucial, but the fans remembered.

"We hope to have something to stop Brown," said Howell.
What he planned to do—or what Landry planned to do—was
to isolate Huff on the Browns' running back with the ball.
Usually, that would mean Brown. Huff would be charged with
halting Brown, a stratagem that spread through the Giants'

community of fans with as much anticipation as the first person who watched the electric light bulb being tested.

The lights on the Stadium scoreboard began shining almost immediately as touchdowns, field goals, and extra points piled up in this final game of 1957 for the Giants. When Webster bulled over from the 1 yard out with fewer than seven minutes remaining in the game, the Giants led 28–27. The 54,294 fans —the season's largest in New York—did not leave. They watched with dismay as the Browns went ahead very quickly to lead 34–28. Then the Giants got the ball and the clock was an opponent as much as the Browns. The crowd began to chant "Go! Go! Go!" and the Giants moved. They got down to the Browns' 26-yard line and then time ran out. For the team and its fans, 1957 ended with a bang. It was a 7–5 year capped by three straight losses, but the finale brought a tingle of excitement to New Yorkers. The big crowd also pushed the Giants' attendance to a record 292,000 for six home games, almost 50,000 a game.

There was football fever out West, too. The 49ers–Lions playoff game was being blacked out to television viewers within 150 miles of San Francisco. There was a tremendous demand for tickets. Promoters organized charters on planes and buses to take football fans to Tahoe or to motels in Southern California, where the game could be seen on television.

The enthusiasm for pro football was building to a crescendo hardly heard only a few years before. And if the Giants' 1957 season ended with the despair of three straight defeats, their 1958 campaign would end in a sort of twilight zone of reality. Football was about to become the great American spectacle.

For the first time, they were New York's only Giants. The Dodgers left Brooklyn for Los Angeles in 1958, while the baseball Giants left the old Polo Grounds for San Francisco. There was one football team in New York and only one baseball team.

That did not mean sports were in trouble. On the contrary, business was booming, as was the economy. Cities in the South were talking about trying to lure big-league sports franchises. The Southwest was also looking to put itself on the sports map.

Although sports were starting to dominate the news, there were still enough outrageous happenings in 1958 in the news world:

A Georgia voter registrar admitted he flunked some Negroes on literacy tests even though he knew they had college degrees. Philip Morris was marketing a new cigarette called Marlboro, and had rehired its once-famous midget, Johnny, who was insured for $100,000 a year in case his voice changed or he grew above 47 inches. Little Rock, Arkansas asked a "reasonable delay" in desegregating its schools.

The United States was said to be ready to defend Quemoy if Mainland China attacked the island. The chances for Governor Edmund S. Muskie of Maine to become the state's first popularly elected Democrat to the Senate were considered good. Jet airplanes began daily passenger service.

A rough-'n'-ready general named Curtis E. LeMay, a good
friend of Arthur Godfrey's and vice chief of staff of the Air
Force, personally piloted a jet to the Far East to tour military
bases. Pope John was the new pontiff and was considered only
an "interim" leader because of his advanced age. Harry
Winston donated the Hope Diamond to the Smithsonian In-
stitution. In the ultimate act of self-hate, the student body of
the University of Houston hanged itself in effigy because of its
disinterest toward the school's football team.

They were a minority of fans. Not only were more people
going to events, and clamoring for different attractions, they
were paying in ways never before believed possible. In Los
Angeles, 200,000 people watched Floyd Patterson knock out
Roy "Cut 'n' Shoot" Harris. But not in person, of course.
Over closed-circuit television. After counting the million-dol-
lar gate receipts, the president of TelePrompTer announced,
"Theater TV will become increasingly important."

Fans at Madison Square Garden rioted after a wrestling
match with Antonino Rocca. Althea Gibson defied Forest Hills
tradition when she ignored the referee and sat down during
the brief break for changing sides. *Columbia, Weatherly,* and
Vim were the United States boats in the trials for the America's Cup, held for the first time since 1937.

A fifteen-year-old chess whiz named Bobby Fischer was on
an international tour in Yugoslavia and unhappy. The Rus-
sians would not let him play their Grand Masters. Back home,
clean, well-lighted bowling alleys were sprouting in a boom of
the sport. Herb Elliott of Australia, the mile record holder
at 3:54.5, was cleared of professionalism after he appeared in
a soft-drink ad. "There was no money paid" was the finding.

West Point unveiled its "lonesome end" on the football
team. The Yanks won the World Series from the Milwaukee
Braves after trailing by 3 games to 1. Vice President Nixon
said there should be a Major League team in Havana. Wilt
Chamberlain made his Madison Square Garden début with the
Harlem Globetrotters. The city was talking about starting a
third major league, reported a lawyer named William A. Shea,
the chairman of Mayor Wagner's baseball committee.

Pessimism was not in the nature of Jim Lee Howell. Yet, what was he to think after his Giants dropped their last five exhibition games of 1958? "This may be my weakest team," he said.

He was at least partly right. For it was to be his lowest scoring Giants team. In fact, the Giants won the Eastern Conference championship even though they outscored only three other teams in the whole league. The difference between their points-for and points-against was only an average 5.25 a game. After their opening game they did not score more than 30 points in any contest the entire season. They averaged only 20.5 points a game. That was the poorest offense by a division winner since the Giants of 1939 had taken the Eastern crown.

So people spoke about the defense more than ever before. The man who ran it was Landry, without hollering, efficiently. Even today, at the heights of a rich career with the Dallas Cowboys, Landry can recall all the Giants' people of those days. He can remember key plays, he knows exactly what people were good and why. Yet, there was a series of accidents —so out of keeping with his ordered view of the world—that led Landry to a business he never was really serious about.

"I really wasn't thinking much about professional football in 1949, when I got out of the University of Texas. I was twenty-four years old then. I had started college in 1942, then I went back in the service for three—I was on a B-17 bomber —and then I went back to college in 1946. I wanted an industrial engineering degree, but they didn't have one, so I wound up with industrial management.

"My defensive strategy was based upon my background. It was based not so much on reaction—which was the basis of most defenses—but on ability to blend players together as a unit to form a strong defense. Most defenses are not that way. If you get hit from one side, you're gonna fight through and go to the ball carrier. We hold. We don't fight through the block. We control an area. That's based, I guess, a lot from my engineering background—you know, coordinating people."

Actually, Landry did not begin his career with the Giants.

He went to the New York Yankees of the AAC out of school. Within a year, though, the Yankees folded and the Giants plucked Landry, Weinmeister, Otto Schnellbacher, and Harmon Rowe from the dead team as their share of the spoils.

Schnellbacher, Rowe, and Landry joined Tunnell in the Giants defensive backfield and the four formed the top of the "umbrella" in the umbrella defense. When Landry took over as defensive coach in 1954, while continuing to play, he moved the Giants' line around to a 4-man line, backed up by 3 linebackers, to create the 4–3 defense that has been dominant since.

"If you weren't willing to sacrifice, you know, sacrifice the ability to make a big play by yourself, then you couldn't work in our system. You had to be willing to work with other people, and everybody would receive the success together. And that's what it was based on."

It was nice having the people who could work in the system in 1958. The Giants that Landry had to work with were: Robustelli, Grier, Modzelewski, and Katcavage on the line; Harland Svare, Bill Svoboda, Sam Huff, and Cliff Livingston as the linebackers; and Tunnell, Jim Patton, Karl Karilivacz, Lindon Crow, and Ed Hughes as defensive backs.

"It was really an exceptional defensive football team, and that was the catalyst. Television made football a nationwide sport then, and this was the first time in professional football that the defense became recognized as a unit. It was the beginning of the chant, 'Defense! Defense!' that's carried through all these years. The Giants' defense was separated from the offense. We did not particularly want it to happen. But it just happened, and they became a great unit. Me and Vince Lombardi had a good working relationship, though. Vince . . . he hated to lose worse than anything in the world.

"He hated to look—you know—bad at all. Any time. A very emotional man. If his offense didn't perform well it could be two or three days before you could talk to him. He was that sensitive."

Even to a fellow coach?

"Oh, yeah. But that was Vince. We understood him. And I got along with him very well. We were good friends. If he was successful he was very outgoing, very emotional. If he was unsuccessful he wasn't speaking to anybody. He had moods. That was one of the things that made him great."

It does not strike Landry as surprising that such an extraordinary number of Giants went on to coaching. He believes it is because they were happy in their work.

"Whenever you have success and you have a good feeling about what you're doing and you like it, you go on to coaching after that," he explains. "The experience has been good. But if you go into a situation where you're always losing, have a lot of rift, that's something you don't want to continue as your life's work. When you do something good, though, it just becomes a part of you. And you continue in that atmosphere."

Since Landry had good feelings about winning, it seems logical to assume that coaching would be his life's work. But again, a sort of accident dictated which road Landry would follow. He actually considered quitting football after the 1959 season with the Giants. For football had always been a temporary situation for Landry.

"You know, I never really thought of myself as a coach—even when I was coaching with New York. I planned to be in business. That's why I took my industrial management degree. I was in business in Houston during the off-season. I was constantly preparing for business while I was finishing up what I thought was just gonna be an assistant's coaching job.

"Then, about the time I was ready to step down as coach and go into business, that's when the Dallas job opened up. I was living in Texas anyway. It was a natural transition. But I hadn't even thought about it before."

What he had thought about was a way to halt Jimmy Brown. And he thought about it not, as most people have believed and as legend embellished, by giving Sam Huff the single job of tailing Brown.

"Our defense was not designed specifically for Sam Huff to follow Jim Brown," says Landry, coolly. "Our defense was designed to stop the offense we were working against. Our defense was based on coordination. You know, people. And Sam was just one of eleven people who were coordinated. Specifically, the front seven was coordinated against the run. He was just one element in that group. But he got great recognition, which he deserved, because in this particular defense he was stopping Jim Brown—who is almost unstoppable. And therefore Sam Huff became the one person that everyone could identify with. He'd be at the point of attack much more than Grier, or Robustelli, or Modzelewski.''

Landry remains proud of that unit. Each member was his private possession. He coached all of them, without assistants, and he told them how to meet every situation and prepared the squad's overall defensive plans. He remembers their attributes well:

Grier: ''He was the one guy on our defense who had more freedom than anyone else. He was a big, strong guy who had a quick charge. He was very hard to control. Therefore, we let him move a lot stronger than most anybody else.''

Modzelewski: ''He was a much more controlled player. He complemented Grier. He covered up for him a lot. Grier made the strong move, with great speed, and Mo covered for him because Grier might have been out of position, he was so anxious. Mo was short, about 6 foot, but great in the hands and arms. Great strength. He could control the blockers, and he would slide up and down the line very well.''

Robustelli: ''He is a very smart football player. He played with the Rams for a long time, and he understood defense. An excellent pass rusher, who eventually became a defensive coach. He was a talented player.''

Katcavage: ''He was a young player, and he kind of grew up with those first successful teams. He was strong and big and aggressive, a very aggressive football player.''

Svare: ''He was a smart player. Him and Robustelli played on the same side, and they worked together very well. Those years, I had no problems with those two because they knew how to handle the point of attack. They were excellent.''

Svoboda: "Like a little Katcavage. He was a tough cookie. Boy, he was really a tough football player, one of the toughest ones we've ever had. As far as really having great technique, well, he wasn't that type. He was more of an explosive type of football player."

Huff: "Sam was a very disciplined player. The thing that made Sam Huff so good was that he would listen, and he would do what was necessary to operate our defense. He was originally a lineman, and he had to switch from that to linebacker, which was a big thing, even in those days. He had to listen pretty close to make sure he had keyed it right, that he was, you know, in the right position. And he learned his job very well. He didn't look it, but of course, he had that little mean streak that you've got to have when you play linebacker. He was tough. He challenged people."

Patton: "A natural. Great range, very competitive. A hitter. A natural for our type of defense. He was a little guy, but he had range."

Tunnell: "Of course, you know, Em was one of the great players of all time. Em didn't know particularly how to play a defense. He knew how to play a ball. I played next to him for many years. He had a real sense of what was gonna happen. He might not have played defense the way it was supposed to be played, but he was usually in the right spot to make the great plays."

Lindon Crow: "A pretty solid football player. A good cornerback who did his job well."

Ed Hughes: "He was the other corner. A smart football player. He's one of my coaches now."

Those years, Landry admits, "we knew we were something special in New York. The city was just on fire. It was amazing the way they supported the Giants. And the defense. This was a brand new thing in pro football, because no one even knew when you played defense until the late fifties."

Could it happen again?

"Jim Lee was willing to let Vince take over the offense and me handle the defense. None of this could have happened unless Jim was willing to let it, and it worked. In fact, it probably never would again with any combination of three men. But it worked out well then.''

The professional athlete has always been jealous of his job. But he was more jealous in the 1950s than today, when there are more than twice as many teams. Fewer than 400 people were major league football players in 1958. There are more than 1,200 now. If a player fails to land a job with one club, there are many others trying to get him. And today, the professional athlete can make a living in so many more sports than he could in the 1950s—there are so many more basketball and baseball teams around. There is pro track. There is pro soccer.

So in 1958, when Pat Summerall joined the Giants, he was eyed by the veterans as every new man was eyed—with suspicion.

''It was a prestige symbol for a kicker to have Charlie Conerly hold for him,'' recalls Summerall, now one of the most popular and busy announcers for CBS. ''Charlie wouldn't hold for me, though. I was a new man and Agajanian was a veteran and I was trying to get Agajanian's job.''

Summerall and Crow joined the Giants from the Chicago Cards in a deal that saw Dick Nolan go to the Cards, along with a first-round draft choice. Summerall was, at least, more versatile than Agajanian. He could play tight end on offense if necessary, and he could fill in on the defensive line.

Summerall's credentials were, kindly, not impressive. In the era of the ''automatic'' extra point, he had a percentage of 95.2, missing 6 of 127 attempts with the Cards. Over that span Agajanian booted at a 99.1 percentage, missing 1 of 123. In field goals, meanwhile, Summerall made only 41 percent of his tries with the Cards—none as long as 50 yards—while Agajanian was compiling a 53.5 percentage.

But Summerall could do other things for his salary. Still, that didn't impress Conerly.

"He just wouldn't hold for me. I guess he didn't know if I was any good or not. So I had the backup holder. Pretty soon Charlie began to see that I was reasonably good, with a strong leg, and I knew what I was doing. I was there every day, too. You see, Agajanian had a garbage disposal business in Los Angeles, which was important because of the smog out there. You couldn't burn garbage. So he was busy during the week, and he only came to camp, which was in Salem, Oregon, on weekends. I kicked against a bunch of guys. The only one I remember was Curley Johnson, who became the Jets' punter.

What business did Pat Summerall have on the football field anyway? The man was born with his right foot backward. The toes were pointing to the rear. In an operation that made the medical journals, the infant's right leg was broken and the foot was turned around. One of the first things Summerall remembered his mother telling him was, "The doctors say you've got a weak right leg, and you can't run with the other children."

Not only was Summerall somewhat of a physical oddity—although he contends, "I never thought about the foot"—he was also an anomaly intellectually. How many place-kickers, after all, had a master's degree in Russian history? From the University of Arkansas.

Kickers were not coddled in 1958. "It was rare that you could get somebody to hold for you," explains Summerall. "It was rare that you could get somebody to run balls back to you in practice. There were not many good holders around. The players almost had the option whether or not to hold. It was . . . almost demeaning to hold. But mostly, it was dangerous. You were squatting on all fours, you could get belted if you were the holder. In Chicago, I never had the same holder for two years in a row. Finally, in New York, I had Conerly all the time."

Like major league baseball pitchers, a kicker can reel off his statistics. He has, in a sense, a won–lost record more than any other performer in football. With Conerly holding, Summerall's field-goal mark with the 1958 Giants was 12 for 23.

The year before with the Cards he was 6 for 17. "In 1959 with the Giants I was Number One in the whole league with 20 for 29," says Summerall.

"You just about had it made with Conerly holding for you. But the big difference was Tom Landry. He was the kicking coach as well as the defensive coach, strategist, defensive line, defensive secondary, linebackers. He and I worked closely, staying late. He would watch films of me kicking. Also, the way Wietecha and Conerly worked on the snap. A center's snap changes from day to day, sometimes it spins more, sometimes less. So they would work every day and in pregame practice. They'd figure if they should be just over seven yards, or just under, because they had figured on how many times that ball would spin between the time it left Wietecha's hands until it hit Conerly's hands. Conerly wouldn't have to do much with it once he got it. The laces would be facing front. I can't ever recall having to kick a ball with the Giants—a field goal or an extra point—where I could see the laces on the ball." In four seasons, Summerall took 250 kicks—138 extra points, 112 field goals.

By amassing 26 percent of his team's points in his first year as a New Yorker, Summerall became an immediate part of the New York scene, joining Gifford, Rote, and Conerly as "Lords of the City." Yet after the 1961 season he was ready to quit to become a high school history teacher in his home town, Lake City, Florida. Then one morning Rote called him to tell about a change in the Giants' television broadcasting crew—John Lujack was leaving as the color man because he was a Chevrolet dealer and the games were sponsored by Ford.

Summerall was not a neophyte in broadcasting. He had been Phil Rizzuto's football season replacement on a network radio sports show. But Wellington Mara advised Summerall not to take the TV job. "I don't think you can make it pay," said Mara. Summerall decided to take a chance anyway. He gave up football and his soft radio job. Another Giant replaced him on the radio—Jack Stroud. The Giants probably had more members in AFTRA than they did in the Players' Association.

Those five straight exhibition losses worried Howell, especially the last two—routs at the hands of the Colts and their cool-handed young quarterback, John Unitas. Perhaps things would improve in the season, hoped Howell. Perhaps that fast, skinny rookie with the sideburns and cowboy boots from Texas Western, Don Maynard, could help open up the Giants' game a bit. Maynard was clocked in 9.6 seconds for the 100. Howell would use him on punt returns and kickoff returns to try to get some excitement back.

As the season was ready to begin, Howell announced he would go with three quarterbacks: Tom Dublinski had been added to the perennials, Conerly and Heinrich. The Giants were also keeping a player named Ken Ford on their taxi list. He was from the Canadian League, a quarterback. The New Yorkers were thinking that in 1959 Conerly would probably be through, and this way they would have three potential signal-callers around.

The Giants opened their 1958 campaign with a big 37–7 victory over the Cards as Gifford scored three times. Since the baseball season was still on in Chicago and New York, the game was staged in Buffalo. For one week, at least, the Giants were tied for first with the Browns, who halted the Rams.

The Giants split their next two games, also on the road, and opened at the Stadium with a 2–1 record. The Browns, as expected, were 3–0, scoring at least 35 points in each game as Jimmy Brown was on his way to rushing yardage that had only been imagined. In their second game the Giants had been victimized by the thirty-two-year-old Van Brocklin, whose passes picked up 238 yards and two touchdowns in an Eagles victory. In the third game, though, at Washington, the Giants had come back for a 21–14 decision. Lombardi put in something new this game. He lined up one of his offensive guards, Bob Mischak, as an end and explained to the officials that he was eligible to catch a pass. Mischak had played end at West Point, but had been a lineman in the pros. He caught his only pass of the season, a 27-yarder, after telling the officials of his plans.

"Don't think you're going to have an easy game just because you're at home this week and you're playing the Cards again,'' warned Lavelle. Grier was out with an injury and Stroud was suffering from asthma and the Cards, cautioned Lavelle, ''aren't the same team that you beat 37–7.''

Meanwhile, a writer discovered Huff and did a story on the young man. ''Being a defensive lineman,'' the story began, ''Sam Huff rarely receives the attention that goes to the glamour boys, the ball handlers.''

There was, however, the subtle beginnings of the distinctive units on the club. For at breakfast the day of the game, Landry softly told his defense, sitting around him, ''Pressure them.'' From the other end of the dining hall, where Lombardi had the offense gathered around, came back an echo, ten times louder: *''Pressure them!''*

There was not enough, apparently. The Giants were upset by the Cards, 23–6, while the Browns won their fourth straight game. Now the Giants were 2–2 and the Browns were 4–0. Already, it looked like a lost season. Worse, Gifford had been injured and was hospitalized. Conerly? He had been booed to the sidelines.

Gifford was in St. Elizabeth's Hospital, but he was given permission to leave for a few hours each night so he could do his nightly radio show.

Heinrich took over for Conerly the following week, and the Giants stormed back with a 17–6 victory over the Steelers. But the Browns also won and were 5–0. The Giants were 3–2. The season was almost half over. In another week, the Browns and Giants would meet, at Cleveland, and a Cleveland victory would virtually assure the tie for Paul Brown's men. And now Heinrich had a sore ankle. Conerly was on the bench. The Giants talked of using Gifford at quarterback.

It was obvious that Jim Brown was the key to Cleveland, and the word key took on a new meaning for the Giants' defense. It was misinterpreted by the majority of fans, though. They read that Huff had been assigned to Brown—that is, he was to chase Brown even, they believed, if Brown was simply tying his laces. That is not quite the way it worked. Huff was to ''key'' on Brown. That meant that he was to watch Brown's alignment and motion. For Landry discovered that Coach Paul Brown worked in a predictable pattern. If Jim Brown, for example, was lined up in a certain way, invariably a specific play would follow. So while Huff "keyed" on Jim Brown, it did not necessarily mean he would chase him. Indeed, Jim Brown might be going in one direction, and Huff would know that was a decoy, that the ball really would be going to Bobby Mitchell—and that was where Huff was to go.

Rarely had one man been such a dominant force as Brown. He ran with the ball for 54 percent of the Cleveland rushing plays. In the first 5 games he scored an astounding 14 touchdowns. In no game did he rush for fewer than 125 yards. He averaged 6.9 yards a rush and 163 yards a game. In fact, he amassed 401 yards more than the Number Two rusher in the league. The Browns were averaging 35 points a game.

This Huff–Brown confrontation, misread as it was, made people recall the first time—and perhaps only time—a true one-on-one situation occurred in the pro game. In 1950 Steve Owen had told John Cannady, the stem of the umbrella, "Marion Motley's your private pigeon." To which the North Carolina-born Cannady replied, "Pigeons make powerful tasty eating."

This game against the 1958 Browns began a string of New York domination over Cleveland that remains fresh in the memory of players and fans. For the Giants whipped the powerful Browns six straight times over the 1958, 1959, and 1960 seasons. In that stretch, the Browns posted an overall record of 22 victories, 12 defeats (including a conference playoff loss), and 1 tie. Six defeats were at the hands of the Giants. Only the Lions, Steelers, 49ers, and Eagles were able to defeat the Browns over that stretch—but the Giants made an art of it.

The string began with the sixth game of 1958 when, dramatically, Conerly returned to the lineup. The man had a sense of history. Of course, his defense helped. On the first play from scrimmage, the irrepressible Jim Brown was belted for a 2-yard loss. He was to gain "only" 113 yards, 50 yards fewer than his average. And he was outrushed by the Giants' full-

back, Mel Triplett, who picked up 116 yards. It was the only
100-yard day for a Giants rusher all season. In fact, 100-yard
games by runners were a rarity for a Giants club that was so
often among the leaders. There was none, for example, from
November 1952 to October 1955.

Conerly played all the way against the Browns, threw for
three touchdowns and became, a week after sitting on the
bench, history's second most productive touchdown passer.
He now had a career total of 140, more than Sid Luckman produced, and second only to Sammy Baugh's 187.

Conerly produced his record before the largest crowd in
the Browns' history—78,404 people. That day, a significant
one for the Giants, also produced a 100,000 crowd for the
Bears and Rams at Los Angeles, and 51,000 people for the
Packers and Colts at Baltimore, in the rain.

The Giants were now 4–2, the Browns 5–1, with a way to go
for the Giants. For their next opponent was Baltimore, atop
the Western Conference with a 6–0 mark, averaging 39 points
a game, with more than 50 points in each of two games and
yielding an average of only 15 points a game.

The game was to attract the greatest crowd in New York
football history—71,163. It is a mark that remains. That week
also launched a career for a young black named Richie. The
career was scalping, and he has become the biggest in New
York.

But in 1958 he was a shoe-shine boy, hanging around a candy
store in the East New York area of Brooklyn known as "triangle." The store was on a triangular-shaped intersection
underneath the last stop of the IRT, at New Lots Avenue. The
block was called Ash–Livone, short for Ashord Street and
Livonia Avenue, which formed the other points of the triangle.
It had been a popular hangout since the late 1930s, when the
Jewish enforcers who worked for Murder Incorporated, as
well as their friends and bookies, would congregate there late
Saturday nights for bagels and lox and cream cheese. It was
an "action" area.

Richie's father was a cop, his mother a nurse's aide at Coney
Island Hospital. His father was kicked off the force after it

was learned he had, according to Rich, "two families." Rich had fourteen brothers and sisters. When he was eight years old he began shining shoes. For the next eight years he worked in a bar on Liberty Avenue, in the heavily Italian area, where Mafia types congregated. One night, sixteen bullets came through the bar window. "They were after Johnny the bartender. They missed then. But they finally got him."

From the age of sixteen until he was twenty-one, he worked the triangle. He had gone to high school for six months, "but had trouble reading. I wasn't stupid. I just couldn't read." Then one day "a Jewish guy" told him about scalping. Richie had been making $60 a week shining shoes. In one hour of scalping at the Colts–Giants game he made $22. "I never shined another shoe," says Richie.

His early scalping method was crude, but like all his successes, deceptively simple. Because he was a polite, light-skinned black who dressed neatly, if a trifle raggedly, he had no trouble picking up tickets at the game. He met a scalper there who told him to stand outside the subway kiosk. He then asked the arrivals if anyone had tickets to sell. He picked up twenty-two, and then sold them to the middle man for a dollar over his cost. Richie figured there must be a way to make even more, to do it himself.

He discovered that some people actually gave him a ticket when he asked if there was one to be sold. Perhaps it was the worn basketball sneakers he wore, or his polite way of asking. But he started to buy tickets in bulk. It was risky for him to pick up more than a few tickets at a time and then return to the head of the line. So he started to employ high school kids. He rounded up an army, mostly from Brooklyn and the Bronx. They were called "diggers," and their job was, simply, to buy tickets for him, then go back to the end of the line and start again. For each ticket they bought, Richie paid them a 50-cent bonus.

The search for tickets became a way of life for Rich. He became bolder. He noticed how many youth groups had tickets to Giants home games, and every Sunday buses would deposit Boy Scouts, Cub Scouts, church groups, handicapped children, prep school youngsters, at the Stadium gates. If there are children around, he reasoned, there must be some who had the mumps, or chicken pox, or were having their tonsils out. That meant that the scoutmaster, or the bus leader, would have an extra ticket, perhaps two or three extra. But Richie had to figure a way to pry the tickets from the leaders. Once they got out of the bus, they probably would head to one of the admissions booths and return the ticket. If he tried to stop them in front of the Stadium, he might be spotted by the cops.

So Rich decided to collar the scoutmasters while they were in their buses on the Major Deegan Expressway. Each Sunday, buses and a thousand or so cars would be idling their engines on the clogged exit ramps waiting to get off the expressway. Rich walked onto the parkway up the ramp, and would knock on the door of a bus. The driver would open the door, Richie would find the youth leader, and in his best Uncle Tom manner, respectfully ask, ''Sir, would you have an extra ticket? I can't afford to buy one.'' Of course, there was always an extra ticket, for indeed, someone in the group would be out with the mumps, or chicken pox, or tonsillitis. Richie was surprised to find that, often, two or three extras would be shoved in his fist. He was also surprised to find that scoutmasters sometimes scalped him. He would chuckle to himself, pay a dollar or two over the face value gladly.

As the Giants, and big league sports in general, grew over the 1950s and into the 1960s, Richie grew with them. He was making as much as $500 on a typical Sunday at Yankee Stadium. But his horizons were greater.

When Pelé attracted more than 40,000 people, the greatest crowd to see a soccer match in the United States, Rich was at one of the Yankee Stadium gates. He made a deal with a ticket-taker. Rich found a thousand fans who were standing at the end of long lines. ''Give me six bucks,'' he told each of them as he escorted them to his special entrance. They each went through, and Rich gave the ticket-taker $3 for every one smuggled in. Rich made $3,000 for himself that great day.

He also, in his words, ''worked the pope,'' during his historic visit to the Stadium. By walking into a hundred churches all over town, and respectfully asking for a ticket to see the pontiff, Richie wound up with hundreds of tickets and turned a $1,500 profit.

His greatest score was the Muhammad Ali-Joe Frazier Superfight I at Madison Square Garden, history's most scalped event. That night he made more than $30,000.

That simply continued a tradition he had established at the Garden shortly after discovering the Giants. When a key Knicks or Rangers game was staged, tickets would be hard to get. But not if you knew Richie. In time, he had more than 100 regular Garden customers. The Stadium had become too difficult to work. Everyone who had a Giants ticket used it. Richie couldn't even bribe youngsters to part with their tickets to the Stadium. So he turned to basketball and hockey and special events. While it lasted, though, the Giants were a beautiful score.

The largest crowd ever to see the Giants play a game in New York did not see Unitas, this time, anyway. In one of the most lopsided games in league history, the previous week's 56-0 victory over the Packers, Unitas suffered cracked ribs. He learned that he would be out for three weeks and his place would be taken by George Shaw.

Be careful of Shaw, Lavelle cautioned the Giants: "Shaw is more dangerous than Unitas. Shaw is the better runner."

Actually, that last sentence was not true, either. Unitas was one of the best running quarterbacks in the league with an average of 4.2 yards a carry. Shaw? His five carries saw him total minus-3 yardage. But Lavelle did not want his boys to think that they were going to skip over the Colts with Unitas out of the lineup.

For Shaw, once the team's Number One quarterback, this was a chance to work himself back in the eyes of his coach, Weeb Ewbank. Unitas joined the Colts in some backdoor fashion while Shaw was the Number One draft choice in the whole league in 1955. Shaw came with star credentials out of Oregon. Unitas, meanwhile, came up to the Steelers that same year and was dropped without even getting into an exhibition game.

Soon, he was playing for the Bloomfield Rams for $6 a game. In 1956 the Colts were looking for an understudy for Shaw. The Colts' Don Kellett, the general manager, phoned Unitas in an 80-cent phone call. By the fourth game, Shaw had been hurt. On Unitas's first play, he was intercepted. Kellett then called for Gary Kerkorian to come out of retirement and join the team the following week. Ewbank had a hunch, though. He kept Kerkorian on the bench and gambled with Unitas. The former bush-leaguer threw a pair of touchdown passes, the Colts beat the Packers and Unitas was a starter. In 1957, his first full season, his marks of 24 touchdown passes and 2,550 yards were the best in football. Shaw threw a total of 9 passes in 1957.

Now Shaw was starting for the first time in two years. He knew that if he did not keep the Colts' winning string going he would shoulder the blame. So he was, perhaps, the most highly motivated man in the game. The Giants knew this was serious business, too. Before the game, Landry had the defense in one room and Lombardi took the offense in another. Howell moved among the units silently. Then he clapped his hands to signal that the meeting was over.

While the clubs were dressing, more than 5,000 Baltimore backers were being brought to the Stadium by special subway cars from Penn Station. The Baltimore fans had come by train to Manhattan, and then with a special hand from the Transit Authority, the rest of the way by subway. This was, after all, only the second winning season in the Colts' history in Baltimore.

One of the more nervous Giants was Summerall. He had already missed two extra points that season and had connected on only 3 of 10 field-goal tries. Of course, he did not know it then, but he was never to miss another extra-point attempt in his career.

The game began a stretch of last minute, can't-be-done, impossible, tingling victories for the Giants that solidified them in the New York scene as firmly as the cornerstone for the Empire State Building.

The 71,163 fans rose (except for the 8,000 fans already in the standing room areas) on the first play of the game, the Lombardi play, when there was an option to Gifford. He took a Conerly pitchout, ran right, and connected with Schnelker on a 63-yard play.

Despite this early razzle-dazzle, the Colts led 14–7 in the third quarter. On a key play, Conerly, hit by two linemen, managed a pitchout to Phil King for a first down. The score was tied at 21 in the final 2 minutes 40 seconds, when Summerall was asked to kick a 28-yard field goal. Webster, Gifford, and Rote had scored the Giants' touchdowns and now it was up to Summerall. He turned to Billy Lott, a spare halfback, and said, "The pressure's killing me, Billy." Nevertheless, he kicked the field goal and the Giants won, 24–21. Meanwhile, the Browns were being upset by the Lions, who had won only one game all season. The Giants and Browns now were tied at 5–2.

The next week the Giants blew a 10–0 lead at Pittsburgh and bowed 31–10, while the Browns were fortunate that the Redskins Eddie LeBaron, the league's top passer, was out with the flu. The Browns won, with Jim Brown setting a rushing mark of 1,163 yards after only 8 games. At 6–2, the Browns had a one-game edge over the New Yorkers, who were 5–3. But in their next three games the Browns faced the last place Eagles twice and the Redskins once. The season ended with a game against the Giants.

In their ninth game, the Giants faced the Redskins. Perhaps they would return to some consistent form with the return of Rosey Brown, who had a cheek fracture, and Stroud, who had a knee injury, and Heinrich, who had a sore ankle. But now Tunnell was hurt after slipping in his bathtub and almost drowning after he knocked himself out.

The Giants won at the Stadium, 30–0, as Summerall found his groove—he had made three straight field goals. Tunnell even returned in the final quarter, just to keep his consecutive appearances streak alive. But the Browns also won, and they were 7–2 to the Giants' 6–3.

While they wait for their next visitor, the Eagles, Well Mara drew up a list of the six top quarterbacks in college.

1—Lee Grosscup, Utah
2—Randy Duncan, Iowa
3—Tom Greene, Holy Cross
4—Don Allard, Boston College
5—Bud Humphrey, Baylor
6—Joe Kapp, California

The draft was coming up soon and Mara made no secret of the fact that he was looking for a quarterback.

The present quarterback, Conerly, could not even bend over to tie his shoes because of a kidney injury, as the tenth game of the season, against the Eagles, was coming into the Stadium.

Webster was honored with a "day" at half time, but it was the defense that took over. The Giants intercepted three Van Brocklin passes (he was to throw only 17 interceptions in the other 11 games) and recovered 3 fumbles, and Huff blocked a Bobby Walston field goal attempt and the Giants won 24–10. Cleveland also won, and the Colts clinched the Western Conference title. After 10 games the Giants were 7–3, the Browns 8–2.

It appeared to be a good week for the New Yorkers as they got ready for their next-to-last game, which would be held at Detroit. In a coin flip with Cleveland and Pittsburgh (which was 6–4) for the playoff sites, the Giants won all the tosses. Thus, if there was a three-way tie for first, the Browns and Giants would play at the Stadium, with the Steelers playing the next week at the winner's field. Meanwhile, Mara got his wish in the draft. He picked Grosscup, who strangely, was not chosen by the nine clubs that picked ahead of New York. The Giants also selected Buddy Dial, an end, and Joe Morrison, described as a "two-way" halfback.

Allie Sherman, who returned to the Giants as a scout in 1957, had raved about Grosscup since seeing him in a stunning performance against West Point. Conerly was asked about Grosscup and said, "I can't play forever." But Heinrich, when asked about the future Giants' quarterback, growled, "He'll have to win it."

Of course, the Giants did not realize it then, but a Katcavage safety in the opening quarter at Detroit would help to propel the New Yorkers toward the playoffs.

Katcavage dropped Gene Gedman in the end zone. It was one of three safeties for Katcavage in his Giant career; he is the only New Yorker ever to get more than one. The Giants also got a touchdown from Conerly, who was well enough, sort of, to play. He tossed to Webster, who had missed a month. And they got a field goal from Summerall. Still, that did not appear to be enough, for the Lions led, 17–12, late in the game. If the Giants lost, they would have no chance to make the playoffs.

The Lions had the ball on their own 44, but they had 21 yards to go for a first down. It was fourth down, and naturally, they were expected to punt. In Yale Lary they had their conference's best punter, with a 42.8 average. Just an average punt by Lary would go to the Giants' 20-yard line, 80 yards from a touchdown. What followed was a controversial play, one of the most unusual in a season that was winding down with controversial plays. For George Wilson, the Lions' coach, did not call for a punt. He called for a fake punt and a run by Lary! The punter had not run with the ball all season. It was, in fact, his only run of the campaign. And it wasn't enough. He gained only a yard and the Giants took over as the fans booed, shocked at Wilson's call.

Conerly immediately hit Schnelker with a 34-yarder. A few plays later, it was fourth down and 1½ yards to go for the touchdown. Gifford took the ball—and scored. The Giants now led, 19–17.

But the Lions came back. They drove back from the kickoff and had the ball on their 18 with eight seconds remaining. Jim Martin would try a 25-yard field goal. Robustelli and Svare argued over which one would attempt the block from their right side position. "I'll go inside," said Robustelli. "Drive my man to the outside and I'll sneak through." Svare retorted, "No, I've got a better angle. Drive my man outside and I'll sneak through.'' Which is what happened. Robustelli pinched the 6-foot 4-inch, 235-pound Jerry Perry, and Svare burst through to block the kick. The Giants won.

The outcome was preposterous to suspicious fans, who had discovered something called a ''line'' and whose football bets were becoming an increasingly larger share of the bookmakers' action. Why would a team fake a punt on fourth down from midfield when it was leading late in the game? The reason, many bettors believed, was because the game was fixed.

Commissioner Bert Bell immediately received FBI reports in which the Bureau's informants contended there was nothing unusual in the betting patterns about the game, nor were any players reached.

So much for that. Now the Giants could concentrate, they hoped, on the final game of the regular season. For dramatically, it would pit them against the Browns at the Stadium. Cleveland was 9–2, the Giants were 8–3. A victory—and nothing else—was needed by the Giants to force an Eastern Conference playoff. If not, the Giants were out of it.

But they had trouble. Summerall had a bad charley horse on his knee. He was convinced he would not play. In fact, he did not even work out all week. Instead, Don Chandler, the punter, drilled all week as the place-kicker for the game.

Most of the 63,192 fans who turned out in a snowstorm were surprised to see Summerall warming up before the game.

''I told Jim Lee I'd be all right,'' recalls Summerall. ''My charley horse was loosening up a bit. So Jim Lee said, okay, but he wanted Chandler to kick off and I would do the extra points and the field goals. It was a slippery field, and he didn't want me running around.''

Slippery or not, Jim Brown enjoyed his biggest New York day. In the very first quarter he scored on a 65-yard run, Groza kicked the extra point, and the Browns led by 7–0. In the second quarter the clubs exchanged field goals, Groza from the 23, Summerall from the 46. At half time, the Browns led 10–3.

In a clutch game, people get nervous. They do the little silly things they do not do for a whole season. Poise and execution —which were the bywords of the New York Jets when they won their big Super Bowl—were the qualities that had elevated the Browns to the top of the Eastern Conference by the last game of the season. In a clutch game, the poised team will not fumble. It will execute its handoffs. It will, in short, do what it has done so well during the season.

But the Browns, who committed the fewest number of fumbles since World War II—only 12 in 11 games—and who were to set a record the following year of only 8—fumbled twice in their most crucial game of the season. People do not remember those fumbles, though. They were to recall Summerall, incredulous at being asked to perform the feat, putting his foot to the ball in a driving snow from somewhere around midfield as the clock ticked away the seconds. For many of the Giants, that game from the frozen Stadium turf has become their fondest memory. It is a more memorable one for them than the championship against the Colts.

The first Browns' fumble led to the Summerall 46-yarder. Then a Milt Plum over-eager handoff attempt was misplayed by Preston Carpenter in the final period. Robustelli recovered. Soon Gifford connected with Schnelker on a 7-yarder to tie the score.

''We got the ball back again, and I tried a field goal from about the 40,'' says Summerall. ''I missed, and I went back to the bench thinking that this was it, we'd blown it. And the guys, particularly the defense, said, 'Don't worry about it. We're gonna get the ball back again.' They pressured the Browns, who had a kicker named Dick Deschaine. He shanked the ball off the side of his foot and it landed around midfield.''

If fate had smiled more at redheads, Webster might be remembered as the hero.

''I told everyone I could beat their left cornerback,'' recalls Webster. ''I had to be the slowest back on the team, but I told Charley I could beat their corner on a deep fly pattern—and the whole huddle turned and looked at me as if I were crazy. But I'd been running down and in, turning patterns, the whole game. I felt he'd be waiting for me to turn. But if I went down, gave him a move like I was going to turn, and instead took off . . . I did it. And I took off, and oh, jeez, I had him beat pretty good, five or six yards. But the ball came out of the snow—I know that's no excuse—and it went right through my hands and I dropped it on the 5-yard line. It would have been an easy 6 points.''

Instead, the Giants still were almost 50 yards away. A third-down play failed and then Howell stunned just about everybody by telling Summerall to attempt a field goal.

"I couldn't believe Jim Lee was asking me to do that,'' says Summerall. "That was the longest attempt I'd ever made for the Giants. It was a bad field, and it was so unrealistic. Most of the fellows on the bench couldn't believe it either. They wanted another pass play.''

Meanwhile, Wellington Mara was up in the press box in the upper stand "sitting on the phones and taking those Polaroid pictures. You know, of the other team's defense. Then I'd drop them in a weighted sock. That Summerall kick was the most vivid play I remember. I was sitting next to Ken Kavanaugh and Walt Yowarsky and we all said, 'He can't kick it that far. What are we doing?' ''

It is credited as a 50-yard attempt but, according to Summerall, "no one knows how far it had to go. You couldn't see the yard markers. The snow had obliterated them. But it was more than 50, I'll tell you that.'' Rote contends he was standing on the 50 "and the ball was 2 yards past me.''

So Wietecha, from about the 43- or 44- or 45-yard line, spun the ball backwards between his knees. And Conerly, who had never once shown the laces to Summerall, took the snap and placed it down and Summerall, perhaps 52 yards away, gave the ball a heck of a shot.

"I knew as soon as I touched it that it was going to be far enough. My only thought was that sometimes you hit a ball too close to the center and it behaves like a knuckleball, breaking from side to side. It was weaving out. But when it got to the 10 I could see it was breaking back to the inside.''

Interestingly, it was a Giant who caught the ball. For the club's Vinnie Swerc, now a front office aide and always a close friend of the team's, was standing behind the goal posts. As it cleared the crossbar he raised his arms—just as the referee did—and was surprised to find the ball coming right to him. He cradled it, joyfully.

The Giants had won, 13–10, to force a playoff with the Browns, with the winner to meet the Colts for the championship. Now, says Webster, "I always tell Pat I made him a hero. If I hadn't dropped that ball, Pat never would have had his chance."

That night Paul Brown ran and reran the films of the game. He believed he had made a tactical error—he ran too much instead of passing. Jim Brown, for example, had rushed for 26 times—more than half of Cleveland's offensive plays. His rushing had been good for 148 yards. But after that initial 65-yard spurt, he had been good for only 83 yards on 25 carries. There had not been enough power in the Cleveland attack. So Brown decided his boys would throw the ball more next time.

Meanwhile, Wellington Mara and his ticket manager, Harry Bachrach, and the secretaries were back in the Giants' offices at Columbus Circle, next door to the Coliseum, stuffing tickets into envelopes. For the Giants had won the toss of the coin and the next game would be in New York in just a few days. And people would start lining up for tickets very quickly.

While Paul Brown revised his offense early Monday morning, the Giants were putting more than 60,000 tickets in properly marked envelopes. For almost the entire week the workers and visitors to 10 Columbus Circle had to wait and wait for elevators, which disgorged thousands of ticket holders. The line stretched from the lobby, snaking outside and around 59th Street, and curling west to Ninth Avenue.

"If we weren't thrown out then," says Wellington Mara, "we'll never be thrown out of any place."

When he was not sealing envelopes, Mara went to St. Vincent's Hospital where his first-born, Jack, was recovering from mastoid surgery. Because Wellington's wife was due to have another child any day, he was the only one able to visit his sick son in the hospital. Through that week he would sleep in the hospital next to Jack, get up early for the team workout, return to the office to put more tickets in envelopes, and then return to the hospital.

If Mara knew how things were going to turn out, he would have skipped the workouts. For the Giants produced one of the finest clutch defensive efforts football has yet seen. The final score was 10–0, and the Giants earned the right to face the Colts for the NFL championship. But no one had done to Jim Brown, or Paul Brown, or the Cleveland Browns what the Giants did that day.

Jim Brown produced the poorest day of his career—a total, incredibly, of 8 yards on 7 carries. And on one play he gained 20 yards so he was minus-12 on his other 6 attempts. The Browns managed only 40 plays the whole game—compared to 80 for the Giants. The Browns gained a total of 86 yards—24 by rushing, 62 by passing. The Giants got their scoring from Conerly, of all people, who upset the Browns in the first quarter by taking an 18-yard lateral from Gifford for a touchdown, and from a 26-yard field goal in the second quarter by Summerall.

This game, as much as any other over the era, symbolized for the Giants and their followers the toughness of their defense and the critical factor it had become in the team's success. The success it had against the Browns—and against Jim Brown, in particular—was remarkable and unmatched by anyone else.

In the 6 straight games that the Giants halted the Browns, Brown managed to score only 2 touchdowns, carried an average of 15.6 times, and ran for an average of 66.5 yards a game.

In 1957, 1958, and 1959, Landry-coached Giants teams faced Brown seven times. He scored only 3 touchdowns and averaged only 76.7 yards a game. Against all other clubs in that span, he averaged 108.7 yards and 1.2 touchdowns a game.

"We just played better under pressure," is Katcavage's explanation.

The 1958 championship game between the Giants and the Colts on December 28 was not the greatest football game ever played. History has a way of perpetuating errors, and indeed, enlarging on them. On the other hand, no one has ever been accused of slander for calling it the greatest game.

"Pete Rozelle always told me that the reason pro football took off was because it happened just at that time, in that season, and it happened in New York," says Mara. "If it had happened in Pittsburgh or Green Bay it wouldn't have taken off."

There were 64,185 people at the Stadium for the historic game on December 28, including 15,000 fans from Baltimore. By now it had been established that, even if a club were sold out, there was no television in the local area. Yet, why do so many people believe they were at the game? They don't fantasize they were there—they believe they were. They can see Huff punching the Colts' coach, Ewbank, on the sidelines after Ewbank punched Huff for a late tackle. They can see a skinny Giants' rookie named Don Maynard take the sudden-death kickoff and fumble it, then recover. They can see Gifford fumble twice to set up a pair of Baltimore scores. They can also see Gifford make a first down—they see him moving past the yard marker—and they see the referee mistakenly place the ball backward 2 feet to nullify the first down. They hear Gino Marchetti screaming because his leg has been snapped by his own teammate, Big Daddy Lipscomb, and they realize that the ball is misplaced because of his screams. And, finally, they see John Unitas, calmly, as an executioner might throw the switch to the electric chair, move his club 80 yards in sudden-death overtime, the first official sudden-death game ever held in pro football.

Some hours before, Ewbank, who might have given Edmund Gwenn a battle for the Santa Claus role in *Miracle on 34th Street,* gave his troops one of those old-fashioned, Knute Rockne, pregame battle sermons.

Marchetti related the scene later: "I heard them all," said Marchetti. "Don't piss in the air when the TV is on you, win this for mother, etc." He heard Ewbank go down the roster and stop at each name, even the great ones, and signal out a reason why that player had to win. He drew on some negative from the player's past. So he told Alan Ameche, "Green Bay didn't want you." He told the 270-pound Art Donovan, "Other clubs got rid of you because you were too fat and slow." He told Unitas, "You were in the minors."

So the Colts charged to a 14–3 half-time lead, a comfortable margin, too, for the favorite players who bet the Colts and had to give 3 points. If the Colts won by more than 3 points, they won their bets. Actually, the Giants had taken the early lead when Summerall hit on a 36-year field goal. But the Colts got second-quarter touchdowns from Ameche, on a 2-yard run, and from the incredible Raymond Berry, on a 15-yard pass from Unitas. Both times Steve Myhra converted the extra points. Berry was simply doing extraordinary things to the Giants' Carl Karilivacz, who could not handle him in the secondary. Berry had the greatest day any receiver had enjoyed in a title game—the most catches (12) and the most yardage (178). The Giants desperately were trying to keep Karilivacz out, but the Colts had too many good options and the rest of the New Yorkers were busy all over the field. They had to worry, for example, about Lenny Moore who, according to Charley Winner, "was the greatest runner ever when he wanted to be."

It was Moore who almost buried the Giants when he opened the game by dashing 60 yards with a Unitas pass. The drive ended, though, when Huff blocked Myhra's 27-yard field-goal attempt.

By the third quarter the New Yorkers were down and in danger of falling hopelessly out of it. Leading 14–3, the Colts got down to the Giants' 3-yard line. Then the Giants held and started to come back. It was, in a sense, a microcosm of the entire 1958 season.

The Giants took over on the 5 after Cliff Livingston dumped Ameche for a loss on the fourth down. Two short runs were followed dramatically by a long toss from Conerly to Rote. Rote traveled 62 yards to the Colts' 25—and then fumbled. But Webster scooped up the ball and made it to the 1, where Carl

Taseff pushed him out of bounds. Then Mel Triplett dived over and the Colts' edge was cut to 14–10. In the fourth quarter Gifford, who was to lose yardage on his other two catches of the day, scored on a 15-yarder from Conerly and the Stadium erupted. The Giants led 17–14.

After some exchanges, the Colts had the ball on the Giants' 27-yard line, virtually a chip shot for Myhra. And then the Giants' great clutch players, Robustelli and Modzelewski, went to work on Unitas. First, Robustelli broke through the 6-foot 3-inch, 270-pound Jim Parker to sack Unitas 11 yards back on the 38. And then Modzelewski pushed the Colts 9 yards farther back by dumping Unitas on the 47. The Colts punted and now the Giants had the ball with only a few minutes remaining. They made a first down on their 34 with just over two minutes left. Up in the press box the writers were voting the Corvette, for the game's most valuable player, to Conerly. It was now third-and-four on the 40 and Gifford, the clutch runner, got the ball.

Gifford swears he made the 4 yards and more. All the Giants on the field will swear to it, too. "Of course I made it," says Gifford. "When you're in the game as long as I was, you know where the first down was, and you know when you made it."

At the moment that Gifford hit that imaginary spot, and perhaps went over, Marchetti snared him. Then the 290-pound Lipscomb barreled in on the play and broke Marchetti's leg with a crack like an elephant stepping over a twig.

"There was a whole lot of screaming, 'get off me! get off me!'" says Gifford.

"The referee was so concerned about Marchetti that he forgot where he had picked up the ball," says Rote. "I saw him pick it up at his front foot. But he put it down where his back foot was."

"His job," says Gifford, "was to mark the football—and not be concerned about somebody getting hurt."

Then the referee, Ron Gibbs, called time to move Marchetti and to make the measurement. Gibbs held his hands up, six inches apart. The Giants were short, it was fourth down.

Now came Howell's decision. A first down would ensure victory. The Giants could eat up the clock. But logic dictated a punt. Chandler, after all, was the league's Number Two punter with a 44-yard average. And logic prevailed and seemed right, for Chandler got off a beautiful spiral down to the Colt's 14-yard line, where Taseff called a fair catch.

Unitas's first two throws were incomplete, and now it was third down, 86 yards away from a touchdown and with only 76 seconds remaining. Of course, that was what made the Unitas legend. Five straight tosses hit, including three to Berry. They now were on the Giants' 13-yard line with 20 seconds remaining in regulation time.

Myhra was not your prototype field-goal kicker. In fact, Ewbank probably had less faith in him than other coaches had in their kicker. For that season Myhra was called on for only 10 field-goal attempts, by far the fewest in the league. He hit on only 4. But he hit this time, for a 20-yarder, and suddenly it was tied up at 17–all and suddenly there was going to be a sudden-death game. Many of the players did not even know there was such a contingency.

Landry knew then that they were in trouble.

"We had it won, and then we let them tie and at that point the momentum completely changed. Whether you can ever pull out a game you had in your hands, and then lost in the last seconds of play, whether you can win it in overtime is questionable," he says now.

Yet the Giants did win the coin toss for the kickoff. And Maynard, who was to perform his last act for the Giants with the sudden-death kickoff (which became a great question for trivia fans), did finally run the ball back to the 20. But on third-and-six, Conerly was 2 feet short and Chandler punted. It was a magnificent kick and Colts took over on their 20, 80 yards away. Unitas did not fail.

Fans, most bettors, and some historians wonder about the last plays. Unitas brought the Colts to the 8 as he stumped the Giants with an attack that just wore down the defense. It was now first down and some fans were asking, "Why not the field goal? It's just a 15-yarder." At that point, a cable was knocked out in the telecast to Baltimore, and a hundred thousand television sets went blank.

Ewbank was thinking, "There's always time for a field goal." And that is why he did not try one then. Fans seem to remember, incorrectly, that it was a fourth-down situation on which the final score came. It was not. On the first down Ameche gained only a yard as Huff nailed him. On the second down, Unitas made everyone in the Stadium groan, including Ewbank. For he threw a pass.

It went to Jim Mutscheller, who snared it on the 1 and tripped out of bounds. Perhaps that play made the bettors wonder if perhaps Unitas wasn't more concerned with the 3-point betting spread than beating the Giants. For a pass seems such risky business in a crowded goal-line situation. Now it was third-and-one. Ameche got the ball, and it was over as he went over. No point-after was attempted as the 15,000 people from Baltimore swarmed the field. Anyway, the game was over. It was sudden-death, not sudden-death plus the point after.

As the Giants left the field Gifford spotted Gibbs, the referee. "I told him that he cost a lot of players money," says Gifford.

What was the referee's reply?

"He nodded, as if he knew."

And Perian Conerly was to recall later that someone else "was driving around in my Corvette."

Vince Lombardi was gone when the 1959 season began. Gone but never to be forgotten. He had moved to Green Bay, where he took over a Packers' team that had won only one game and had been outscored by almost two-to-one.

Lombardi's place as offensive coach was taken by Allie Sherman, the slight, boyish, resident genius of the T-formation in the pro ranks. In a sense, the coaching change was one of heart for brains. Sherman's arrival—or was it Lombardi's departure?—began a different trend for the Giants. Yet for the rest of that magic decade, the results stayed the same.

It was a sports year that saw the opening of Aqueduct, the Big A, Baghdad-on-the-Subway. Perhaps the bettors should have seen the omens: there were 428 windows to sell tickets and only 310 to cash them. Another giant sports conglomerate was in its infancy that year, too: Jack Nicklaus. At the age of nineteen, he won the United States Amateur Golf Championship. Still more precocity was exhibited by a trim left-hander for the (now) Los Angeles Dodgers, Sandy Koufax: eighteen strikeouts in a victory over the Giants. The feat tied Bob Feller's Major League mark. Back East a wild pitcher named Ryne Duren, whose unpredictable image was enhanced by his glasses—the lenses were so thick they resembled the bottoms of Coke bottles—was starring in relief for the Yankees. Frankie Carbo was arrested as an undercover fight manager. The Dodgers' desertion of Brooklyn for the Golden West paid off: They played in the World Series against the White Sox, and 92,000 showed up to stare at the 252-foot left-field wall.

But all was not fun and games. Herbert M. Stempel admitted he got the answers in advance on the country's big quiz show "21." A Soviet rocket hit the moon near the Sea of Tranquillity. There were 150 gangs in New York, police reported. In Montreal bandits stole 75,000 Salk anti-polio shots. Carol Burnett was starring off-Broadway in *Once Upon a Mattress*. Uptown, people were going to see *Room at the Top, Wild Strawberries,* and *Gigi.* Television viewers stayed home at night to see "To Tell the Truth" and Bishop Fulton J. Sheen. A teenager named Salvatore Agron was picked up in a West Side playground murder. Papers called him the "Cape Man."

Funny that it should take Charlie Conerly all those years to make it as the top quarterback in pro football. This, after all, was supposed to be his last year. Now, almost forty years old, his best friend, Frank Gifford, was challenging him in training camp. Gifford wanted the job as quarterback.

An even more imposing challenge was coming from Lee Grosscup, the heroic, dashing figure from the University of Utah, possessor of a series of imposing "stats."

But Grosscup always wanted to be a writer, an ambition also harbored by his father, a post office worker. Because Grosscup attempted to write something about football, his career was headed in a direction that, it appeared now, was impossible to alter.

The Giants were in training camp and Grosscup was preparing for the College all-star game against the champion Colts in Chicago. Some months before Grosscup had written a series of engaging, if not especially absorbing, letters to Murray Olderman, then a feature writer for the NEA news syndicate. The collection of letters was edited and published in *Sports Illustrated*. The article ran more than 3,000 words, virtually all about his college days. But it also contained the following, which took up four lines in the story:

> Impressions on the N.Y. Giant Football players:
> Great bunch! Fine gentlemen, very spirited, close
> knit, good drinkers, great physical specimens.

The words "good drinkers" sealed his fate. From the moment he reported to training camp he was an outcast. Even today, some of the Giants recall that he had written some "damaging" things about them. That was the extent of the damage.

He had some other things wrong with him: his hair actually touched his collar. He listened to classical music. He dressed with a sort of hip flair. He was, in short, not like the other guys.

Perhaps he thought he was on his way in his first exhibition game appearance. The first time he threw a pass he hit Joe Morrison with a 55-yarder for a touchdown against Detroit.

"Now," Huff told Grosscup, "you're about ready to write another letter."

Lee Grosscup now lives in Alameda, California. He is a reformed alcoholic and a reformed drug user. A major source of his income comes from selling health foods.

"Do I look back over those years?" he asks. "Not really. I had come from the beaches of Santa Monica to the mountains of Utah, and all of a sudden there I was in the Big Apple. They call me a one-game all-American. But I had led the nation going into that big game at West Point, when the Eastern press saw me. I was throwing at 72 percent, the best percentage in NCAA history. I set the record. It only lasted ten days. Don Meredith then broke it."

The record was to last as long as any of the dreams that Grosscup had over the years.

He was sent to the taxi squad in his rookie season of 1959. He threw a few passes in 1960 and 1961 for the New Yorkers.

Then, Norm Van Brocklin, the coach of the Minnesota Vikings, was unhappy with a rookie quarterback named Fran Tarkenton and wanted Grosscup, but the Giants wanted too much for their young quarterback and the deal fell through. Finally, he was picked up by Minnesota for $100 on waivers, when the Giants cut him. The Vikings cut him, too, and he wound up with the New York Titans in 1962, the club that became the Jets.

In the 1962 season's opener, the first two times he threw the ball for the Titans he threw touchdowns. He played 10 minutes the next three games after injuring his leg. A year later he was with the Saskatchewan Roughriders in Canada.

In 1964 the San Francisco 49ers tried him out, but as soon as he arrived in town a story in the *Chronicle* perpetuated the myth of what he had written. The *Chronicle* story read in part of Grosscup's writing ''unfriendly stuff which made enemies of the men he played for and with.''

His reputation had hurt him during his short stint in Minnesota, where Van Brocklin, once an agitator for players' rights but now the leading exponent of conservatism, had thrown up his hands when Grosscup told his center to snap the ball on ''deuce'' instead of on the count of ''two.''

Grosscup, of course, flunked his one-game trial with the 49ers. It seemed everything he did was doomed by his teammates to fail. He played for five sequences—penalties were called against his team on four. The fifth, a long pass, was dropped.

But he was able to hang on with the Oakland Raiders' taxi squad the following month. The next year he was dropped and became a member of the Hartford Charter Oaks of the Continental League, whose opponents included such stalwarts as the Newark Bears. One of his receivers went to a psychiatrist, it was said, to cure him of a bad habit of dropping passes.

''I don't know what started it,'' says Grosscup, now calm, seeing things plainly. ''Maybe it was me, the English major, coming out of Utah, the Number One draft choice with a no-cut contract. Sam Huff, for example, found out I was making $12,000—a thousand more than he was making as an all-pro.

"Maybe I was five, ten years too soon. It was definitely a period of nonenlightenment among the jocks. When I came up I had no basis for communication with anybody. I felt funny talking about classical music or literature."

But the greatest conflict was between Sherman and Grosscup. Sherman, the smallish left-handed quarterback from Brooklyn, had his own ideas of what a quarterback should look like.

"He was supposed to look like Charley Conerly, leathery," recalls Don Smith, the long-time publicity director of the club. "He thought you were supposed to have lines in your face. That made you a good quarterback. Allie used to ride the kid unmercifully.

"Another one who used to get on him was Heinrich. I remember once we were arriving from someplace or other and the players got out of the bus and there was Lee's wife and baby. She was wheeling the carriage. And Lee gave her a kiss and then he started to wheel the carriage back to the car. And Allie turned to me and said, 'Will you look at that? That's my quarterback. Wheeling a baby carriage.' Lee just didn't have the image for Allie. Now, I saw Heinrich some time ago and he said, 'Whenever I think of Grosscup I think of him wheeling that carriage.' "

Grosscup understands—now. "Allie had funny little things. He thought the quarterback should room with the offensive linemen. Because they were the guys that protected you, so you should make friends with them. There was this kid out of Utah named Don Erickson, and I wanted to room with him because he didn't know anyone on the team. I had thrown to him at school. But that was one of the things Allie had against me."

Was the story about Van Brocklin really true? Did he get upset because Grosscup had said "on deuce" instead of "on two"?

"Oh, sure. All I was trying to do was have some fun, and Van Brocklin said, 'We don't want any more of this Madison Avenue bullshit.' "

With the Giants, Grosscup remembers he was constantly

being embarrassed, singled out for mistakes in front of other players. "I just wasn't in the mold he wanted. What I really should have said was, 'Allie, I really think you're a goddamn creep, and I'll punch you right in the face if you ever say this to me in front of a crowd again.' I think that's what he wanted me to say. I had one blow-up with him, finally. We were on the sidelines, and it was one of those days when Conerly got hurt and Tittle got hurt and he was stuck with me. And they were just beating us up—it was the Colts. Marchetti was doing a dance on me. Everytime I came off Sherman had something to say to me, and finally I took off my helmet and threw it down and told him everything I could think of. I just had this tantrum and all my venom came out. Some of the veterans told me they wanted to applaud. But the next year I was traded."

Years of degradation were to follow.

"In 1968 I became a PR man for the Oakland Raiders. Just your average flack. I'd disappear and not reappear at all. I had a drinking problem. What I did about that was just stop five years ago. I was really into booze and pills. I went into uppers and downers and in-betweeners and things of that nature. Kind of a walking pharmacologist. After that I slid into broadcasting but hit bottom in 1970 from drinking and pills.

"I went into therapy and got involved with an alcohol recovery group and quit drinking one day at a time. And after six months of sobriety I got into nutrition and started selling food supplements, and I created my new business and started getting more jobs. I do A.B.C.; I'm a male model; I do commercials. My health food company is called New Life."

Still, there are times he remembers an incident here or there fondly, such as going into P. J. Clarke's, and Warren Beatty and Natalie Wood were waiting for a table, but he was ushered right in.

He also remembers, in his last year as a Giant, going in against Washington while his club had a big lead. His first two passes were intercepted and Tittle came over and told him to throw some short percentage passes.

"So anyways I got a little march going and finally threw a touchdown pass to Shofner. And I got this standing ovation from 65,000 people, and I remember I went over to the bench and just sat there. And I was listening to this noise and I started to shake. And then I started crying. The tears just popped into my eyes and I just started sobbing. It was . . . really . . . it was something; I can look back on it and be able to say, 'Well, at least I had that. I know what it is to have a standing ovation in Yankee Stadium.' ''

Nineteen fifty-nine was the year of the arm—Conerly's—and the foot—Summerall's—for the Giants. Never before in pro football had a kicker meant so much to a top-flight club as the once-backward-toed Summerall did to his team. For Summerall accounted for a remarkable 31.6 percent of the Giants' points that season.

The Giants now had not only New York virtually to themselves for football—Columbia was the only college in the area to field a major team—but the pro team was becoming the darling of New England, too. In Connecticut and Massachusetts and Maine the Giants were the ''local'' team. In fact, Lombardi's first meeting against his old Giants was an exhibition up in Bangor, Maine. The Giants won that one, 14–0, as Sherman's offense, with a new man-in-motion series, stumped the Packers.

Grosscup was cut just before the Giants' opener, while the club was staying at Disneyland. Huff was not supposed to play in the first game, against the Rams. In the last exhibition game he had gotten a concussion.

''Who asked you to leave the hospital?'' asked Doc Sweeny, the club physician.

''I did,'' replied Huff.

The Giants beat the Rams, 23–21, on three field goals by Summerall, and the season was off and indicating which way it would go. The only difference was that the Giants would give up so many points just once more.

The Rams had halted the Giants all five times the teams had met previously. But they never saw Conerly play so well. He completed 21 of 31 tosses and gained 321 yards. His key pitch was a fourth-and-one that hit Schnelker on the 18 to set up the winning field goal.

But the next week the Giants fell to .500 when the Eagles handed them their worst defeat since 1953—a 49–21 drubbing. Those 49 points were virtually a third of all the points the New Yorkers yielded that season. In the final 10 games they were to give up only 100 points.

The third game continued the trend against the Browns, a 10–6 victory. Jim Brown rushed 22 times and got only 86 yards. Another kicker shone for the Giants this time. Chandler averaged 54 yards for 8 punts, including out-of-bounds bull's-eyes on the 4, 5, and 6.

The victory whetted the appetite of Stadium fans for the New Yorkers' first home game of the season. With a 2–1 mark they were tied for first with Philadelphia—which was coming to town. And a crowd of 68,783—which was the second greatest in New York history—turned out to see the Giants win 24–7. Finally, they were "making the crucials," in the lexicon of Allie Sherman. The game marked the first touchdown, after 80 games, in the pro career of Svare. He picked off a Van Brocklin pass and ran 70 yards.

Svare was one of those players that came in a series of trades with the Rams that appears to have been a continuous string. It has gotten so twisted that Svare today is not sure how the deals worked.

"When I was coaching the Rams later on we tried to piece it together," he says. "But it just got too complicated. Let's see. Herb Rich preceded me. Then I went. Then Andy Robustelli was involved. There were lost of contingencies. I was one of the parts. I believe Stan West was involved. Eventually a guy named Charlie Toogood.

"The Rams came up with Del Shofner. The Giants gave up a lot of draft choices. All I know is we tried, and we just couldn't figure it out. To this day."

Svare started as linebacker for the Giants. From his arrival in 1955 until his retirement following the 1960 season, Svare was on the right side; Huff was in the middle; and Svoboda, then Livingston, was on the left.

''There's no question in my mind that the players of those days would have played for nothing,'' he says. ''You have to understand that pro football in the early fifties hadn't really caught on yet, and most of those guys—they just didn't do anything in the off-season except hunt and fish. We were very happy playing professional football. You never heard about people being unhappy. My relationship with Huff was excellent. I think that the whole Giants' team was the most unselfish I've ever seen. But the offense was underestimated. It was efficient. I think, though, that the publicity our defense got helped the offense because the other clubs underestimated it.''

The defense ran itself in 1960, the year that Landry quit. Robustelli was the player-coach of the line. Svare was player-coach of the linebackers, and Patton was player-coach of the secondary. Sherman did not like that arrangement, though, and wanted Svare to be a full-time coach in 1961. Svare moved along. He wound up as head coach of the Rams, then returned to the Giants as an assistant, then moved with Lombardi to Washington, and then to San Diego, where he became general manager and head coach.

He was one of the half-dozen people from Wietecha's photograph to become a head coach. The job with the Chargers soured, though, after reports of drug abuse filtered out.

But in those Giants days, as he says, ''you never heard about people being unhappy.''

While the Giants prepared for their fifth game, at Pittsburgh, the organizer of the American Football League, which was due to start play in 1960, was angry. ''They are attempting to sabotage us,'' charged Lamar Hunt, when the NFL announced its plans to expand and bring Dallas into the league. The American League had already planned to bring in Houston, which would have given it the inside track in Texas.

In beating the Steelers 21–16, there were further symbols of the Giants' powerful defense. For Huff collared a fumble by Larry Krutko and slashed over 5 yards for the decisive score. Then in the closing seconds, the Steelers were halted on the 6-yard line. Tom Tracy, the East's Number Two runner, was stopped three straight times on runs to the right, Katcavage and Grier's territory.

And so it was only natural that Huff made the cover of *Time* magazine, the first time in pro football history a defender made it to that particular Olympus.

At Giants' games fans chanted, like a locomotive gathering steam, "Huff Huff Huff Huff . . . Huff Huff Huff Huff." This time another spectacular standing-room crowd, 67,837, saw Lombardi's return to New York as he brought in his Packers, who had won their first three games, then dropped a pair.

For this game, Sherman's offense was more potent than Lombardi's. Twice, Webster crossed the goal line. Summerall kicked a pair of field goals from the 49. People, packing into the standing-room sections, uncomfortable, began fighting. They set bonfires, they tossed beer. But it was a minor uprising. After all, their team had won.

Despite the loss, Lombardi remained a hero to his team. The Packers had won only once the year before. After winning their opening game, the Pack hoisted Lombardi on their shoulders. In a sense, he never touched ground again.

After half a season, the Giants were 5–1, a game ahead of the 4–2 Browns and Eagles. The New Yorkers were leading everyone in halting the run, yielding only an incredible 2.7 yards a carry. But their next opponents were the Chicago Cards, who led in rushing with a 5.3-yard average. And the Giants did not have Conerly, who was suffering with a bad ankle.

No matter. Summerall was about to begin his stretch of improbable scoring. For the Giants, league leaders, began a stretch that would see them play 171 minutes and 23 seconds —the equivalent of virtually three games—without scoring a touchdown. Yet, that long drought, stretched over two full games and part of two others, would see them lose only once.

Summerall was the Giants' offense in Game 7, for Conerly
was sidelined with his bad ankle. But the defense embarrassed
the Cards. The offense did not get a touchdown. Summerall,
though, kicked 3 field goals—from the 37, 49, and 20—and the
Giants won, 9–3. The Cards, who had scored 153 points in
their first six games, were held to only 1 field goal. They
rushed for only 108 yards; they gained only 63 in the air.

It was the same scoring situation the following week—3
field goals by Summerall were all the Giants' managed as they
bowed 14–9 to Pittsburgh. Again, Conerly was out. The loss put
the Giants and Browns in a tie for first with 6–2 records.

The New Yorkers' next game was against the Cards—but
at Bloomington, Minnesota, where the citizens wanted to prove
they could support NFL football. While the Giants were preparing for this game, the fledgling American League staged
its first draft. Lamar Hunt estimated that the total team pay-
roll would average about $350,000 a club. The top players, he
said, would get about $20,000 apiece.

Conerly, who had seen what had been his most successful
season begin to stagnate, was pushing himself in practice. ''I
gotta play, I gotta play,'' he repeated over and over as he
hobbled on his bad ankle. He knew Charley Conerly Day had
been set for the week after this at the Stadium. He wanted to
play in that game.

Again the old pro returned. He tossed a pair of touchdowns
against the Cards after coming in the second period for Heinrich. The Giants won, 30–20, and the young general manager of
the Rams, Pete Rozelle, asked someone:

''Thirty points? Did Summerall kick 10 field goals?''

Not quite. He had kicked 3, though, as his streak of scoring
the New Yorkers' last 28 points ended.

Charley Conerly Day became exactly that. There were
60,982 fans at Yankee Stadium and the old man did not dis-
appoint them. He threw for three touchdowns as the New
Yorkers picked up their biggest score since the 1956 championship in a 45–14 victory over Washington. Better still, Conerly
received $25,000 worth of gifts, and Perian Conerly finally

got her Corvette. Now the Giants had clinched at least a tie
for the conference title. They stood at 8–2. They could clinch
the title by halting the Browns next week.

Howell posted this sign to make sure the Giants would not
be overconfident against Cleveland, which had lost consecutive
games 21–20 and was feeling miserable:

REMEMBER
PAST PERFORMANCES
MEAN NOTHING
THE BROWNS ARE COMING
AND THEY WILL BE—

Burning
Revengeful
Obnoxious
Well Fired Up
Nasty
Seeking Salvation

Perhaps.

Howell forgot that the same thing might have been said
about the Giants' fans. For now they and their team were at
the peak of their powers. Enthusiasm for the club had never
been higher. Even the Giants' public address announcer, the
courtly Bob Sheppard, who was also the chairman of the
speech department at John Adams High School, was moved
to write a poem:

These are the four that carry fear:
Robustelli, Katcavage, Modzelewski, and Grier!
These are the three that runners find tough:
Livingston, Svare, and husky Sam Huff!
And these four make the passers reluctant to throw:
Nolan and Lynch, Patton and Crow!

About 10,000 bleacher seats and standing room tickets went
on sale at 10 o'clock on the morning of the Browns' game,
which signaled the end of another sort of era. For the 68,436

fans included the last standees the Giants would have. The New Yorkers demolished the Browns, 48–7, holding Jim Brown to 50 yards in 15 carries. And then, with the game almost over, a thousand fans left the stands and began to stream over the field. They tore down the goal posts—a ritual that had been the preserve of enthusiastic college students—and they surrounded the Browns' bench. Paul Brown shouted to his players to get out, quick, and the Browns dashed for the locker room.

Sheppard, who only a few minutes before had brought titters to the crowd when the Giants' Dick Modzelewski stopped the Browns' Ed Modzelewski (he announced, "Modzelewski no gain . . . tackle by Modzelewski"), now broadcasted, "This game will be forfeited unless the fans leave the field."

"Actually, I had no authority to say that," recalls Sheppard. "But I had to think of something." The next day's newspapers spoke of the "near-forfeit."

After twenty minutes order was restored. Considering it appeared that half the Stadium had been drinking, that was pretty good time to restore normalcy. The fans had reason to be happy: Conerly threw another 3 touchdowns, completing 14 of 21 for 271 yards. Gifford scored twice. And the defense held the Browns' passing attack to only 36 yards. The Giants had clinched their title, again. They had attracted 389,603 fans to their six home games, an average of almost 65,000 fans a game. It was their best average, and one that would never be broken. For that last game also convinced Wellington Mara to do away with standing room.

The last game of the season, against Washington, was of interest only to Pat Summerall. He went in as the league's leading scorer with 84 points. He did kick a field goal and 3 extra points in the 24–10 victory, but his 90 points fell short. Paul Hornung of the Packers wound up with a big finale and snared the scoring title. The Giants, though, had become the first team in their division to win as many as 10 games since 1953. And Conerly produced a completion average of 58 percent (113 of 194 for 1,706 yards).

The 1959 season ended as the 1958 season had—with a Giants–Colts championship. This time, Howell was taking no chances. He closed the practice sessions to Baltimore newsmen. Coach Weeb Ewbank of the Colts retaliated by closing his workout to New York reporters. ("All they have to do anyway is ask me what happened," explained Ewbank. "I won't lie to them.")

It seemed strange business after such a successful season for both clubs. In Conerly, the Giants had the top quarterback, statistically, in the league. He was supposed to have been finished. Even his best friend had tried to take his job. Instead, Conerly had responded under pressure by gaining an average of 8.8 yards an attempt and by setting a league record by having only 2 percent of his passes intercepted. Through the 12-game season, only 4 of his 194 passes had been picked off.

The championship was attended by frenzied Baltimore fans, and one of the followers was Vice President Richard Nixon. Just the day before the game he had received good news: Governor Nelson Rockefeller of New York announced he would not seek the presidency. Nixon was a happy man.

So were the Colt fans, at the end. Summerall, of course, had taken care of all the New York scoring and the Giants led by 9–7 going into the third quarter. They did not go for a fourth Summerall field goal on the Colts' 28, though. It was fourth and a yard. The ball went to Webster; he was halted, and the Colts took over. They went on to trample the Giants. Johnny Sample intercepted a pair of Conerly passes, including one for a 41-yard touchdown, Unitas threw for 2 touchdowns, and scored one himself, and the Colts repeated as champions 31–16.

Yet the Giants had played with Rote suffering from a concussion and with Patton out after the second quarter. Father Dudley was sad when he turned to someone on the bench and said, "I have failed in my job. I was supposed to stick with Rote and not let him play." Instead, Rote talked Doc Sweeny into permitting him to get back in.

Four final-period Baltimore touchdowns sealed the Giants' fate. When the game was over, Summerall was sitting in front of his locker rubbing his eye.

"Something must have got in it," he said.

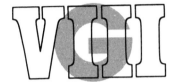

Yes, there really was an American Football League. It opened in 1960. And not far from the Stadium, right across the river, in fact, at their old Polo Grounds, the Giants could see the birth of a club called the New York Titans.

The National League, meanwhile, had altered its long-time setup. A new team had been created, the Dallas Cowboys, and placed in the Western Conference. The Chicago Cards kept their nickname but moved to St. Louis. And Wellington Mara became the league's king-maker by breaking a deadlock in the voting for a new commissioner by suggesting Pete Rozelle for the job. But Tom Landry was now with Dallas, leaving the Giants without the man who created the sport's finest defense.

Meanwhile, there was expansion in other sports, too:

Baseball was taking in four cities from the expiring Continental League, including New York. There was expansion of money as Wilt Chamberlain signed a three-year deal with the 76ers for "the highest contract in sports." That gave him more than the $85,000 a year the San Francisco Giants paid Willie Mays. Billie Jean Moffitt, a sixteen-year-old from Long Beach, California, won the Philadelphia women's grass court tennis title. A sendoff for the Olympic team was staged at New York's City Hall. The team included a light-heavyweight boxer from Louisville with the charming name of Cassius Marcellus Clay.

A different sort of international competition occurred when a man named Francis Gary Powers was shot down in his spy plane over the Soviet Union. Che Guevara of Cuba was on the cover of *Time* with the title, "Man to Watch." Princess Margaret's butler quit over an argument with Anthony Armstrong-Jones. A magistrate in Queens traffic court took a woman to task because she appeared in court in slacks. Payola hearings opened in Washington. "The Real McCoys" were fun viewing over home television, but *Psycho* frightened the nation in movie theaters.

Before a preseason game against the Bears, Sam Huff was wired for sound. A television documentary called "The Violent World of Sam Huff" would be shown and elevate Huff to the top of his profession in the minds of football fans across the United States. "Hit Huff and get on TV," one of the Bears said before the game.

Howell had divided the defensive coaching duties among his three top defenders. Landry was gone, coaching the Cowboys. Howell really did not want to coach any more. In fact, after 1956 he had begun to entertain thoughts about giving it up. What more was there left to do?

Beyond that was his personality. "About the fourth or fifth year I stopped being enchanted with the job," he explains. "It became just a job. I felt you had to win, and when you didn't it was such a letdown. When you did win, you were supposed to. So the kicks were gone. And then I found that I would get snappish at home. I just wasn't as happy about things as I used to be."

He might have had a happier exit as coach. But for the first time in their great years, the Giants were hit with a series of injuries to key people. Luck, or avoiding injuries, had always been a factor in a dynastic stretch. This time, the Giants had neither luck nor health.

They did have Doc Sweeny, though, to minister to them. If there was one constant that characterized the Giants in addition to a Mara, it was Francis J. Sweeny. He was from the tape-an-aspirin-on-it school, an old-fashioned M.D. who did not believe in surgery, as a rule, and who would be insulted if one of his players suggested that an orthopedic man be brought in as a consultant. Doc Sweeny found 1960 to be his busiest year with the club.

Mention Doc Sweeny and people smile. It is a warm smile, with a hint of the beginning of a chuckle. Don Smith, who took over as the Giants' image maker in 1959, remembers Doc Sweeny well.

"One of the great all-time characters," Smith begins. "He was my roommate on the road, and I knew him pretty well, but I don't think I could do justice to the guy if I wrote a book about him. He was a guy from the Prohibition days, taking dum-dum bullets out of rum-runners.

"He was a baseball fan of the Giants under John McGraw, and when the football Giants came into existence and moved into the Polo Grounds, he came with the franchise."

Actually, Sweeny also was the brother-in-law of Steve Owen. And he was the physician of the Manhattan College basketball teams from 1925 until his death in 1966. But it was as the Giants' team doctor that the public knew him.

"I used to have to hide the scotch at night," recalls Smith. "He drank a lot but never while working. At 1:30 in the morning he'd be blind-eyed, but at 6:30 he'd get up with his little bag like nothing ever happened, like there hadn't been a fifth of Dewar's. Doc had two hates—the Bears and the Eagles. Blind, passionate hates. One of the Bears was giving him a hard time, maybe Bulldog Turner. Every time they passed they'd give Doc the finger."

Doc got even. For one of the Bears gashed his lip and a tooth protruded through the lip. There was no team doctor for the Bears so Doc Sweeny was called in. He did emergency surgery, not really a big deal.

"But as a finishing touch," says Smith, "Doc took one stitch and stitched it through the guy's tongue to the side of his mouth. And as they wheeled the guy off, Doc said, 'Let that son of a bitch give me any talk now.' "

He was so excitable that generations of Manhattan College

students remember a short man running up and down the sidelines of the basketball court shouting at officials at a bad call,
which was a call that went against the Jaspers. That man with
the black bag was Doc Sweeny.

"One day at Fairfield University, where we were training,
a priest had an epileptic fit on the running track. Doc was
sleeping. I went to get him. Doc didn't want to get up. Anyway,
Doc got there and John Dziegiel and John Johnson, our
trainers, were holding the priest. One had his tongue, the
other had his hand and there were hands all over the place
and Johnson shouted for Doc to get the priest's pulse.

"Doc reaches in and grabs a hand and says, 'This guy's
healthier than I am.'

" 'Damn it, Doc,' says Dziegiel, 'that's my wrist!' "

Sweeny would have been viewed as a curious antique by doctors for today's clubs. The old man just did not believe in
putting a player under the knife.

"I remember when Charley Conerly had something with his
elbow and he could not pass. This was 1956 or 1957, when
Charley was the meal ticket. Some orthopedic guy thought
they'd have to cut the elbow, and Charley would be finished
for the season.

" 'Ah, these guys, all they know is cut,' Doc said. 'The old
days, we'd never cut. Let me call in a dentist.' And he called
in this old guy whose name, I swear, was Doctor Croaker. And
Croaker says that Conerly had an abcessed wisdom tooth. He
drained it and in a few days his elbow was okay. Doc Sweeny
didn't know what it was, but he knew they shouldn't cut that
guy's elbow. Doc Sweeny was a seat-of-the-pants guy."

From the beginning of the 1960 season he was having trouble
getting Alex Webster back to health. Webster had a bad knee
from an exhibition game injury and could not play. It was a
strange preseason for the New Yorkers, who staged games in
Toronto, New Jersey, Kentucky, and New Haven. Until then,
there had never been a pro game at the Yale Bowl. They
broke the amateur stranglehold in a game against the Lions
that attracted 50,120 fans.

The Giants opened their regular 1960 season at San Francisco with a 21–19 victory but they lost Conerly. Conerly's arm began to swell and George Shaw replaced him. The injury made Conerly, nearing 40, reflect on his career. This was, after all, the season after his greatest triumphs.

"When I win," said Conerly, "they say I'm an old pro. When I lose they say I'm an old man."

Not only were Webster and Conerly now out, but Chandler was hurt making a tackle and would not return for a month. So now Summerall was practicing punting along with Gross-cup, Rote, and Bill Kimber. But none of the above won out: Conerly got the honor. Although he could not play, he could punt and hold for the place-kicking Summerall.

George Shaw, another would-be replacement who was doomed to failure, replaced Conerly in Game 2, the opener of the transplanted Cardinals in St. Louis. Without all these key regulars, the Giants still won 35–14, as Shaw starred with 4 touchdown passes, including 2 to the versatile Joe Morrison. Conerly, meanwhile, hung up 5 punts for a 39-yard average.

While the NFL was getting over the early part of its expansion season, the AFL was proceeding smoothly in its first year. After three games the veteran George Blanda led the young league in scoring.

Perhaps inspired by the old Blanda, Conerly returned from an injury, replacing Shaw late in the third game against the Steelers.

It appears that, perhaps, it was too late even for the old hero. For with exactly 60 seconds remaining the Steelers lead 17–12. The New Yorkers were on the Pittsburgh 42. And Conerly tossed a high one aimed for Gifford. On the 6-yard line Gifford leaped for it, but the Steelers' Fred "the Hammer" Williamson, who was to make a bigger name in black exploitation movies, grabbed it instead. But while the Hammer was descending, Gifford pulled it out of his hands and skipped over the remaining 18 feet. Another Giants victory. Not only that, they were in first place, undefeated with 3 victories, leading Philadelphia (2–1) and Cleveland (2–0).

More people than ever before had seen the Giants play because all the victories were on the road, and that meant they were on television in New York, where they would make their 1960 debut in Game 4.

But first, Mayor Wagner proclaimed it New York Football Giants Week, and he invited the team to City Hall for the proper ceremony.

Since few people in the mayor's office are sports oriented, the Giants' publicist, Smith, was asked to look over past proclamations and write something suitable for Wagner to present. What he did made the Titans pound their fists and scream in agony.

For the proclamation that Mayor Wagner read to the co-captains, Robustelli and Rote, began: "Whereas the Giants are New York's major-league football team. . . ."

Just about now Huff was becoming as famous as any player who had worn a New York uniform. The documentary on Huff and football was perhaps the first network show on pro football. It made Huff a household name, and a synonym for power and, yes, brutality. For the viewers heard Huff screaming and wailing through the transmitter attached to his helmet.

In bars, he was being tested by loutish drunks who wanted to see just how tough this coal miner's son was.

"Are you prepared to die?" he would ask them.

"What do you mean?" was the reply.

"Because if you're not prepared to die," Huff would say, deliberately, his voice even, "then you had better walk away."

In the stands, binoculars would sprout when the Giants' defense took the field. The fans cared, oh, a little for a fine Giants run, but they cared even more for a Huff crackling tackle or for a quarterback sacking by Katcavage or for a blocked punt by Robustelli, the league's best at that. The Giants were not big. But they were just about the smartest team around, and each member of the defense was extraordinarily tough.

Even Dick Nolan, the lightest man with Patton at 180 pounds, was admired for his toughness by Huff.

"I once saw Dick Nolan bring down Jimmy Brown by himself," remembers Huff.

"I'd key on Brown, and make the tackle or slow him enough so that we could gang-tackle him. One time I got knocked away and I couldn't get over to the hole, and Jimmy broke through. Dick came up and gave him a shot and really stopped him. I thought Dick was dead. I went over and said, 'Great tackle, Dick. Great tackle. I'm sorry I couldn't help out. But, jeez, did you get him!'

"And he said, 'Get him? Hell, I couldn't get out of that sonofabitch's way.'"

Despite all these hard-nosed Giants, the home opener for the New Yorkers was a disappointing 24–all tie with the Redskins, and the next game was worse, a 20–13 loss to the Cards. In his return, Webster was able to run only once, for 2 yards.

Yet, the New Yorkers continued their dominance over the Browns as the midway point of the season was reached. For before the largest crowd to see the Browns in Cleveland, 82,872, they halted the Browns 17–13 while limiting the runners to a net of 6 yards. Katcavage, having a big season in fumble recoveries, had one that cut Cleveland down near the end. Once again the great Jim Brown was limited—this time to 29 yards in 11 attempts. It was his worst day of the season, in which he would go over 100 yards 7 times.

The Giants also managed to win the seventh game, over Pittsburgh, and with a 5–1–1 mark, to trail the 6–1 Eagles. The Browns are 5–3. Gifford, now the greatest career scorer in Giants' history, was at the top of his game. He got 3 touchdowns against the Steelers, and Summerall kept those last-second victories as the norm with a field goal 30 seconds before the end of game.

But Rote, who led the league in catches with 19 after only 3 games, suffered a broken finger. He would wind up with only 23 more in the last 9 games.

The key to the 1960 season was approaching. Two straight games against the first-place Eagles, first in New York and then in Philadelphia.

Why do so many people swear they were also at the game in the Stadium, when Chuck Bednarik, it appeared, was leaping for joy after almost killing Gifford, giving him a brain concussion, and sending him to the sidelines for a year? Yet ask a fan and he'll tell you how he remembers Bednarik waving his arms and leaping and laughing. The fan probably also saw the riot at the Browns' game in 1959 or the sudden-death championship in 1958 or the field goal that Summerall kicked in the swirling snow.

More than 20,000 fans were turned away from the Eagles–Giants game for first place at the Stadium, as 63,571 got in. Someone counted 72 fans on the roof of one apartment house across the street. A special cop at the game died of a heart attack. And Gifford nearly died of an extraordinary tackle.

The Giants led 10–0 at the half, but then Van Brocklin tossed for a score and a field goal tied it with fewer than five minutes remaining. The Giants were moving, though. They had a third down and inches to go. The handoff from Shaw to Mel Triplett was bungled, and Jimmy Carr of the Eagles picked it up and raced 38 yards for a score as the Eagles led, 17–10.

Back came the New Yorkers, with Shaw moving closer by connecting with Schnelker. Then Shaw looked for Gifford as time was running out. He hit him with a pass and Gifford caught it, then dashed for the sidelines to go out of bounds to stop the clock. Bednarik, one of the top linebackers in the game, angled over on a collision course. The 235-pound Bednarik smothered Gifford inches from the sideline, the meeting making a sickening "thwack" that nauseated the players nearby. Bednarik did not see Gifford fall in a heap, near death. But he did see the loose ball, in play, bouncing around and he saw an Eagle teammate recover. And he started to jump up and down, pumping the air with his fist for joy.

Later, Bednarik (who was to send Gifford a basket of fruit in the hospital) went over to the Giants' bench to ask about Gifford.

Doc Sweeny, 5 feet 5 inches, picked up his bag and charged Bednarik. "I'll kill you!" shouted Sweeny. "I'll kill you!"

Not only was Gifford through, the Giants discovered they had also lost Katcavage for the season with a broken shoulder. So it was not surprising that the next week they blew a 17–0 lead at Philadelphia, in their last shot at the title, and lost by 31–23.

They blew another lead the following week, in their first meeting with the Landry-led Cowboys. Dallas had dropped its first 10 games. But they hung in after a 21–7 New York lead, recovered 5 fumbles, and tied the Giants, 31–all.

Some respectability returned in the next-to-last-game, played in a Washington snowstorm with the snow half a foot thick under the players' shoes. The Giants rushed for minus-1 yard, yet they won by 17–3.

After the game, Howell formally announced his retirement. Everyone knew it would be his last season, but he wanted to tell the public now, before the finale at the Stadium against Cleveland. Also, there was a chance the New Yorkers could finish second, if they could beat Cleveland. If they did, then they would go to a new game called the Runner-up Bowl at Miami.

The Giants team was not young any more. Already, some fans were beginning to wonder whether the New Yorkers should begin revamping the club. Ten players—more than a fourth of the team—were at least thirty years old.

The Giants would have liked to rebuild with Vince Lombardi.

"We tried to get him," admits Wellington Mara. "But he told us he'd never come here if there would be any problems with his Green Bay contract. They didn't want him to leave, so he didn't."

The Packers were about to wind up on top of the Western Conference in only Lombardi's second year with the club. Howell, though, could get no better than a third in his final year with the Giants. The Browns won 48–34—scoring 27 points in the final quarter as the Giants again collapsed late in the game—and took second place.

Showing his age, Conerly admitted, "I started to get awfully tired that last quarter."

Yet it had been a great era under Howell. In seven seasons there were three conference titles, one league championship. There was a legacy of success, 53 victories, 27 losses, 4 ties. Howell, the easy-going farmer, was going to retire to the front

office as the Giants looked for a new leader to take them deep
into the 1960s. There was, perhaps, a certain symbol of change
that last week. For as the Howell era ended—an era that began
with Howell playing in the 1930s—another sort of symbol for
sports began. An insurance man named Charles O. Finley was
given permission to buy the Kansas City Athletics.

Allie Sherman was a man for the jet-aged 1960s.

He used the modern tools available to coaches—television, computers, scientific analysis, cause and effect. He was the logical man for the job of head coach of the New York football Giants, especially since Vince Lombardi was not available.

Allie knew the "people." If he was not quite family—he did not go to the same school as the Maras and certainly not to the same church—he was loyal to the team. He knew everyone and he was successful.

It was obvious that 1961 would be one of those transitional years that marks an athletic team. Gifford had retired, forced there by Bednarik's terrible tackle. Conerly was past the one-more-year syndrome. Grosscup remained untried as he continued on his treadmill. Alex Webster was just about washed up, too, people believed. His knee injury had limited him to 22 carries the season before.

These were dark problems for Giant fans. But in the world at large there were other diversions.

On the news front, senators rushed to get a bill requiring a life sentence for hijacking an airliner. This action followed the seizure of a plane by a man and his son. Newton N. Minow, chairman of the Federal Communications Commission, characterized television programing as a "vast wasteland." Pres-

ident Kennedy announced he had made an agreement with
Vice President Johnson whereby the vice president would
take over if Kennedy were incapacitated.

The United Nations Secretary-General, Dag Hammarskjold,
died in an African plane crash. Russian astronaut Gherman
S. Titov was the first man to orbit the earth. The Reverend
Billy James Hargis, an anti-Communist preacher, got a net-
work radio show. People were reading *To Kill a Mockingbird,
Franny and Zooey,* and *The Making of the President 1960.*
They often watched Alexander King on the "Jack Paar
Show," and on Broadway they were watching Robert Morse
and Rudy Vallee in *How to Succeed in Business Without
Really Trying.*

Meanwhile, the sports world was buzzing about the creation
of the New York Mets, whose first selections a year before
their 1962 rookie season included Jay Hook, Gil Hodges, and
Elio Chacon. Sugar Ray Robinson, forty years old, beat Denny
Moyer in a comeback bid. The last of the two-hand set shoot-
ers, Dolph Schayes of the Syracuse Nationals, set a National
Basketball Association mark by appearing in his 683rd straight
game. The Redskins were given permission to play in their
new municipal stadium after they promised no racial discrimination. They drafted their first black player, Ernie Davis
of Syracuse—then traded him. Warren Spahn became the thirteenth pitcher to win 300 games in the major leagues. Sal
Durante, a fan, caught Roger Maris' 61st home run ball in
the Stadium and mulled over the Yankees' offer of $5,000 for
the ball.

Allie Sherman looked good as he sat in the board room of
the money management company he was now associated with.
He chatted easily, in an offhanded way. The smiles came
quickly. Strange, to think of him as the frenetic, intense leader
of 5 tons of prime-beef players, prodding them to Eastern
Conference championships in each of his first three seasons
with the team.

The tenth year of Sherman's contract had ended, a $50,000-

a-year sinecure that had guaranteed continuity to the Giants' dynasty. But the early days were happy days for him, and they are fun to recall. They were days recalled by half a dozen novelists in books such as: *A Stone for Danny Fisher, The Amboy Dukes,* and *Goodbye, Columbus.* Here is how Allie Sherman remembers them:

"I was born in Brownsville, Brooklyn, U.S.A. on William Street. Then we lived on Sheffield Avenue; then we moved to the New Lots section. I had a lot of fun at Tiger's Field. You had to stake your field. I went to P.S. 202 then 149, the junior high school Danny Kaye went to.

"We moved to Eastern Parkway, near Troy Avenue in the Crown Heights section, and I went on to Boys High. On Saturdays and Sundays I used to go back to the old neighborhood to play ball. You see, I couldn't make the Boys High football team. I was kind of small. Wally Mueller was the coach. When I got to the pros, he wrote me a letter telling me how 'smart' he was not picking me. Mueller had seen me and said, 'What are you doing, son?' And I said, 'I'm going to try out for the football team.' And he said, 'You're kind of small. Why don't you try out for the handball team?'

"I never played football in high school. But I made the handball team. And on Sunday mornings I'd take the subway to the Parade Grounds and play big-time football with the Dukes.

"We didn't have the money to send me to an out-of-town college. I was out of high school when I was fifteen. The only thing I knew about out-of-town colleges was what I saw in Jack Oakie films. That was just a dream, you know . . . beautiful campuses. I went to Brooklyn College. You didn't need money to go there, just a high enough average to get in. We had a single-wing football team there. I couldn't run as well as most tailbacks, which was my position."

Then the T-formation came in, and Sherman's life was changed and his future mapped. Why did football take so long before it got around to the T?

"Football," says Sherman, "is supposed to be so creative, innovative—conceptually, formation-wise, tactically—yet it's got a great deal of imitation. If a guy hits with a style people take it and try to understand why. And that's what happened to me. My coach at Brooklyn College was a nice guy, Lou Oshins. But we weren't doing well. We'd play Panzer—a physical education school—Cortlandt, Ithaca, Wagner. We'd measure our success in first downs."

And then one day when little Allie Sherman was up in the Catskills working at a summer job, a package arrived from Coach Oshins. It was part of a book on the T-fromation put out by Clark Shaughnessy, George Halas, and Ralph Jones.

"It was a big spiral book called *The Modern T-Formation with Man-in-Motion*. Each week Oshins would rip out a chapter and send it to me. Cripes, I would take the pages out and put them down on a rock and stand behind the rock. This was a new concept, the quarterback under the center, a spinning, half-reverse pivot. I always had a ball with me that summer.

"When I got back to Brooklyn that fall we were a big success. I had a real feel for the T. In those days, you took the ball and if you just wiggled an elbow the defense would send four guys flying after the fake. Cycles. It takes time for the defense to catch up with a new offensive concept. A lot of the NFL teams went for the T but not a lot of colleges. And then the war came. I got a questionnaire from the Eagles. This was something. Who ever looked at Brooklyn College play? Oh, once I got some attention. That was when the Brooklyn Dodgers football team practiced on our field and we had a scrimmage against them. I threw seven straight balls, completed seven. So I got some attention out of that. And then in my last college game, a real big game. City College. Big rivalry. Benny Friedman was their coach. You know, when I was a freshman I was the quarterback of the first Brooklyn College team to beat City College. I was a big hero then. They pulled the goal posts down at Lewisohn Stadium.

"Anyway, this last game, we played at Brooklyn College, across Bedford Avenue. I scored two and I threw two—after we were losing by twenty-one-oh at the half. We win it, 28–21. I got more writeups. And then I got the questionnaire. I don't

say it was that game that made the Eagles send me the questionnaire. Quarterbacks were scarce. But I got it, me from a
school where we never played with new football cleats. We
used to get some of Fordham's and NYU's old shoes. Recon-
ditioned football cleats. I filled out that questionnaire from
the Eagles in a hurry.

"When I got to camp—this was in 1943—they had 12 guys
trying out for quarterback. Among them was a guy who just
got out of prison. Then, there was Bill Hewitt, one of the
great defensive ends in pro football, a guy who played without a helmet. He was trying out, too. There were other guys,
one of them a sandlotter. And I made it because I knew how
to handle the goddamn football better than anyone else under
the center."

There were many ironies in Allie Sherman's career as a
pro quarterback, but the most ironic was the way he was
treated by his coach with the Eagles, Greasy Neale, and
Sherman's search for an image—the very same problems
which caused trouble in his relationship with Lee Grosscup
almost twenty years later. But later it was Sherman who was
the coach dissatisfied with the ways of the young quarterback,
and it was Sherman who wanted the young quarterback to
conform to a norm.

"I had no concept of pro ball when I started. The first time
I lined up on defense—you played two ways then—I lined up
15 yards back of the line of scrimmage. 'What the hell are
you doing back there, you little shit? Get back in the ball
game,' Greasy yelled at me.

"The old guy scared the hell out of me. I don't think I
slept one night in six weeks. You were so worried then about
getting cut. One night after practice—we practiced at night,
because a lot of guys held real jobs during the day—Greasy
saw me sitting around feeling sorry for myself and said,
'What the hell you doing there looking like that?' And I said,
'Coach, I don't think I'm doing any good here. Night and day
you're always criticizing me. I'm not complaining, but it
seems I do most everything wrong.' He looked at me and

said, 'Listen, son, I want to tell you something. The time to
start worrying is when you don't hear from me. I pick on
you because I care.' "

Although Sherman admits today that what he felt for
Neale was "hate, like every kid does who thinks he's good
enough but doesn't play," he became enamored of the life-
style of football players. More importantly, he became enamored of an attitude, or of a style or tone, of a certain sort
of person: the laconic hero-jock who took things as they came
and had a built-in coolness. Also, these new teammates had
size; that is, they were big. To Allie, in fact, they were bigger
than life.

"I loved it, the whole scene. I'd watch films at one in the
morning with Neale, and I was absorbing things: percentage
moves, how to evaluate defense, how to evaluate offense. And
my mother used to say, 'What kind of business is this for a
Jewish boy?' But my folks were good about it. My first year
I made $125 a game, and we played ten games. Twelve hun-
dred and fifty dollars. By the end of the season my father
was sending me money.

"But I wasn't treated differently. I never heard Jewboy.
But they did make fun of my New York accent. That's an old
joke, like mother-in-law jokes. Any guy from Brooklyn, he's
supposed to say 'dese dems and dose.' But my job—I was the
quarterback—was to get in good with them.

"I think I began to talk like they did. I liked it, that whole
scene. I didn't like Brooklyn and New York. My roommate
was the biggest guy on the team, Elbie Schultz, 6 feet 4 inches,
one of the big people."

Sherman was, perhaps, 5 feet 11 inches tall and weighed
perhaps 170 pounds. He tends to exaggerate the size of his
teammates.

"Our captain was an all-American out of Michigan, Al Wistert. You know what his size was? Only 6 feet 2½ inches, all
of 226 pounds [actually, Wistert was 6 feet 1 inch and 215].

"Schultz attracted every broad for twenty miles. I shagged
along with him. I had a great thing going. What did New
York have for me? What did Brooklyn College have? A nice

little quadrangle. But that's about it. Not like the Jack Oakie movies. I used to stay in school late and fantasize that I was away at college.''

In his Southern accent—actually, more of a Brooklyn drawl —Sherman explains what happened when the reality of his situation finally hit him. For once he got to the pros, there was no more day-dreaming.

''I'd diddle around a scrapbook with plays. I had to compensate. I made up my mind I'd be the best goddamn ballhandler there is, and I'd know as much about quarterbacking as there was, so I don't have to throw the big 40-yard pass too often.''

His knowledge of the T brought him to the attention of the Giants' Steve Owen in 1949, when Owen was contemplating going to the T and was faced with the problem of converting Charlie Conerly from a single-wing quarterback to a T-formation player. So Sherman left Philadelphia, where in five seasons he had thrown a total of 135 passes, and returned to New York. When Owen told him, ''I don't know a damn thing about this T. It's your baby,'' Sherman said he felt ''nineteen feet high.''

In Philly he had roomed with ''defensive guys and offensive linemen because I wanted to get a feel of what they did.'' In New York he was supposed to be the architect of the Giants' blueprint to help them move into pro football's modern age.

But after the 1953 season, when Owen was let go and Allie did not get the head-coaching job, Allie decided to leave for Canada where Winnipeg had offered him a three-year contract. Lombardi replaced Sherman in New York as head of the Giants' offense. And Allie had to explain to his wife what life would be like in Canada.

''I had to orientate my Joanie to this,'' he says. ''I told her, 'This is a small town. This isn't New York. There'll be people gravitating toward us, and you've got to have the same feel and same receptions for everybody. You've never been out of New York. Jewish people out of New York are more clannish. They're a minority and they're going to want to dominate all your time. But you're not just in Winnipeg representing the Jewish faith. You're the head football coach's wife and I'm the head football coach.' "

After three years in Canada, Winnipeg wanted Sherman for a five-year deal. He did not want to "commit" for that long. Back he came to New York, and back he went to the Giants, where he served as a scout. And then one day he got a pair of phone calls—one from Lombardi and one from Howell.

"I'm going to the Green Bay Packers," Lombardi told him. "I want you to come with me. We can put this Green Bay team across." Later, Howell called Sherman and asked him to take over the offense because Lombardi was leaving.

"It was 1959. I told Jim Lee, 'You and I don't think alike. I scare you a little. But it's got to be the way it was when Vinnie was here.' "

He meant as far as control. But Sherman could sense that it would not be quite the same as far as talent went. He could see that "Gifford and Webster were growing old," and that the team ran more than others "and that wears you down." Allie Sherman knew he had to open up his offense. He needed a younger quarterback who could throw the damn ball well enough to strike fear into the opposition, which would allow his aging players to score without killing themselves.

The best game that Lee Grosscup ever had with the Giants was an exhibition against the San Francisco 49ers before the 1961 season. Yes, the Giants saw a quarterback in that game they felt would be their answer. But the quarterback they were looking at played for the 49ers—Yelberton Abraham Tittle.

He was thirty-five years old, with a monk's bald spot, and he had asthma. He was also a steal. For the Giants acquired him by trading a young guard named Lou Cordileone, which prompted Cordileone's classic question when he was told he had been traded for Tittle: "Just me?"

It was a busy time just before the 1961 campaign. The Giants got a writ forbidding a bar in Hackensack from show-ing their home games (the bartender owner had hooked up a huge antenna which picked up Philadelphia's station). Webster, meanwhile, was attempting a comeback.

"Before the season started I went into the coaches' office," recalls Webster. "I turned around and looked at the board and saw the depth chart and got a little upset. My name wasn't even on it. I walked in to see Jack Mara. We were very close. I wanted to know what the story was. I didn't even go to see Allie. Mara told me not to worry about it. You see, I always had a one-year contract. They told me they would let me know if they didn't want me. They didn't tell me that. So I made up my mind to get in the best shape. I had that terrible season in 1960. I went over to Rutgers University and got a group of exercises, and I'd go there two, three times a week to work out. I didn't even report with the veterans. I came to camp with the rookies.

"In our second exhibition game we played the 49ers and I had a pretty good day, a couple of touchdowns, a lot of yardage, and from that day I became the back on the right side and Kyle went to the flanker spot. And 1961 marked the first time I played the right side the whole season."

So now Sherman had his "young" passer, an exciting, versatile player who could also run, and he had a healthy Webster who appeared to be better than ever. Now he needed the final ingredient in the bomb. That turned out to be a tall, skinny fellow with ulcers whom the Los Angeles Rams were unhappy with: Del Shofner. He was an outstanding receiver with the Rams until an injury cut his effectiveness, and then the Rams just forgot about him. The Giants, though, remembered. He would be the first fleet receiver they had within memory.

The season had now expanded to 14 games with the addition of the new Minnesota Vikings. There were 14 clubs in the NFL now, and the Dallas Cowboys moved into the Giants' Eastern Conference. The New Yorkers' season tickets' sale had reached 45,000, and all those ticket holders were to get a treat. For the first time, the New Yorkers were going to open their schedule in September at the Stadium.

Tittle would not be on hand. He had injured himself in his first appearance with the Giants in an exhibition game. So

Conerly started against the Cards and by the end of the game
was hearing an old chant: "We want Grosscup." When Grosscup finally made his appearance he was only 3 for 11, and the
Giants were beaten 21–10.

As if an opening home loss was not bad enough, the Giants
then had to play four straight games on the road. Yet that did
not hold the terrors it would have for most clubs. For the
Giants were one of the finest road clubs in the history of
sports. From 1956, the year of their first title under Howell,
through 1960, they won 22, lost 8, and tied 1 on the road. That
is, they won almost three times as many games as they lost. At
home over that stretch they were 18–9–1, winning twice as
many as they lost.

And the New Yorkers proceeded to show why they had done
so well on the road. The poise and execution of their veteran
players again came through. But it was Tittle especially, who
shined in his début. He replaced Conerly. He clicked with 10
of 12 passes. They were good for 123 yards. He discovered he
liked tossing to Shofner. And Webster came through with a
59-yard run. The Giants stopped Pittsburgh 17–14. Shofner,
after his first two games with the team, was already leading
the league in the number of catches. He continued his lead in
Game 3, a 24–21 victory over the Redskins, as the Giants
helped Washington open their new stadium. This time Tittle
again replaced Conerly and rallied the team from a two-touch-
down deficit. Shofner had snatched 8 passes for 103 yards,
Webster had rushed for 98 yards of 20 tries, and Tittle had
completed 24 of 41 passes, good for 315 yards and 2 touchdowns. And the Giants were tied for first with Dallas, Cleveland, Philadelphia, and St. Louis, all at 2–1.

Now Tittle would get his first starting assignment for the
Giants. It appeared that, finally, the man had been found to
replace Charlie Conerly. It was a search that had started in
1948, Conerly's rookie season, and had ended thirteen years
later.

One of those quarterbacks who had hoped to replace Conerly, Sam Etcheverry, appeared against the Giants in their
fourth game against the Eagles. The Eagles had scored 80

points in their first three games. But the Giants' defense held them to five first downs, 28 yards rushing, only 6 completions in 21 passing attempts. The New Yorkers scored a 24–9 victory.

In the last of their four straight road games, the Giants broke the color barrier at Dallas hotels and then went on to win 31–10. It was marked by a record equaling 102-yard interception return by Erich Barnes. He liked to pronounce his first name EE-rich. But Bob Sheppard, the Stadium's public address announcer, pronounced it Eric. "I always thought that Barnes mispronounced his own name," Sheppard explains, "and I made sure to pronounce it right."

A gala crowd of 63,053 saw the Giants return to the Stadium sporting a 4–1 record and tied with the Eagles for first. The opponent was Los Angeles and Tittle led the Giants to an early 10–0 lead. But their attack stalled and they trailed 14–10 late in the game. In came Conerly, replacing Tittle. The place went wild. For Conerly had spent seven straight periods on the bench. It is the dramatic sort of situation that he had been through a dozen times and the fans had lived them with him. And he delivered, tossing touchdowns to Rote and Shofner in a 123-second span of the final period. The Giants won, 24–14. But they lost to the Cowboys on Kyle Rote Day the next week when Allen Green, who made only 5 of 15 field-goal attempts all season, made good on a field goal with 83 seconds left. The Giants now were second at 5–2 while Philly was 6–1.

It was half a season. Gifford was the new scout who warned the players and press and fans about the impending opponent. Retirement had not been as much fun as he had thought it would be. He did his TV and radio and scouting chores, but whenever he could he picked up a football and practiced with his old teammates. He did not take a chance running with the ball, mind you, but he ran patterns and enjoyed catching passes from Tittle.

Tittle's favorite was Shofner, 6 feet 3 inches and 185 pounds, and so slender that his teammates told him he should be nailed to the ground during a stiff breeze.

From the time he starred at Baylor and got the reputation as the Southwest Conference's finest all-round player since

Doak Walker, he had been a big man on his teams. He set a
Baylor mark of 6.2 yards a carry. As a sophomore he was
among the conference leaders in seven categories: rushing,
receiving, punt returns, kickoff returns, interceptions, punting, scoring. He got letters in football, baseball, basketball,
and track. It seemed only fitting he should finally play for
the Giants, because they originally had him, sort of. He became a Ram in 1957 because the Giants had traded their top
draft choice to Los Angeles for Robustelli. The choice the
Rams exercised was Shofner. In 1958 the Rams put him at
end, and he led the league with 51 catches. They were good for
1,097 yards, 8 touchdowns, and an average of 21.5 yards a
catch. In 1959, only Raymond Berry had more catches. But in
1960, injuries, dropped passes, and contract problems kept him
in the background. And suddenly in training camp, in 1961, he
was being beaten in wind sprints, which upset Coach Bob
Waterfield. He was ripe for a trade.

He blended in immediately in New York. His injuries ended.
For the first time the Giants had speed. His style was a sort
of smooth stream. He would be in stride almost immediately,
effortlessly, and suddenly he was gone. He also had tremendous control of his body, and when he went up for a ball his
arms resembled a cherry picker as they moved, as if on hinges,
behind him or sideways or straight up to pluck a ball out of
the air. A strange combination, Delbert Martin Shofner and
Yelberton Abraham Tittle. But they brought a new, thunder-
ous term to the New York sports fan—the "bomb." It was
the long pass on a simple "fly" pattern—that is, Shofner
just flew—that would connect for a long gain, or invariably, a
touchdown. In a three-year stretch with Tittle, Shofner caught
185 passes. They were good for 3,439 yards and 32 touchdowns.

They went to work on the bomb in Game 8 of 1961, against
the Washington Redskins. The Redskins had dropped 15
straight games. But according to Gifford, in the best Jack
Lavelle tradition, he warned everyone on Tuesday, "We have
a hell of a job on our hands Sunday."

So on the first play of the game, Tittle and Shofner connected for a 38-yard score. The Giants went on to win 53–0.

It was the game that Grosscup came in, hit Shofner for a score, and heard the fans calling his name and then sat on the bench and cried. It was a game in which Modzelewski and Katcavage each tackled quarterback Norm Snead for safeties. It was such a good game that Coach Sherman, in his best Madison Avenue explication, said, "Continuity-wise, it was the best."

The victory brought the Giants' record to 6–2, while Philly was at 7–1. But the teams met in the ninth game, and when it was over Tittle had again starred, along with Shofner, while the Giants' defense had held the Eagles long enough for the New Yorkers to jump to a 38–7 lead.

Tittle now was receiving national recognition with a day that saw him complete 75 percent of his passes—18 for 24, good for 307 yards and 3 scores. Shofner, meanwhile, snared 8 passes, and the defense intercepted Sonny Jurgensen 3 times. It was a 38–21 rout, and the clubs were tied for first with 7–2 marks. This time Shofner had snared a 32-yard bomb.

For their tenth game the Giants received two dozen plays in the mail. Fans were making suggestions following the Pete Previte Special. Previte, the Giants' locker-room attendant, had suggested to Sherman that the two fastest Giants, who happened to be Barnes and Patton, be split wide on offense and just fly for a pass. Tittle then connected with Barnes for a 62-yard score. Now fans were sending in diagramed plays, one of which put fifteen Giants on the field.

The Giants did not need any new plays, as they stopped the Steelers in their next game 42–21. Dick Lynch, who was to lead the league with 9 interceptions, picked off a pair against the Steelers. Again, Tittle picked up more than 300 yards and completed 3 touchdown passes. Webster was among the rushing leaders and the explosion of 133 points in 3 games is the greatest such stretch in the club's history.

Even the powerful Browns were victimized as the Giants brought their mark to 9–2. Jim Brown did gain 72 yards on 17 first-half rushes, but in the second half he was thrown for minus-4 yards on 3 carries. The Giants were 9–2 after a 37–21 decision and now faced the Packers.

At no point before in Giant history—and perhaps not since —had the fan interest been as high. Now motels began to advertise that their television sets could pick up the blacked-out Giants' home games. Thus began one of the stranger chapters in the history of sports in this country: a stream of hundreds, perhaps thousands, of people leaving their homes on Sunday mornings for a day at a motel that had a television set that could pick up the Giants' games. So in Eastern Long Island, in Westchester, and in Connecticut, where the motels with antennae facing in the right direction could pick up Hartford, which would be televising the Giants' games over channel 3, motels that would have been virtually empty started to fill up.

Not only that, but a whole world was built around the telecast of the Giants' games. In the middle of one motel quadrangle, there was a high school band playing marching songs. And there was someone selling hot dogs! And there was even a man hawking a program!

"There would be twirlers, there'd be a half-time show on the lawn, tailgate parties, a football buffet," recalls Don Smith. "They'd even have a film of the Giants' highlights. There would be a football breakfast; there would be a local football coach with a question-and-answer session. This whole thing would start at nine in the morning, and the motels, like the Stratford in Connecticut, would give you a special game-day rate.

"There were probably as many Giants fans in motels as at Yankee Stadium. And some guy invented an antenna that would rotate and you could pick up games from another state over your home television. But the motels would give you your money back if you couldn't get good reception of the games. One guy told me the football-watching in motels was knocking the hell out of the shackup business."

So, fans watched over television as the Packers halted the Giants in Game 12, 20–17, pushing the New Yorkers into a tie with the Eagles at 9–3. The victory clinched the Western title for Green Bay in a rough contest with 147 yards in penalties, 102 to the Pack. The Giants' Huff picked up some reverse yardage on his own, though, by elbowing the Packers' great runner, Jim Taylor. "We're even now," says Huff.

There was still another road game, perhaps the biggest of the year. It was at Philadelphia. Tittle was ineffective and he was replaced by Conerly in the second period with the Eagles ahead. Conerly did it again, with 3 touchdown passes to Shofner. One of the key plays was a roughing-the-kicker penalty called on the Eagles while Chandler was attempting to punt. Most people in the place claim to this day that Chandler was never hit. In any event, the penalty that followed positioned a Giants score, and the Giants broke their tie with Philadelphia in a 28–24 decision. Perhaps, said some of the Giants, Bednarik would not say those nasty things about Huff any more, such as calling him "an overrated hillbilly."

In their last game of the regular season, the Giants faced the Browns at the Stadium, and all they wanted was not to lose. A tie would ensure the Eastern championship no matter what Philadelphia did. And a tie is what they got, thanks to a dropped pass by Mel Renfro on the 7-yard line in the final quarter. So a Tittle-to-Joel Wells score in the first quarter and a Milt Plum-to-Frank Clark toss in the third took care of the scoring. It was lucky for the Giants that Renfro dropped that ball, for the Eagles wound up winning with 28 seconds remaining. The New Yorkers ended with a 10–3–1 mark while Philadelphia was 10–4. Since ties are thrown out, the Giants won with a percentage of .769 to .714. It meant that the Giants would face the Packers for the title. It meant Sherman versus Lombardi for the first time.

In Green Bay's long football history, which began way back in 1921, it had never been the host to a championship game before. Now they were calling their city "Titletown U.S.A."

It had been a cold winter in Green Bay. For weeks, the field had lain under a blanket of hay and tarpaulin to keep it from

freezing. The Packers' style was the run, and the more man-
ageable the field, the better the Packers' chances were. It was
20 degrees below zero the day before the game. It had, in fact,
been miserable all week, and now the Eastern press and the
national magazines for the first time focused in on Lombardi
and his practices. They saw men playing without gloves in
that weather, but they did not hear the players complain. And
Lombardi smiled through his alligator teeth at the weather.

The Giants fielded eight players from the Eastern all-star
team: Robustelli, Katcavage, Huff, Barnes, Patton, Tittle,
Shofner, and Webster. But they got slaughtered 37–0 as the
country watched incredulously over NBC, which had paid a
record $615,000 for the telecast. It was as perfect a game as
a team ever played, championship or regular season. For the
Giants were held to six first downs. They were held to 31
yards rushing. They completed only 10 of 29 passes. The
Packers intercepted 4 of Tittle's passes as he was embarrassed by completing only 6 of 20 tosses. This began a string
of 3 straight championships in which he performed below his
expectations. Webster, who had a remarkable comeback during
the season, with 928 yards and a 4.7 rushing average, gained
only 19 yards on 7 carries.

When it was over, the head of the New York Titans, Harry
Wismer, said he was "sorry" the Giants lost so badly. Then
he challenged them to a charity game.

The bald man has an honest face. He walks up to the room clerk in the New York Hilton and says, "Key for 3725, please."

"What's the name?"

"Tittle."

"Any identification, sir?"

Once, not that many years before, the bald spot would have been enough.

That doesn't faze Y. A., though. He is in a hurry as he rushes for an insurance meeting and now, in his room high in the hotel overlooking Radio City Music Hall, he is scurrying about his room getting his clothing ready.

"What do you think? Is this too sporty?" he asks as he fingers a wide-striped tie. "Maybe I ought to take this one. It's more conservative. This is New York, you know."

In about 27 seconds Tittle has leaped into his trousers, buttoned his shirt, selected his tie, smoothed his jacket, buffed his shoes, and put his change and wallet in the right pockets.

Finally, he drops into a chair—as if landing via parachute—and is ready to reminisce.

"Do those years have magic?" he repeats. "Yes. New York was like—I can't even describe it to you. I played football on the West Coast. But New York City, it's really the most glamorous of all cities as far as teams that win. What I'm saying, I couldn't explain in a thousand years to the 49ers' players. Being in New York on a winning team there is this . . . charm . . . and especially if you win or if you have a lot of money. One of the two. The worst thing to be in New York is to be a loser and to be poor.''

Tittle was neither. He was set after that magical first year, when he intruded on New York's love-hate relationship with Charlie Conerly. For Tittle there was only love. For he showed them skill that Conerly rarely approached, and he showed it to them immediately: 163 completions in 285 attempts for 2,272 yards. There were 17 touchdowns and a completion percentage of 57. It was the finest quarterbacking Giants fans had ever seen.

It did not go with the name. Yelberton. Is that a name for a quarterback? There have been Chuckin' Charlie Conerly. Slingin' Sammy Baugh. Broadway Joe Namath.

''I haven't the slightest idea where that name comes from,'' he says. ''I know that I'm a junior. Yelberton Abraham Tittle, Junior. My father was English and I know Yelberton was a section of England. You see a lot of those names in Devon. My son's name? It's Mike.''

And that is all he knows—or wants to talk about—when the subject of his name is brought up. But he loves talking about throwing. He speaks of it so easily, which seems strange, because he is now such an established, successful businessman in California it often seems as if the Giants were a minor part of his total life, like one high school football game. Yet, he speaks easily of what it was about.

''You see, me and Shofner both came here at the same time. One was a passer and one was a receiver. And we both were traded from West Coast teams. So that put us both in the same bag. I'd never thrown to someone with the speed he had—along with such a good pair of hands. Normally receivers that have tremendous speed don't have very good hands. I don't know why. It's true, though.''

There was a professionalism about the Giants then, a willingness to work for the victory they always expected. There was also a deep pride and sense of self.

"Shofner was a receiver," says Tittle. "He was proud of that. He was no blocker or tackler. He could punt very well, but he didn't want to punt. We had a hard time keeping him as Chandler's backup punter in practice. You see, Del was a pass-catcher. I was a PASSER."

He capitalized the word with his voice. It was an attainment he was proud of, and it was one he had come by the long way. It started for him in Marshall, Texas, on October 24, 1926, a whistle-stop town near the Louisiana border. He played college ball at LSU, part of the state educational system that was Huey Long's pride and joy. In fact, the coach before Tittle played at Louisiana State was fired because he didn't permit Huey Long to give a half-time pep talk. Y. A. played for two seasons at LSU, averaging 54 minutes a game on offense and defense. His finest moment came against the big state rival, Tulane. He completed 32 of 38 passes, with a string of 12 straight. His most embarrassing moment? The day he intercepted a pass against Ole Miss. Legend has it that it was Conerly's pass he intercepted. As he was running for what he hoped was a touchdown, his pants fell down, and he tripped.

"It's probably a better story with it being Conerly's pass," he says. "But I don't think it was."

His first pro club was in the old AAC with the Baltimore Colts in 1948, and he promptly set a record against the New York Yankees, smashing four AAC marks in a game that saw him pick up 346 yards. This sudden notoriety also sparked interest in the origin of his name, and among the reports were that his lineage was traced to brothers who came over on the Mayflower. One was named Yelberton, the other Abraham. Also, it was said, the Tittles had an estate in England, which Y. A. Tittle, Senior, unsuccessfully laid claim to. And, finally, Yelberton was a French name which got to England during the Norman Conquest.

Interesting names were part of Yat's life. His mother's name was Alma. He had a sister Huline. His wife's name is Minnette. His favorite receiver was Delbert.

Delbert was far in the future in Y. A.'s rookie campaign.

Another year with Baltimore was followed by his longest stretch—from 1951 to 1960—with the 49ers. They were, mostly, years of success for Tittle. Despite 8 seasons at .500 or better, the 49ers never finished first. And Coach Red Hickey switched to a shotgun offense, in which he wanted the younger John Brodie as his Number One and Billy Kilmer as the back-up quarterback. Tittle, the bald eagle, was expendable.

So in his first year with the Giants, when he was the league's most valuable player, he tasted his first division championship and he discovered New York.

More titles followed in 1962 and 1963, but not the league championship. So in 5 title games—with Baltimore in 1949, against Detroit for the divisional playoff in 1957, and in 3 with New York—Tittle wound up on the losing end.

Yet he was confident when 1964 began. For 1963 had been his most magical season: his first as official head of the quarterbacks, a season in which he threw for 36 touchdowns and completed 60 percent of his passes.

"How," he wonders as he sits in his hotel room now, "could I be so good in 1963? Throw 36 touchdown passes. Then nine months later I could be washed up?"

No, that does not seem right. It must have been injuries to him and other key players. The good years, though, were something else.

"It was," he concludes, "a fine group of prideful men."

The 1962 sports world saw some changes as dramatic as the Giants underwent: Sonny Liston knocked out Floyd Patterson in the first round to win the heavyweight title. Buzzie Bavasi of the Dodgers said Leo Durocher was disloyal to Manager Walter Alston and "there's no room for both of them on this club." Durocher had simply told friends the Dodgers would have won if he had been manager instead of coach. The American League rookie of the year was Tom Tresh of the Yankees. The Mets helped Casey Stengel honor his fiftieth year in baseball by dropping a doubleheader at the new Polo Grounds.

Jimmy Piersall jumped into the stands at Baltimore when a fan called him a "fruitcake."

Meanwhile, television fans were taking in "Sing Along with Mitch" and, in New York, Allie Sherman's show called "Inside Giant Football." Vaughn Meader sold 200,000 albums in a month; the album was called *The First Family.* Francoise Sagan gave birth to a boy. Donald "Deke" Slayton, a member of the space program, was grounded by a heart problem. A TV show, in which a mystery guest completes a set of questions, drew the following clues: Q.: The thing I hate to do is ——. A.: Lose. Q.: You could never get me to ——. A.: Quit. Q.: If I could be a moment in history, I'd be ——. A.: President. The mystery guest was Richard M. Nixon.

In 1962 Charlie Conerly, Kyle Rote, and Pat Summerall retired. But Gifford decided to try a comeback. He would not do it as a running back but from a new position, flanker. No sense having those defensive linemen take another pop at his head. It had taken him a year to recover from the last one.

The Giants' kicking now would be handled entirely by Don Chandler, who had not place-kicked since high school. But he had a strong leg and, figured the Giants, they could bring in their old hero, Ken Strong, to teach Chandler the art.

Through the early part of the season, Gifford was unspectacular despite having Rote as his teacher. The transition from running left to right presented Gifford with a different rotation on the ball and a different perspective.

The Giants' offense was unspectacular in the opener, as it bowed to the Browns 17–7, and was halted twice inside Cleveland's 11-yard line. Undaunted, the New Yorkers roared back the second week of the season in a remarkable game. The Eagles' Sonny Jurgensen threw 57 passes, he completed 33, he gained 381 yards—but the Giants won 29–13. For Y. A. and Del were embarking on a season that would see Shofner average 21 yards for every ball he caught. Against the Eagles he snared bombs of 69 and 56 yards. Jurgensen had thrown a touchdown on the third play of the game, so Tittle and Shofner connected for a score on their third play.

Meanwhile the Giants' defense blocked 3 field-goal attempts and made 3 interceptions.

In their third straight road game, Erich Barnes intercepted Bobby Layne in the end zone with fewer than 2 minutes remaining, and the New Yorkers held to a 31–27 decision over Pittsburgh. Gifford was returning, finally, to form as he snared 4 passes. It was also a 4-touchdown day for Tittle.

For the third straight game the opposition opened the scoring, but for the third straight week the Giants won on the road in a 31–14 trouncing of the Cards at St. Louis. The incredible Yat, who would wind up the season as the Giants' fourth-leading rusher, rambled over on a 21-yard run for the tie-breaker. Now after four games the Giants had a 3–1 record, and played, finally, at home. But the Redskins, who had posted a 1–12–1 mark the season before, led the conference with 3 victories and a tie in 4 games.

Game 5 was a disappointment for the team and its Stadium fans. The Giants blew their home opener to the Steelers 20–17, as Johnny Sample covered Gifford tightly, Shofner was injured (he seemed to leave every week with a different ailment), and Tittle was sacked repeatedly by Big Daddy Lipscomb and Ernie Stautner. Now the Giants were 3–2 while Washington was 3–0–2.

As they prepared for their sixth game of the campaign, against the Detroit Lions at the Stadium, Chandler continued to get place-kicking pointers from Strong.

He was doing tremendously. Although his punting average had slipped, he was making better than 60 percent of his field-goal attempts. He was doing it despite repeated differences with Strong, who believed the only way to kick a field goal was the Ken Strong way.

The memory of the education still makes Don Smith chuckle.

"All place-kickers are crazy," begins Smith, whose job was to present the New Yorkers' most clean-shaven face to the public. "They're crazy, but I guess Chandler might have been the sanest of all. He was strong-willed, independent. Ken

Strong. Poor Ken Strong. He was a great kicker, a great athlete, but maybe thirty years too soon. He played for $55 a game. Don Chandler was making $25,000—a grand a minute of playing time. And Strong was strong-willed. He would always think he knew more than the guy he was teaching.

"But Chandler would say, 'Heck, I'm better than this guy. Why should I listen to him?' Chandler would kick six for six right through the uprights and Strong would say, 'You're not locking your ankle at impact.' And Chandler would try it Strong's way—and miss. It was like bringing in a guy to teach Tittle how to pass.

"He had a super-powerful leg. My God. His leg was so strong. We'd be sitting bare-footed in the locker room and he'd grab you by the leg with his big toe and the other toe! He could hold you so tight with those two toes it would hurt and you couldn't get away."

Following Summerall was not going to be easy. Summerall's field goals had won 9 of the 35 games he played in during his four seasons with the Giants. Chandler was a known quantity as a punter, of course. Smith once figured out that in clutch situations, behind his own goal line, Chandler had averaged 51 yards a punt.

Once, the Giants swear, he kicked a ball in a 1961 preseason test against the Packers that traveled 107 yards in the air. He took to field-goal kicking as expertly. For in his very first campaign, in 1962, he led the league in averages by kicking 19 of 28 for a 68 percent mark. He continued kicking with New York through 1964, when he came into conflict with Sherman. He wanted time off during the week and planned to commute from his cattle ranch on weekends.

"You are either a professional football player or you are something else," Sherman told him. And in 1965 Chandler went to the Packers where he was reunited with Lombardi. He went on to star in the 1968 Super Bowl victory with 15 points against Oakland.

Now in 1962, though, he had a problem: what kind of shoe should he wear? You wore one sort for punting, another for place-kicking. So Chandler had two pairs of shoes on the bench. A high-topped shoe with a squared-off toe was good for place-kicking, kickoffs, and extra-point attempts. It helped lock the ankle. And for punting he used a low-cut, streamlined job. He would change shoes nine or ten times a game. For speed, he experimented with a zipper-shoe to help him get in or out of a shoe quickly. This was especially important if the Giants were near midfield. Would there be a punt? Or would the Giants cross into the opposition's territory and go for a field goal?

In Game 6 of the 1962 season they went for a field goal in the third quarter, Chandler made it and it was the difference as the Giants halted the Lions, 17–14. The Giants' defensive character showed against the Lions. In the game, Huff blocked a kick, and with 20 seconds remaining, Barnes deflected a pass from Milt Plum that was headed for Gail Cogdill on the goal line. Then Lynch blocked a field-goal attempt and the Giants' victory was on the board. In fact, the Giants did not lose another game in the 1962 season; they wound up winning their last 9 games.

The upset (the Lions had lost only once) gave the Giants a 4–2 mark, but it kept them behind the undefeated Skins, who had won four times and lost twice. But in the continual dramatics that surrounded the Giants of this era, their next opponent was Washington.

The game attracted so many people that a thousand cars were parked at the Polo Grounds, where the Titans were playing and where Titans' officials were stunned into believing it was their game that was attracting the fans. But no, after parking in the Polo Grounds' lot for $2, the Giants' fans walked over the 155th Street Bridge to the Stadium to see their heroes. Meanwhile, at the Stratford Motor Inn in Connecticut, 158 rooms were booked by 500 people. The Connecticut Turnpike was filled with cars heading for motels, with some of the drivers coming from 100 miles away, in deepest Long Island. Drivers would open their windows and shout to people in the car alongside, "Going to the game? Wanna share a room?"

Those in the motels and those at the Stadium were lucky. They saw what just might have been the finest quarterback performance in history. For Tittle connected for 7 touchdowns, completed 27 of 39 passes (including a stretch of 12 straight) and gained 505 yards through the air, and the Giants swamped Washington in the Skins' first defeat, 49–34. Only two other quarterbacks—Sid Luckman of the Bears and Adrian Burk of the Eagles—had thrown 7 touchdowns in a game.

Why didn't Yat go for eight?

"It would have been bad taste," he explained.

In the game, Shofner snared 11 passes for 269 yards, getting a record for yardage for the Giants and equaling Gifford's mark for catches; Walton scored three times, Morrison twice, and Shofner and Gifford once apiece. The Giants at one stretch scored 3 unanswered touchdowns and led 49–20.

That wide margin was probably the major reason Tittle did not go for the mark, even though his teammates told him to. Years later, Tittle explained his reasoning again by saying, "If you're leading by so much, it just doesn't sit right with me to fill the air with footballs. I'm the quarterback. It would be showing off."

The New Yorkers moved into first place the following week by halting the Cards, 31–28, while the Skins lost to the Cowboys. Funny, but a week after that performance of 7 touchdowns, Tittle had his worst day as a Giant—8 completions for 31 yards. Shofner made only 1 catch for 13 yards. So the Giants won on a flea-flicker—a Guglielmi-to-Andy Robustelli score.

The home stand was over and Game 9 found the Giants at Dallas, playing a Cowboys' team that had scored, 41, 42, 24, and 38 in their last 4 games. But a 24-point second period led the Giants to a simple 41–10 victory. For the first time all season Gifford carried the ball, on a double reverse with Webster, and scored. The Cowboys were hampered, meanwhile, by a change in their style. Landry had employed a shuttle-quarterback system—Don Meredith and Eddie LeBaron would come in on alternate plays with a play from Landry. But LeBaron was hurt and Meredith had to run the whole show. He was no match for Tittle, who was back on the beam with 3 scores, including a 37-yarder to a new receiver, Aaron Thomas.

The Giants put away the title in their tenth game by wrecking the Skins, 42–24. Yat set a club mark of 25 touchdown passes in a season.

The man in charge of warning everyone about the impending game was none other than Tunnell—don't get overconfident in Game 11, even though the opponents are the Eagles, who lost 49–0 the week before. He followed in the tradition of Lavelle and Gifford in his scouting report with his comment. But first, he committed a boner. He told the press that he really did not know much about the Eagles' offense "because they weren't out on the field long enough." Suddenly, Sherman gave him a sidelong glance which Tunnell, who had tremendous peripheral vision, picked up. He knew he had displeased his coach, so he quickly added, "But the Eagles will be loose next Sunday."

So they were. It was a miserable, snowy, rainy day. Chandler had missed 20 of 25 field-goal attempts warming up before the game. But Chandler set a Giants record by booting 4 field goals in a 19–14 victory, a victory secured when Modzelewski and Katcavage halted Theron Sapp on a fourth-and-two late in the game, and in the final minute, knocked the ball out of King Hill's hands. Meanwhile, on the Coast, Agajanian had come out of retirement at the age of forty-three to kick a 49-yarder for the Raiders of the AFL.

Another week went by—and Chandler again kicked 4 field goals. This time the Giants halted the Bears at Chicago, 26–24. It was a momentous event that led the writer for the *Times* to begin his story this way: "Don Chandler walked across Lake Michigan today . . ."

But the editors did not like the lead and asked him to do another one. This one began: "With the stealth of Lamont Cranston, Don Chandler . . ."

The *Times* in those days checked questionable leads with someone in the "bullpen," the place where the man in charge of the day's paper would be sitting. That day the tweedy Harrison Salisbury happened to be in the bullpen.

"What," he was asked, "do you think of this lead with Lamont Cranston?"

"I don't know who Cranston is," replied Salisbury. "I don't follow football."

Chandler, walking across Lake Michigan or disguising himself as the Shadow, showed 18 field goals in only 25 attempts.

But if people do not recall the end of the 1962 season too clearly in New York it is because there were no newspapers in town. There was a strike that shut them down and led to the death of four of them. To compound the football fans' frustrations, the Giants wound up the season with two home games, so fans could not see their heroes on television either. Not only were these games blacked out, but the championship game against Green Bay was also at the Stadium, and therefore, blacked out.

The Giants wound up the regular season with a 17–13 victory over the Browns and a 41–31 decision over Dallas. By season's end, Tittle was the leader in touchdowns with 33, and Shofner had averaged 21 yards a catch and scored 12 touchdowns by snaring 53 passes for 1,133 yards. Gifford averaged 20 yards a catch in his great comeback season.

The cover of *Time* the week of the title game was filled with Lombardi's grinning face—or was he gritting his teeth? Across the cover it said, simply, "The Sport of the 60's." And the Packers, who were seeking to supplant the Giants as the next dynasty, won the championship at the Stadium before the largest crowd since standing room was done away with—64,892. In the thirty-mile-an-hour winds and fifteen-degree chill, Jerry Kramer kicked field goals of 26, 29, and 30 yards and the Pack won 16–7. More important than the field goals, the Packers' defense allowed the Giants past midfield in the first half only twice. The line swarmed over Tittle, permitting him only 18 completions in 41 attempts. His longest was only 18 yards as the blitzing Ray Nitschke dumped him often.

The Packers led 10–0 at half time on a Kramer field goal

and a Jim Taylor 7-yard run, following recovery of a Phil
King fumble. The Giants' only score, in the third quarter,
came from the defense when Barnes blocked Max McGee's
punt and Jim Collier landed on it in the end zone. The score
was cut to 10-7, and perhaps the Giants might have moved,
especially after the Packers punted on their next series. But
the kick was dropped by Sam Horner, recovered by Green
Bay, and that was that.

Yet there remained a fond memory for Giants fans. Taylor,
who rumbled for 85 yards on 31 carries, was bitten once by
Huff. Anyway, he said he was, which meant Huff could bite
through a helmet. It was probably the most famous action of
Huff's career, one that was to follow him, lead to nasty letters
from fathers of young boys, and bring chuckles to him and
Taylor today.

At the end, though, the Giants simply were not good enough
for Green Bay.

It seemed to Sherman that there had to be some changes
made in the Giants—or at least the beginning of some changes.

Rosey Grier was the first of the core to be plucked out. He was traded on July 8, 1963, to the Rams for John LoVetere and a high draft choice. This meant the break-up of the defensive line that had played together for seven seasons. Grier, Modzelewski, Katcavage, Robustelli—they were such familiar names; they had been together for a generation of football fans that grew up in the sport's most productive era. Somehow, it would not be the same. Yet there were still the others, and above them all, was Tittle.

There were other magical names in sports in 1963, when a Giants age would be nearing an end. Out in San Francisco, Willie Mays still roamed the outfield, and he got the 2,000th hit of his career against the Los Angeles Dodgers. Roger Staubach was the quarterback leading Navy. The new man on the New York sports scene was Cleon Jones, who joined the Mets out of the suburbs of Mobile that produced Hank Aaron and Ernie Banks.

An astrologer predicted big things for a boxer named Rubin "Hurricane" Carter. He had been born, after all, under the same sign of Taurus the Bull as Gene Tunney, Sugar Ray Robinson, and Joe Louis. Ralph Houk was promoted by the Yanks to general manager, and Yogi Berra was to take over the team for 1964. The Mets drew a million people in the old Polo Grounds; they became the first tenth-place club to make that statement. A Labor Day crowd of 71,675 at the Big A bet a world record $5,569,646 to watch Kelso.

You could still make money in the stock market, too, although AT&T was $123, down about $40 from 1954. A young black writer named James Baldwin was warning the country in his book *The Fire Next Time,* but you could have a smile on your face by taking in *The Thrill of It All,* with Doris Day and James Garner. Madame Nhu termed President Kennedy an ''appeaser.'' A bomb killed four black girls in a Birmingham church. The *New York Mirror* was folded by the Hearst Corporation. The Kennedys made news still: *P.T. 109* was showing in movie houses. Mrs. Kennedy took an Aegean cruise aboard Aristotle Onassis' yacht *Christina.*

Pro football—and the Giants—thought they had seen booming times. They had not seen anything yet. For the exhibition games alone attracted a record average of more than 40,000 fans a game. NBC paid $926,000 just to televise the championship game. The Giants saw their season ticket sales swell to 58,000—making a ticket the most popular season's seat in the world.

Often, the ticket manager, a genial man who never showed the strain, named Harry Bachrach, needed the wisdom of a Solomon.

''We had a divorced couple,'' he recalls. ''Oh, it was a very messy situation. He wanted the season's seats and she wanted them. So as part of the settlement they each got a seat. But they did not want to sit near each other. I put them on opposite sides of the Stadium.''

Luckily for the fans and the Giants, the team did not have to face the Packers in the regular season. But in an exhibition game the Packers scored their seventh straight victory over the Giants as 42,327—a record crowd in Green Bay, a city of 62,888 —watched the game. Among the spectators was Paul Hornung, who received a standing ovation when he was introduced. That was the only hand he would get that year. He had been suspended by Rozelle for gambling, along with the Lions' Alex Karras.

In another preseason game, at Palmer Stadium in Princeton, it was like the 1930s. Raccoon coats sprouted in the parking lot before the game as tailgate parties were revived. The Giants had brought back a college atmosphere, perhaps beginning a few years before when they started a regular series of games at the Yale Bowl. Now, martinis were mixed in the rear of station wagons, silly college beanies were worn, pennants were waved, and fans were eating pâté, pumpernickel, and pop while waiting for the games to start.

As usual, the fans had to wait a while to see their darlings at home. The Yankees had commandeered the Stadium, where they were en route to their fourth straight championship. So the fans watched on TV as Tittle returned to Baltimore and to the field he had begun on fifteen years before. They saw him toss 3 touchdowns, wiping out an 18-point deficit, and they saw him run for a score—before he got busted up crossing the goal line. Still, the Giants halted the Colts 37–28.

It is obvious what Tittle meant to the Giants when the offense fell apart the next week because he did not play. For the first time in 123 regular season games—since the days of Steve Owen—the Giants were shut out. The Steelers won 31–0 as Guglielmi's passes managed to gain only 63 yards. A week later, Tittle was back, and of course, the Giants swamped the Eagles 37–14. Not only did the offense move again, with Morrison plunging for 3 scores as Webster's replacement, but the defense pulled down 5 interceptions. Then the Redskins became the New Yorkers third victims, with Yat throwing for 3 scores, amassing 324 yards, and relaxing in a 24–14 decision.

After 4 games the Giants were 3–1 and trailed the Browns, who were revamped and 4–0. Cleveland was being led by Blanton Collier after Paul Brown was fired. Collier was running more diverse plays around Jim Brown, who was averaging 8.5 yards a carry.

Since the next game was at the Stadium, there would be certain rituals followed. The players would spend the night together at the Hotel Manhattan. Allie Sherman believed in togetherness. Then, each Giant would scrounge around for tickets. They were permitted only one apiece, with the option to buy six more. But since the team's following was so intense that 3,000 fans had to watch the 1962 championship at the Stratford Motor Inn, then it's obvious even ten tickets a player would not have been enough.

Andy Robustelli probably got hit for tickets more than any other player. He had a business in Connecticut, he lived nearby, he had been around for a while, and he knew more people than anyone else. He was also the director of the defense.

These days Robustelli is director of operations for the Giants, the only man since Wellington Mara got out of college in the Depression to decide who will play for the Giants.

There is a bulkiness about him but not a hugeness. His hands, though, are enormous and they appear as if each could palm two footballs.

Actually, it's remarkable that anyone ever heard of Andy Robustelli. Now, more people know him than ever heard of the school he attended.

"Arnold College was a very small physical education school before the war," he explains. "After the war it grew, like most colleges. I had a chance to go to Villanova, but my high school average had been only about a C-plus. They wanted me to go to prep school. But after two and a half years in the service I didn't want to go. I wanted to go to college. Arnold was nearby. Now it's part of the University of Bridgeport.

"Fortunately for Arnold College, Yale had a bad football team then. Arnold was a small school of about 250 boys, maybe 100 girls. We played the Coast Guard Academy and Northeastern and Wagner College. I was a better player than most kids at the school. I was an offensive and a defensive end, too, and I did a lot of things—I blocked some punts in key situations; I made a lot of touchdowns.

"I was a good small-college player. The best game I ever had was up in Winooski, Vermont, against St. Michael's. I caught a couple of passes; I played linebacker. I was 220 pounds and could always catch a ball and run with it. So for a small college, I got a lot of recognition. Also, we had a good publicist. His name was Tufie Maroon, used to write for the *New York Sun*. I used to make the Little All-America teams, you know—second team, third team Little All-America.

"I was drafted by the Rams on the nineteenth round. The reason they drafted me, they told me, was because I blocked a couple of punts. On the strength of that alone they figured I was worth a shot. I played with the Rams through 1955. At the end of 1955, Sid Gillman drew up a blueprint, a statistical list of what a player is supposed to be—how tall for his position, how much he should weigh. He got rid of eighteen or nineteen guys. Anyway, my wife was expecting a baby and he wanted me in camp in 1956 and I told him I was going to be a little late because my wife was expecting a baby. He called me a few days later and said, 'Get to camp or I'm going to trade you.' I said, 'If you want to trade me, then trade me.' I thought he was bluffing. He wasn't.

"The next day Wellington Mara called me up and said, 'You're twenty-nine years old. Do you think you can play for us for a while?' I played for the Giants until I was thirty-nine years old. I knew I could play for the Giants at the age of twenty-nine. You see, just about that time they started space exploration, and I noticed that all the people in the space program were thirty-six, thirty-seven. To tell the truth, the last four years, when I was also the defensive line coach, I played better than ever."

Robustelli became an instant hero for the Giants. Luckily for him, they trained in his first year at Winooski, Vermont, the scene of his greatest college game.

"That made me more important than any Giants player. The people in Winooski all remembered me from college. I also had been a baseball player in college. I used to hit the hell out of the ball against St. Mike's all the time. There was a fence in centerfield about 500 feet away, and they still remember that over all the football I played. I hit that fence."

Outside of Winooski, people got to know about Robustelli because he hit football players very hard. He was the most consistent member of the defense.

"I could play under pressure. I remember in field-goal and punting situations I scored a lot of touchdowns. Once with the Rams—Babe Parilli was playing for Green Bay. He called for a lateral. I picked it up and ran for a touchdown, but they called it back. He tried the same play and this time I picked it off for a touchdown again. I don't recall how many touchdowns I scored, but they were in key situations. I was the guy that if you needed somebody to do something—you needed to block a kick—I just had the ability to play under pressure. I rarely got nervous. I didn't get excited before a game or after it started.

"I used to listen to the quarterback's cadence. A lot of guys disagree with me. But I know that people form habits. A quarterback will usually repeat himself in a certain situation. He might go on "three" or "two" or "one." I remember in my rookie year I blitzed Otto Graham. I was listening to him and I picked up his cadence. I picked up a fumble and ran 60 yards to the 1-yard line."

The reason that Robustelli could block kicks so well and recover fumbles so well was because he has the ability to make an instantaneous decision that was uncannily accurate.

"I look at the films now," he says, pointing to a room where his coaches are engrossed watching and rerunning films of each player, "and I can make up my mind immediately about how good a player is. These other coaches are looking at the films a long time. I can sit and watch the Olympics—I'm not an egotist—but there's certain things you see. I watch the skiing and I can tell you who's going to win. I can see the flaws. I don't ski, but the timing's important. You watch a beautiful golf swing, except for that Mexican—what's his name?—and it's all timing and rhythm."

But why were the Giants a better clutch team than most?

"Because we believed in each other more. Look, I played nine years with the Giants. Never missed a game. Modzelewski missed one game, but not, I don't think, during the whole time we played together. We played with a unit that played together all the time. We didn't want—we were afraid—to have substitutions, afraid they'd take our job away. We just didn't want anybody else to have a shot at it, so we stayed in there all the time.''

It is unreal to hear Robustelli confess that his linemates— those bruising, cool, efficient belters—were worried about their jobs. But Robustelli explains what it was like for him:

''I'm not the kind of person who says to you, 'Hey, take my job.' The hell with you. I'm going to fight you all the way. It's like when I was in business. I didn't join the trade associations. I don't want to be a member of a union. I want to be a free guy. I want more than you. I'm not a socialist.''

No, indeed. After 1964, when ''I had to make a decision which way I was going to go,'' he decided to go into business. His travel agency expanded, and he become as successful behind a desk as he had been at the line of scrimmage.

''Then Wellington asked me to come out one Saturday to talk. I didn't think about what I was getting into. I shouldn't have taken this job. I'm a guy that works all his life to build a business and I've got travel agencies and property in the Dominican Republic and in Vermont. And I haven't been able to look after them since I came back to the Giants. I mean that logically I shouldn't have come back with all those other things. But I just felt I had to come back.

''Now I've tried to upgrade the Giants' front office. I've found the modern ballplayer is different. We've become free individuals, but you can get hurt by that freedom. The player isn't conditioned these days to take criticism from—they call it his peers now. That's why there's very few leaders in today's football.''

Finally, Robustelli makes a statement that probably sums up his attitude toward the game he loves, as it sums up his attitude toward life:

''I don't believe you can go out and be motivated enough to hit a guy and after you hit him you help him up. Look, I have compassion for people. I'm a human being. But if I hit you, heck, get up yourself.''

Neither Robustelli nor anyone else stopped Jimmy Brown in the fifth game of the 1963 season. Brown amassed 209 yards on runs and passes, and Cleveland scored a 35–24 victory. They were undefeated with a 5–0 mark while the Giants were 3–2.

A week later, Robustelli, the defensive coordinator, helped his club roar back as it started its final march to its final title—at least the final one for a generation of fans. The Giants trailed the Cowboys at the Stadium 21–17 at the half, and Robustelli decided on a bold plan: to blitz Eddie Le-Baron. It was a dangerous plan because the clever little Le-Baron could dump off short passes or work some running plays that could make the Giants vulnerable. Instead, he was dumped 3 times in the second half for losses totaling 41 yards. Lynch intercepted a pass and scampered 82 yards for a score and Y. A. completed 19 of 32 passes. The Giants won 37–21.

This set up still another meeting between the 6–0 Browns and the 4–2 Giants.

Few quarterbacks have ever put together the season that Tittle was enjoying. In the five games he had played he had thrown for 14 touchdowns. He was the leading passer based on a compilation of percentage of completions, touchdowns thrown, percentage of interceptions, and average yards gained for each pass. Tittle had gone 74 passes without an interception, and before that he had a stretch of 70 straight.

The prospect of a Giants-Browns battle—one that could be the decisive game of the season if Cleveland won—attracted the largest crowd ever to see the Giants play any place. There were 84,213 at Municipal Stadium, a concrete circle built twenty-five years before by the Works Progress Administration.

Since this was a clutch game, and on the road, it meant only one thing—a Giants victory. And suddenly the New Yorkers were only a game behind the front-running Browns, thanks to Chandler's 4 field goals, a defense that held Brown to one of his worst days as a pro (40 yards in 9 runs) and Tittle's completing 21 of 31 for 214 yards. Tittle did not go for the bomb, under orders from Sherman, and instead sliced up the Browns with a short passing game. He was so efficient in directing the team that the first seven times the Giants had the ball, they scored either field goals or touchdowns.

The Giants' rushing game, which had become more or less only a memory, picked up with Hugh McElhenny gaining 53 yards on 13 carries, Webster amassing 53 on 16, and Phil King rushing for 49 yards on 10 tries.

One reason why Tittle was having such a beautiful season was the number and quality of his receivers. Conerly was never blessed with speedy receivers, although he did have some clever ones. But he threw to three consistently over the years. Now Tittle had eight he had confidence in: Shofner, Gifford, King, Morrison, Joe Walton, Aaron Thomas, Webster, McElhenny.

Tittle employed most of them in Game 8, a 38–21 victory over the Cards at St. Louis, for which he left his sick-bed a few hours before game-time, and of course did brilliant things: 4 scores, 17 of 28 passes for 295 yards. His slants, draws, sweeps, and, finally, bombs, gave him a first-half mark of 14–19 and 246 yards.

It was back to the Stadium for Game 9, and more motel madness. The Giants toppled the Eagles, 42–14, but 5,000 people stayed after the game with their eyes fixed to the scoreboard. They were waiting for the result of the Cleveland–Steelers game. While they waited, they discussed Y. A., who had hit 7 different receivers against Philadelphia and had a 13–15 first half. While they talked they saw the result go up— Pittsburgh 9, Cleveland 7. The Giants were tied for first with a 7–2 record.

Then the Giants took over first by themselves. While as many as nineteen people crowded into a room at the Pickwick Motor Inn in Plainview, Long Island, the Giants took their fifth straight game, over the 49ers, 48–14. They held San Francisco to 34 yards rushing. It was not a happy time for the 49ers' coach, Jack Christiansen, especially after Glynn Griffing rubbed it in after replacing Tittle by hitting Gifford with a touchdown pass with less than 2 minutes remaining.

"I hope," said Christiansen, "the Giants lose all their remaining games."

A few days later, the Giants showed compassion. They hired Steve Owen, who was sixty-five years old, to be a college scout. His last job had been with the Syracuse Stormers of the United Football League.

But the Giants fell in the esteem of much of the public—as did the entire league—when all the games went on as scheduled a few days after President Kennedy was assassinated. There would be no television of any games, decreed Rozelle, but there would be games. It seemed to most people unimportant that the Giants bowed to the Cards, 24–17. They now stood at 8–3, along with Cleveland and St. Louis. The Steelers had a 6–3–2 mark.

For the first time in their trips to Dallas, the Giants, with five blacks on the 38-man team, stayed at a downtown hotel. This togetherness did not appear to help them in the first half as they trailed 27–14. They came back with 20 unanswered points in the second half to pull out a 34–27 victory. They remained alive in the first place battle, a truly extraordinary race in which any of four clubs could win.

The next day their thoughts wandered from the race, but just for a bit. The Giants made their first choice of the draft, and it was Joe Don Looney, a product of four different colleges in two states who was dropped by Coach Bud Wilkinson of Oklahoma at the request of his teammates.

"We're not interested in his past," said Howell, in charge of the Giants' scouting.

On the fourth round of the same draft, the Giants chose Matt Snell of Ohio State, which insulted Snell. Anyway, he appeared to be impressed with the Jets' new president, Sonny Werblin, who had taken the trouble to come to Ohio to see him personally.

But the Giants' top running back, Alex Webster, had a sciatic condition that, it was feared, would keep him out for the remaining two games. That put too much pressure on Tittle, said Sherman. Meanwhile, the Giants lost Snell to the Jets, né Titans.

The Giants returned to the field in their thirteenth game. Before a Stadium crowd that was being driven wild, they scored 44–14 over the Redskins. Huff, Lynch, and Katcavage scored as the defense picked off 7 Washington passes and recovered 3 Washington fumbles. Meanwhile, Pittsburgh beat Dallas and suddenly, the Steelers could win the whole thing. For their record was 7–3–3 while the Giants were 10–3.

But if Pittsburgh won the finale, at the Stadium, their record would count as 8–3, since ties don't count, while the Giants would be 10–4. And Pittsburgh would have a winning percentage of .727 to the Giants' .714.

Although the Steelers had been in the league for thirty years, this was only the second time they ever had a chance to win a conference title by winning a game. Perhaps this would be their day. After all, some other establishments were obviously on the way out. Why, the Yankees had their worst attendance in eighteen years, despite winning another baseball championship and scheduling 34 home night games for the 1964 season. And in gangland, a young, up-and-coming mobster named Joey Gallo was arrested for plotting against the old man Profaci. Even that great old car company, Studebaker, was closing its plants. So, many a youth movement was under way—begun, perhaps, by the spirit of President Kennedy, who had replaced the much older Eisenhower. Now in the ads, the man drinking was not a gray-haired patriarch. He was a young artist who told his woman, "As long as you're up, get me a Grant's."

Meanwhile, over at the Polo Grounds, the Jets were preparing to play their last game there. Down in Alabama, the football team's young quarterback, Joe Namath, was suspended for disciplinary reason by Coach Bear Bryant, who once got so angry at Namath that he hurled his locker out of a second-floor window.

The final game of the 1963 season—the final game for a championship Giants team in Yankee Stadium—brought 63,240 fans to the colossal park. The president of Parke-Bernet Galleries, Louis J. Marion, was there with a chance, he said, ''to be a rowdy Mr. Hyde after a week of being Dr. Jekyll in the galleries.'' The head of Bergdorf Goodman, Andrew Goodman, would make it part of his Sunday itinerary that included the 21 Club and El Morocco. It was, he described, ''a pulsy way'' to spend a Sunday afternoon. And the mayor of Stamford, Connecticut, Walter Kennedy, would show up with one of his major public relations accounts, the president of White Tower hamburgers. They were joined, invariably, by Peggy Cass, Arlene Francis, the entire Archdiocese of New York (it seemed), every broker on Wall Street, and all the account executives on Madison Avenue.

There was, perhaps, something special about this final delirium. For in their fashion, the Giants did it again. But first was the pulse pounding. There was a 16–0 lead. But by the third period the Steelers had cut it to 16–10, and the Giants were in danger of giving up the ball. They had the ball on their own 24-yard line, 76 yards from a score. It was third down and 8. Tittle searched for Gifford.

Tittle, of course, would rather have had Shofner. But Shofner had been hurt in the second period. An incomplete pass would give the ball to Pittsburgh, probably near midfield. Tittle went back and saw Gifford cutting over the middle as he was supposed to. But the ball was thrown too far ahead and too low.

''I dived for the ball and I thought, 'Well, we blew it,' '' recalls Gifford. ''I stuck out my hand just to make the motion of going through with it—and the damn thing stuck in my hand. It was the stupidest thing you ever saw.''

Yes. Gifford somehow had managed to snare the ball. He got up looking stunned while most of the 63,240 fans went crazy, sensing that this had saved them. And indeed it had. It gave the Giants a first down on the Pittsburgh 47-yard line.

Over on East Tremont Avenue, at Tyrone House, fire inspectors walked into the bar, which was packed with 150 people who were able to see the game, because atop the building

was an antenna facing Connecticut. The inspectors cleared
out half the patrons.

The lucky ones inside, along with the fans at the Stadium,
saw the Giants go on to a 33–17 victory—and their third
straight Eastern title, their fifth in six years, a record four-
teenth overall. Y. A. had thrown 3 more touchdowns, breaking his own league mark and giving him 36—a mark that
remained one of the oldest in the sport.

The championship game, against the Bears at Chicago on
December 29, was not that far from the site of the first Giants'
5:30 Club. The club was an informal drinking get-together of
press and coaches, and it symbolized the Giants' togetherness
of those years.

Now, many years after the last title, Wellington Mara gets
out from behind his desk to greet warmly a visitor who is asking him to relive those days. That's easy. For the Giants are
among his earliest remembrances. The team remained such
an important part of his life that he did not even marry until
he was thirty-eight years old.

"Doc Sweeny, of course, was the one who started the 5:30
Club," recalls Wellington. "It was 1939, at Superior, Wiscon-
sin's state college. Doc and the trainers and the coaches and
the press and a fan of ours from the Cotton Exchange. We
began by calling it infield practice. They had a bar set up on
the piano. It was in the dean of women's room. I often wondered what she thought all those circles on her piano were.
But it was a nice custom. In fact, Vince brought it with him
to Green Bay. But it's gone by the wayside now."

What do you remember about the beginning?

"It was 1925 and I was nine years old. And I remember my
father standing outside of church on Sunday morning and
telling some friends, 'I'm going to try to put pro football
over in New York this afternoon.'

"I remember going to the game with my mother and sitting
in a lower-stands box in the shade. This was early October,

and I guess it was quite chilly and that night my mother told my father, 'From now on, if Well wants to sit on the bench you'll have to put the Giants' bench on the sunny side of the field.' And that's why we were always on the sunny side of the field at the Polo Grounds.

"I also sat on the bench that first game. And I remember our coach, Bob Folwell, shouting 'Jappe' to one of our linemen: 'Jappe, get in there and give them hell.' And I remember thinking to myself, 'Boy, this is a real tough bunch of fellows.' "

Of course, young Wellington was hooked. For life, as it turns out. He became, in time, the patriarch of a Giants' family that took its cue from him. He did not swear. He did not believe in embarrassing the team by word or deed. Those that did were gone. It was a simple as that. Yet he never told his coaches how he wanted his players to behave. In the words of Don Smith, "Wellington's very presence gave the players the cue for the way they should behave."

"This family atmosphere just worked out naturally," says Well. "We were a real family organization. There was my father, Jack, and myself. And that was like Howell, Landry, and Lombardi. I used to handle the personnel, and Jack handled the business side. Jack always thought I was extra-liberal in paying the players. So once we let him deal with Conerly, the last contract Charley ever signed. I had a golf date and Jack said, 'I'll handle him.' I always felt Jack had a kind of secret yen to see how well he'd do with Charley in contract talks.

"I don't remember the figures, but it was by far the biggest contract Charley had ever had, and it was more than I was prepared to give him, and Charley said to me, 'I've been dealing with the wrong brother all these years.' "

Mara laughs with a short, punctuated giggle. And the memory of that contract brings a shock of recognition. For he discloses:

"You know, when Jack died—well, we haven't done much since. I really think the problem was that it took me too long to realize I couldn't do both jobs. I did the hiring of personnel and I took care of the business. He died in June 1965. And just about that time the personnel situation got more involved and more complex. I'm completely out of personnel now. That's why I hired Robustelli. I hated to give it up, and I don't know that I have expertise on the business side of this thing. But there's just things the president of a football club has to do. And I thought it could run the way it had. But it just didn't work out that way. I gave Allie a long contract because I felt the most important part of the operation was the head coach. I felt he was the best man available and I had secured that end of the business for ten years. I gave him a contract from 1965 to 1974.

"It's easy now to look back. Allie believed the team was never going to be good enough to win the whole championship. He said we'd never be better than second best. I think he felt that maybe they were jaded or had gone as far as they were going to go."

Did Wellington agree with the deals that broke up the club after the 1963 season?

"Obviously I did, because I could have stopped any of those deals. But I didn't sense the era was ending."

Neither did the millions of fans who watched the 1963 championship game from Chicago, even though there was some obvious disintegration of the club. But the Bears were the finest defensive outfit in the league. The 144 points they gave were 62 points fewer than anyone else. It was the most efficient defense anyone had seen since the 1944 Giants. It was a good enough team to lead the league in 17 different defensive categories, a club that had lost only one game, that had beaten the second-place Packers twice for their only losses of the season. And the Giants? They were a terrific offensive machine, going over 400 points for the first and only time in their history. They amassed 448 points, an average of 32 points a game.

But that strange—was it jinx?—that the Giants had in playoff games after winning their 1956 league title hampered them again. For the third straight year, too, Tittle was ineffective in the title game. With more than 15,000 people watching over theater-TV in blacked-out Chicago, and another 45,801 on hand at the game, the Giants actually scored first by taking advantage of a Billy Wade fumble on their 17-yard line. The 83-yard march was capped by a 14-yarder, Tittle to Gifford, and the New Yorkers led 7–0.

They could put it away, for on their next series the Bears' Willie Galimore fumbled on his own 31-yard line. Now was the time for the bomb, the Tittle-to-Shofner specialty that deflated the opposition. And Tittle spotted Shofner in the end zone. The ball pierced the 20-degree air and hit Shofner in his hands—like an icicle. He dropped it. And that was that. For the Bears intercepted a Tittle screen—1 of 5 interceptions against the old man—and ran it back to their 5. Then Wade sneaked over for the score, and the game was tied. In the second period Chandler kicked a 13-yard field goal to give the New Yorkers a 10–7 half-time lead. But Tittle had been hurt, and he could not plant himself to pass in the second half. Another screen was intercepted, this time by Ed O'Bradovich who took it to the 14. Wade soon went over again and that was the final: Chicago 14, Giants 10. For the first time all season Tittle and Shofner had failed to connect on a pass. Y. A. had completed only 11 of 29 passes.

Now, years later, Y. A. asks, "How could I be washed up just nine months later?"

The Giants' ripe decade had ended, although not many people realize an era had ended, too.

One day, early in 1964, Jack Mara walked past Don Smith's office and said, "They've gone too far."

"What is it?" asked Smith.

"They've traded Huff," replied Jack Mara.

Huff went, and so did Modzelewski. Within a year, Shofner had quit with ulcers, Y. A. for injuries, Webster and Robustelli for coaching, Gifford to television, and Chandler to Green Bay.

Who could explain to the new, young Giants what it was really like? Who could tell of the significance? Of the after-game dinners, of the pats on the back at Toots Shor's, of the vacations together at Grossinger's, of the feeling before the game that no matter what mistakes they might make on the field, somehow, someone would come along for the Giants and make it right? What happened to the happy-ending family sagas that used to be played each Sunday?

Another amazing insight from Wellington Mara, revealed perhaps for the first time:

"I think that the Jets coming in when they did contributed to our bad years, because we tried to do everything for the short term rather than the long haul—we'd trade a draft choice for a player, figuring he'd give us one or two good years. We didn't want to accept how the public might react if we had a bad year or two or three.

"In other words, it was a question of misplaced pride. The fans would have stuck with us anyhow. They did stick with us through all the bad years. In the past we had been able to fill in—a Robustelli, a Modzelewski, a Walton—we added people like that. That was fine when we had a great nucleus. But after 1963 we kept trying to add without realizing the nucleus wasn't as strong as it had been. Like I said, it was a question of misplaced pride."

Finally, there is another insight:

"We realize now the terrific hold that these players had on one another. Individually, maybe none of them were great. But as a unit—they were that great."

Index